KALAYLA

UNRAVELING TANGLES

ESSENTIAL INFORMATION FOR THE READER

Before I wrote *Kalayla*, I thought writers who said their characters talked to them were exaggerating, hallucinating, or fibbing. I found out they weren't when it happened to me. Having the characters in my head was aggravating and exhausting. I needed a break, and although I knew I hadn't resolved all the characters' issues, I felt as if I'd done my best. I assumed that ending and publishing the book would be acceptable.

I was wrong. I didn't understand that I had entered into a covenant with the characters. I didn't realize they would feel abandoned and betrayed because I hadn't finished telling their stories. I didn't expect their response to be insistent and demanding.

The fact of the matter was I loved the characters, related to their struggles, and hadn't meant to disappoint them. So, I recommitted, fully aware that they preferred late-night conversations, and sleepless nights would follow. I listened attentively and researched topics of concern to them. Outspoken characters continued to speak their minds, and to my delight, previously voiceless characters revealed their complicated and tangled backgrounds.

I concluded I couldn't simply write a sequel to *Kalayla*. I had to rewrite the story and incorporate what I learned, which I did in *Kalayla Unraveling Tangles*. The book was a fascinating and joyous collaboration that showcases the complexity of the characters' lives. I thank my family and friends, who encouraged me to persevere, and I am grateful the characters are satisfied and comfortingly silent.

Exploring the dynamics in Kalayla's extended family encouraged me to think about my life's tangles and pose a question for myself and the readers. How do we unravel our tangles with kindness and help ourselves and others find a constructive way forward?

KALAYLA'S FAMILY TREE

Bold indicates characters who are important in Kalayla's life.

PARENTS
Maureen O'Rourke   Jamal LeeRoyce

GRANDPARENTS
Kevin & Colleen O'Rourke   Harmon & Lucinda LeeRoyce

GREAT GRANDPARENTS

Colin Doyle	Harmon LeeRoyce
Mary Margaret Doyle	Yolanda LeeRoyce

Other family that appears in the story:

MAUREEN'S SIBLINGS	JAMAL'S SIBLING
Colin, Leah, Kate	**Clarence**
Kieran	
(Kalayla's cousin)	

Notes:

- Maureen's mother (Colleen) and Kalayla's great grandmother (Mary Margaret) moved from Belfast, Ireland to South Boston, MA after the death of Kalayla's great grandfather (Colin).

- When Colleen married Kevin O'Rourke, she moved from South Boston to Brighton, MA where Maureen was born.

- Maureen moved to Cambridge from Brighton, MA when she married Kalayla's father, Jamal. Kalayla was born in Cambridge, MA.

JEANNIE NICHOLAS

KALAYLA

UNRAVELING TANGLES

PRELUDE

BELFAST, IRELAND, 1960

The girl tucked her chair against the right side of the bed, her ear almost touching the lips of her father's disfigured face. His voice was hoarse, barely audible, each word a painful effort, "I'm done," Colin Doyle said, gasping for breath.

His daughter, Colleen, knew he would say more if he could. She waited, as she'd been waiting for six endless days.

Colleen had been afraid long before the lads carried her broken father home. Time and time again, she heard her mother, Mary Margaret, warn him to be cautious and to watch his words. Colleen had experience skirting Belfast's danger, and she knew her mother was right. They lived among enemies whose smiling faces could turn to snarls with the slightest provocation. Despite her mother's pleas, the daredevil side of Colin refused to rein in its cockiness.

Colin was a magician with machines, crooning to them softly, fixing any broken or improperly balanced. He believed his talent protected him. The Protestant bosses at the linen factory called Colin the devil Taig—as if his ability had its source in hell. Worse than that, Colin and Mary Margaret were Catholics in a sea of Protestant workers, any one of whom might repeat Colin's arrogant taunts to the B Specials, the part-time constable police force in Northern Ireland.

Everyone knew Colin Doyle was on the list of suspected IRA members. He was a burly, brash man who danced on the narrowest of ledges as if he considered a Catholic taunting the B Specials a schoolyard game.

"No worries," he'd tell Mary Margaret, pulling her close. "They'll not be so foolish as to come after me."

But one night six days ago, they saw the chance and did. Colin had gone with the neighborhood lads to the Horse Trough Pub, but when the others left, Colin waved them off. He'd won a few pence arm wrestling and would stay on to see if his luck would hold.

In the wee hours, Mary Margaret sent word that her husband hadn't come home. The lads went searching and brought what was left of Colin back to her and Colleen. "IRA scum" was smeared in the blood on her husband's chest, his mangled body a showpiece of brutality.

Mary Margaret knew what she had to do. Colleen would be ten soon, the age when children went to work in the linen factory. Mary Margaret's childless sister and husband lived in South Boston in the United States, and they offered Mary Margaret and Colleen a place to live. Mary Margaret had no other choice. She couldn't pay the rent, and it would be too dangerous for any friend or relative to take them in. They would stay in Belfast until after Colin had a proper Catholic burial.

Mary Margaret stowed her grief in her apron pocket and went to the linen factory every day from six a.m. to nine p.m. as Colin would expect her to.

While her mother worked, Colleen sat alone beside the body that had been her father. She knew he would expect her to be brave, but every sound was terrifying. When they found out Colin wasn't dead, would they come to finish their work and kill her, too? Or would they use her as their whore the way the neighborhood girls said they did if they caught you alone?

Later, when Colleen took her da bread and milk for his noontime meal, he took a ragged breath and said, "No food, no water. Our secret."

Colleen closed her eyes and dug her nails into her clenched fists. She understood it had to be their secret. Her mother would never allow Colin to starve himself. She'd say it was a mortal sin, and the timing and manner of his death were God's choice, not his.

Her da would scoff at that idea. Although Colin went with Mary Margaret and Colleen to mass every Sunday and on Holy Days of Obligation, he mocked church teachings with the same regularity. He told his daughter that sins were nothing more than a deck of cards in a game of make-believe. Colleen listened wide-eyed, trusting the handsome man who carried her on his shoulders, taught her to sing, spun bedtime stories of goblins, fairies, and dragons, and knew everything.

The battered body beside her bore no resemblance to that Da, but Colleen heard the echo of his tenor's lilt in the ragged voice, and that was enough for her. She could do what he wanted. After all, she was nine years old, the miracle child, the one of five who lived. Three sisters died before she was born, and one brother after. Mum said the factory's damp, foul air and ever-present coughing sickness made her womb unhealthy. Colleen had been strong enough to survive, and she was strong enough to set her father free to sing again.

SOUTH BOSTON, MASSACHUSETTS/SOUTHIE

Colleen hated Southie more than she hated Belfast. The landscape in Belfast had been familiar, the tension as commonplace as the insults hurled by Catholic and Protestant kids across divided streets. The girl's fear was monotonous and ever-present.

The landscape in Southie was unknown, a deafening source of terror. Noise from planes, trains, sirens, horns, and trolleys mingled with shouting adults and crying children. Teenage gangs wandered without defined boundaries. Music blared from their transistor radios and competed with record players from the Project's open windows. Any step might trigger an invisible booby trap. The girl's fear was intense and ever-present.

Her aunt's and her uncle's flat was in a Catholic enclave in the Old Dominion Housing projects, three-story brick buildings near a traffic circle and park. Neighborhood kids invited Colleen to go adventuring, but what if they were like her da, whose willingness to take risks had gotten him killed? When they grew tired of her excuses and stopped asking, she didn't care. Colleen stayed observant, alert, and close to home.

Colleen's mother wasn't willing to settle for life in a housing project. Her sister was satisfied to be a part-time seamstress and pleased that her husband had a steady job as a postal worker. She didn't have a daughter to spur her to a better life.

If Colin had listened to Mary Margaret, they would have moved to Cork or Dublin before Colleen turned three. But he didn't, and she was left to deal with the consequences of his myopic vision. She'd had her fill of factory work and knew she could sell her domestic skills.

City Point was less than a two-mile walk from the Old Dominion projects but light years away in gentility and prosperity, with mansion-like houses as beacons beckoning to a better life. With a subtle hint of arrogance, Mary Margaret spun a tale about her previous employment to the mistress of the grandest house, who hired her on the spot. The mistress could casually brag that she'd hired a household staff manager recently employed by the royal family to maintain their Belfast residence.

Mary Margaret told Colleen that night, "I'll learn all I can about gentry life. God helped us get this far, Colleen. The rest is up to us."

Colleen didn't brag or preen in front of the other girls in the ensuing years. She made the honor roll but didn't brown-nose the teachers. She helped classmates who struggled with math or English. Colleen's aunt and uncle became surrogate parents. Her aunt enjoyed sewing school clothes for her, and when Colleen was old enough to attend Catholic mixers in Boston, her aunt added flattering tucks, ruffles, and ribbons. Colleen's uncle was a quiet, unassuming man.

Colleen realized she couldn't marry anyone mercurial like her da, whose firecracker mouth got him murdered. She needed a steady, solid man to raise a family without fear.

She was nearly eighteen when she met Kevin O'Rourke, an auto mechanic saving to buy a garage or two if things went as he planned. Kevin was down-to-earth and safe. He wanted three or four children and a home to welcome them and their friends. Colleen could build a life with him, and he wouldn't shatter it.

SUMMER 1999

LENA MANERO BARZETTI

THAT GIRL

I'm not one of those old biddies who mind other people's business instead of her own. But, there are some people it is impossible to ignore, and that girl, Kalayla, was one of them.

The first time I saw Kalayla was mid-June last year. I was walking back from Mickey's Market on one of those perfect sunny days that made you believe you could live happily ever after. *The National Scoop* headline, "*Princess Diana's Death Revealed as Hoax,*" made the same promise.

Kalayla was ahead of me, half swaggering, half strutting in a way so familiar I thought I must know her. I ruminated on it until I realized my twins walked like that when they were showing off, which was pretty much from the minute they got up until they went to bed.

How often had I seen those two boys swagger, strut, or taunt each other? Mikie would dare Jimmy, "Bet it takes you more than 20 seconds to shimmy up that streetlight." Jimmy would dare Mikie, "Bet you can't get five bucks panhandling between here and home." Off they'd go, running, laughing, shoving and punching.

The blast from a horn jolted me out of daydreaming, or I'd have bumped right into Kalayla. She was staring into Hanson's Book Store window, and her saucer-sized green eyes briefly glanced my way.

I pegged Kalayla as a Cambridge street kid scraping her way from one meal to the next, an old hand at trash picking and layering up with everything she found. That day, she wore three layers on top with a mishmash of colors and designs; a rope held up the baggy capri-length pants that would have been shorts on someone taller. A beat-up blue-and-red baseball cap with the brim turned backward squashed down her kinky orange-brown curls. She was an inch or two shorter than my five feet two inches, and I couldn't tell how old she was. Most teenage girls wanted to show off their bodies, but Kalayla didn't.

After that, I saw Kalayla everywhere I went. She was always by herself, and I wondered why. The only way my four boys were alone was if they were going to or coming from someplace where other kids were hanging out. Even my boy Mark, who was always getting in fights, had plenty of friends. If I were that girl's mama, the fact she was alone so much would have worried me.

* * *

About two weeks later, I was walking back from buying milk and eggs at Mickey's Market when I saw Kalayla talking to Maureen, the red-headed woman who waited tables at Eddie's Eatery. Eddie's was across from my apartment building, and sometimes I stopped by to chat. Maureen was friendly and cheerful but didn't blab personal stuff like some folks. Eddie told me she was a widow with a daughter.

I watched Maureen kiss her on the forehead and go into Eddie's. The girl had the same huge green eyes and delicate features Maureen did. Maureen's skin was ivory, and the girl's was light chocolate, but she had to be her daughter. She crossed the street and went into my apartment building. I hurried to see where she was going, but she had disappeared when I arrived.

I didn't just live in the building. I owned it and the building where Eddie's was located. They were the first properties Joey and I bought after we married, and our families solidified their business partnership by forming Manzetti Properties. Joey didn't turn out to be much of a husband, but his family knew all the angles when it came to rehab and construction, and my family was skillful and shrewd at buying and marketing real estate.

My job was to locate vacant buildings or properties the owner was interested in offloading quickly. I kept my eye out for local contractors. It was good public relations to involve them in small tear-downs or rehabs and leave the big jobs to Joey's crews. My office was at our corporate headquarters, and I still worked one or two days a week.

My brother Dominic was a financial wizard who'd been pretending to train his son and daughter to take over from him for the last three years. When I asked Dom if he knew anything about the girl and her mother,

8

he laughed and said, "Have you been walking around with your eyes closed, Lena? Those two moved in across the hall from you."

Well, I never! When they moved in, I must have been volunteering at Helping Hands Shelter for Women, having supper at Dom's, or out with my best friend, Carlotta. That girl didn't come across as if she wanted to keep a low profile, but Voles hunkered down underground would have gotten my attention faster than those two.

A few days later, I saw Kalayla on our landing, staring out the window like a lost soul, and it wrenched my heart. I'd looked out the window many times and wished I'd see Jimmy or Mikie strutting down the street. But no amount of wishing could bring them back from the dead. And no amount of wishing changed the fact that the girl reminded me of them. When we finally did speak, it was no surprise the first thing out of her mouth was a smart-assed comment, like my twins would have made.

When my boys were growing up, Lotta repeatedly told me to wash the twins' mouths with soap. She never raised kids, or she would have known you can't stick a bar of soap into a child's mouth, no matter how tempted you might be.

THE OLD LADY

That crabby old lady would swear I never paid attention to a word she said, but she'd be wrong. Her name was Lena Barzetti, and I called her crabby 'cause that's what she was ninety-five percent of the time. She was seventy-two years old, and boy, did she look it. I was exploring the new neighborhood that summer and got to know her.

It didn't get dark until late, so I could be out without flipping Mama out. Our building was on a corner with a light, about halfway between Harvard Square and Arlington. Massachusetts Avenue had sidewalks. I could walk on one side of the street until I got bored, then cross the street and walk back on the other.

I liked meeting people who were walking their dogs. Pets weren't allowed in our building. I told Mama it'd be easy to sneak in a dog or cat, but she lectured me about not doing anything to get us kicked out of the apartment—as if I would!

Second Time Clothes, White's Fruits and Vegetables, and Mickey's Market were within a few blocks. You could get your nails or toes done at Tammy's Tips or your hair straightened at Creative Clips. Magneson's Flower Shop owners were friendly, but my favorite place was Clean Duds Laundromat.

Regulars there knew better than to go on an errand while their laundry was in the washer or dryer. I earned an easy buck sitting with my feet propped up on the windowsill and reading a book like I owned the place. I kept an eye out for anybody with an empty basket or bag who acted like they were lost while they checked the place out. I'd give them a big smile and say, "You need help?" That cleared out the shifty types pretty fast.

One day, when I was standing on the landing between the third and fourth floors of the apartment building, staring out the window and planning my afternoon, I heard slow footsteps coming up the stairs. That was when I met old lady Lena.

The weird thing was she only wore black. Her dress, socks, and shoes were all black like she worked at a funeral home, and that was her uniform. She was dragging a couple of duffle bags. If she collapsed, I'd be stuck dialing 911.

She stopped when she got to the landing, and I saw that the bags were full of black clothes. She must've come from Clean Duds. She had to be dumber than dumb to live on the fourth floor of a building with no elevator. Besides, anybody smart would've taken small loads instead of everything they owned.

If I felt like starting a conversation—which I didn't—I might've pointed that out.

The old lady said, "Little girl, if you don't have anything to do, I can give you some work."

Dumber than dumb, like I thought, right?

"If it looks to you like I'm hanging out here waiting for a job, you need glasses. And I'm not a little girl. I'm twelve years old."

She stared at me long and hard. "Well, maybe you want to be an architect, and you're staring at those buildings to get ideas. Good view from up here."

I gotta say that was worth a laugh. "Nah," I said, "I'm just planning my day."

"Then how about helping me carry this laundry?"

"My mama told me not to talk to strangers or carry laundry for them. A good-looking girl like me has to be real careful."

She stared longer and harder this time. Anybody could see I wouldn't be crowned queen of the apartment building, even competing against people like her. Maybe her eyesight was lousy.

"Well," she said, "I'm interested in your muscles, not your looks or mouth. I'll give you a Coke for pay."

"I don't like Coke. I'll take a root beer."

"All kids like Coke, and I don't have root beer. I have lemons, water, and sugar to make lemonade. I can throw in a few cookies. Will that satisfy you?"

"What kind of cookies?"

She rolled her eyes like she couldn't believe I'd ask that, but I wasn't lugging laundry for plain old sugar cookies.

"Peanut butter—fresh made."

"Fine!" I said, heaving one bag over each shoulder.

Her apartment was the same as ours, but it was almost empty. Every wall was white, and there was nothing, not one thing, on them. The window shades and the rug in front of the sofa were white. The couch and chair were white. Everybody knew you'd have to wash or clean all that white every other day. Nobody but a rich person could afford that, and she sure didn't look rich.

She said, "Don't stand there gawking. Put the laundry bags in the closet in the spare room."

That'd be my bedroom at home, but I couldn't tell what it was for her. The walls, window shades, and rug in the middle of the room were all white. A small wooden table and a straight-back chair were near the window. Maybe she lived someplace else and came here 'cause she liked Clean Duds. I dumped the bags on the floor in the closet but felt like I'd messed things up.

She was in the kitchen mixing the lemonade, and I decided I better find out how crazy she was before I had any. So, I said, "Do you live in a monastery and just keep this place to store stuff?"

She gave me a big-time stare and said, "That smart mouth must get you in trouble at school. What would you know about a monastery?"

"I read a book that said the walls are white, and they give you a chair, a bed, an extra robe, a pair of shoes, and a box to store them."

"Is that a fact? So, you read books?"

"Yeah. What of it? You never met a kid who reads books?" Why wasn't she asking me the usual stupid adult questions like how I was doing in school and how many brothers and sisters I had?

"That would be an example of the mouth I was talking about. I've got a lot of books you could look at if you wanted to."

Why'd she think I'd want to read her crummy old books? I thought about leaving until she brought out the peanut butter cookies. I tasted one and decided to stay long enough to eat a few.

"You can call me Lena," she said. "And I suppose you have a name."

Did she think my parents named me Girl like some jerks named their dog Dog?

"Sure, I got a name. It's Kalayla."

"Ka lay la," she repeated slowly. "That's unusual and pretty. Is it a family name?"

"Nah. My mama thought it up. She's smart about some things."

I drank a lot of lemonade that summer 'cause the old lady asked me for help every five minutes. Sometimes, she annoyed me so much I wanted to spit, but I wasn't giving up free lemonade and cookies.

I didn't mind 'cause Mama wasn't home much. We got a car last year, and she cleaned houses before her four-nine shift at Eddie's. Standing on the landing, I could watch her serving customers or clearing tables. Sometimes, I'd go over to hang out and have a snack.

Mama attended classes or did art projects when Daddy was alive instead of working. She didn't have a studio now. Even if we had room for one, she was too busy working.

***

When summer came, Mama decided we should spend more time together and have Sunday morning talks. We'd sit at the kitchen table while she drank coffee, and I'd fix whatever I felt like eating. Mostly, Mama asked me questions, and I tried not to lie too much. Sometimes, I had to 'cause she was hyper-nervous about what I was doing and where I was going.

This morning, she said, "Are you going to the library today?"

I never told her the library was closed on Sundays during the summer, so I said, "Haven't made plans yet, Mama. Is there something you want me to do?"

"Well, no, but if you're going out, you might want to change your clothes."

Cow turds! Even the old lady didn't bug me about how I dressed, and she bugged me about plenty of stuff. Someday, I might try going naked to see if Mama liked that better!

Sometimes, Mama got going on how important family was, which was weird 'cause her family died in a gas explosion, so I never met them. Mama seemed nervous when we visited Daddy's family, so I decided she liked talking about family more than being with it.

After Daddy died, his brother, Clarence, thought he'd do us a big favor and drop by to see us. He bragged about how good he was at getting good car deals and offered to find one for us. Clarence always made her nervous, so when she asked me what I thought, I said, "He'll get us a car when he gets a real job."

"Layla, I wish you wouldn't say things like that about Clarence."

"It's the truth, so why shouldn't I say it?"

"He's your uncle, and you should be respectful."

"I am respectful. I never called him a butthole to his face, did I?"

Mama sighed like she wished I'd shut my mouth, but she knew I wouldn't.

For once, Clarence did what he said. He found a blue Ford with eighty thousand miles and not too many scrapes and dents. He kept bragging about how it had a fine American engine, and he had detailed it himself. I got sick of hearing that, so I said, "Wow! You mean you did something besides sit on your butt?" I took off before he could slap me. Mama started cleaning houses after we got the car.

* * *

My grandparents lived near Inman Square in Cambridge. After Daddy died, Grandma told everyone that Mama was exhausted and needed to rest, so we stayed with them. That was a bunch of bull. Mama wasn't exhausted. She had a nervous breakdown. Grandma knew it; I knew it, and so did everybody else.

Staying with them would've been okay, except they dragged me to church. I wanted to tell Grandma they should take Clarence instead of me, but she would've said I was rude.

When Mama finally got back to normal, she got a job at Eddie's, and we moved to a smaller apartment. Mama said decorating the apartment would be her art project, but everybody knew fixing up an apartment wasn't the same as having a studio.

It was kind of funny, but once we moved to the new apartment, the person I saw the most was the old lady. She liked Clean Duds and dropped by every day with her iced coffee. I decided her life had to be pretty boring if all she had to do was take up my valuable time.

She'd pull up a chair and say something like, "Too hot to be out," when it was just as hot inside as it was out. Clean Duds had a couple of standing fans chained to the wall, but all they did was blow around hot air and make a lot of noise.

Mama told me that black absorbs the most heat of any color. So, on one of those broiling days, I said, "If you're so hot, why are you wearing black?"

She gave me the icy stare routine. "What color I wear and why I wear it is no business of yours!"

Fine! It would serve her right if she fried!

When the old lady wanted me to do stuff, she'd ask if I wanted to earn a Coke. That turned into a joke, and I'd say, "I'll have a vanilla Coke float with chocolate ice cream, thanks."

I got used to the whiteness in her apartment, and in a way, I kind of liked it. It was like a blank page, and you could decorate it any way you wanted. A small bookcase in the corner of the living room had photos of some boys. Mama had pictures of her, me, and Daddy everywhere, but Lena's place wasn't normal like ours.

One of the photos was of a beautiful woman standing in water a little above her ankles at the ocean. Her dark-brown hair was blowing around her shoulders, and the wind whipped her dress so you could see her legs. Two little boys were building a sand fort on the shore.

I pointed at the photo and said, "Is that a friend of yours?"

"A friend? That's me you're looking at, Kalayla, in my younger days."

I covered my mouth to keep from snorting. I almost said, "Yeah, a couple hundred years ago," but I already had her lecture on being polite memorized.

In another photo, the same woman held the two little boys to keep them from squirming away. Two older boys stood straight as statues beside them.

"Are those your kids? How come I never see them here?"

The old lady didn't say anything for so long that I thought she might've gone deaf. Finally, she said, "I had four sons, and those photos were taken when they were little. You better go home, Kalayla. Your mama's likely waiting."

THE MAMA

That girl was sticking her nose into places she shouldn't, like asking me about my boys. What good would come of me telling her two of them were dead, that I didn't know if the third was living, and the fourth was a big-shot businessman who thought I was as desirable a mother as a field of poison ivy.

I decided I better get to know Kalayla's mother. The fact I'd done a lousy job raising my boys meant I could give her plenty of good advice on what not to do.

I bagged a batch of Lotta's cookies the following Sunday afternoon and went to Maureen's. When she answered my knock, her smile was genuine, "Lena! I'm so glad it's you! Please come in. Kalayla's at the library; she'll be sorry she missed you. I hope you'll like what I've done to the apartment. I'm an artist, well, not a real artist. I mean, I've never earned any money with my art. Oh, do come in!" Maureen asked Dom if she could choose wall colors and do the painting herself. Of course, he said yes because he wouldn't need to pay our painting crew. Dom's knee-jerk reaction was to pinch every penny, nickel, dime, and quarter any way he could. The joke was that he didn't know how much Maureen loved color! The entire apartment would have to be repainted when she moved out, and Dom would be on his high horse about that!

The wall colors reminded me of tropical fish with their brilliant colors. Two of the kitchen walls were yellow, and two were orange. The cushions, curtains, and wall decorations were a mixture of stripes, polka dots, and geometric shapes in yellow, orange, green, and white.

"Maureen, I don't know what to say except what you've done is just plain wonderful!"

"Oh! I'm so relieved you like it. When Layla told me your apartment was all white, I was afraid you might ask us to repaint every room."

"The house I lived in before I moved here was full of color. You should consider being a home decorator instead of waiting on tables and cleaning houses."

"Oh, I'd love that, but I don't have any formal training or experience, and I don't have a college degree. I started on one, but—."

If Maureen had gone on instead of stopping abruptly, I might have found out more, but instead, she gave me a tour of the apartment. Every room was unique, and her creativity was unmistakable.

When Maureen told me Kalayla was at the library on a Sunday afternoon in July, I knew I'd come just in time. I decided to get to know her before pointing out that her daughter was prone to altering the truth when it suited her.

After we settled in the living room with coffee and Lotta's cookies, Maureen started talking again.

"I'm so glad you came, Lena. I can't chat when I'm working. I wouldn't want Eddie to think I was wasting time."

"Don't you worry about Eddie. He'd cut you some slack. Is this your first job?"

"Oh dear, is it that obvious? I didn't work when Jamal was alive. I enrolled at Rhode Island School of Design as a part-time student, and took one or two classes each semester. It was taking forever, but I loved it. Our apartment was big enough that I had a studio, and after I had Kalayla, I put her crib there and later her pack 'n-play.

"When she started crawling, she was so quiet that I'd lose track of her. One day, I found her in the kitchen with everything from the bottom cupboards strewn on the floor. Jamal put on baby-proof cupboard locks and gates across the doorways. That worked until she figured out how to climb over them.

"When Jamal died, my life changed completely."

I took a sip of coffee and waited for Maureen to go on, but she'd run out of steam. She fiddled with the handle of her mug until I said, "Your family must have been a big help when your husband died."

Stricken was the only way to describe Maureen's expression, and I knew I'd stumbled onto a right big sore spot.

"My family? No, they didn't help, but my in-laws were good to us. Lucina and Harmon would have helped us move, and Jamal's brother, Clarence, would have, too, but I wasn't sure if that would cause problems."

I didn't bother asking why Maureen thought having Jamal's family move them in might be a problem. It was 1999, but the idea of whites and blacks getting together still rubbed some folks the wrong way. It wouldn't have bothered me, but Maureen might've found out the hard way that not everybody felt like I did. You could never tell when bigotry would come around the corner and hit you in the face.

Uncle Clarence must be the black guy I'd seen who stopped in and left about ten minutes later. When it came to helping, you'd think an uncle would do more than a drive-by on the way to somewhere else.

Before I could say anything, Maureen said, "Kalayla told me she sees you at Clean Duds. I'm glad I have the chance to ask you. She's not getting into any trouble, is she? I mean, like hanging out with the wrong kids?"

Huh! I wished Kalayla had friends, and her mama was afraid she'd find the wrong ones!

"As far as I can tell, she doesn't hang out with anyone."

"That's a relief. Kalayla told me you have four boys. I bet they were a handful! I'm having a hard time with one girl. You must be so glad they're all grown. How are they doing?"

I admit that stopped me. Everybody knew about my family, and I never had to explain why, when, or how things happened to my boys or my husband.

I could have told Maureen my twins joined the Marines during the anti-war protests. I could have told her my second son, Mark, had disappeared from the face of the earth about fifteen years ago, and I didn't know if he was alive. I could have told her I worried that my oldest boy, JJ, had become a clone of his dad, which was the worst thing he could have done.

Eventually, I said, "My oldest, JJ, runs the construction side of our family business. My second boy, Mark, moved out West. I'm not sure where he is or what he's doing. The twins, Jimmy and Mikie, were the youngest. They were killed in Vietnam less than a year after their dad died."

The color drained from Maureen's face.

"How awful!" she said. "Now I understand why you wear black. Oh dear, that didn't come out right. I just meant I'm so sorry."

Yeah, everybody was sorry, especially me.

Talking to Maureen made me think about Joey, how he loved high living and being the top man, how he bragged that his boys were like him, and I hoped they weren't.

Joey said acting out was healthy for boys because they needed to prove themselves. He said the trouble they got into was good, harmless fun. I believed him until I realized not all the fun was harmless.

I was sure Mark was doing fine in school until I got calls saying he wasn't.

"Mrs. Barzetti? This is John DiSilva, the principal at Mark's school. I'm calling about an incident at lunch today. Mark smashed another kid's piece of pie in his face."

I knew Mark had a temper, but I'd never seen it get out of hand. Joey told me all boys fight with their brothers and that I should ignore it. So I did, but picking a fight outside the family was different.

"My Mark?" I said. "That doesn't make sense. You must have him mixed up with some other boy."

"I don't think so, Mrs. Barzetti. He's sitting right here in my office. You can ask him yourself."

There was no doubt it was Mark's voice saying: "Yeah, Ma, I ate the lunch you made me. I wasn't going to eat his pie. But the kid is an ass-hole and does stuff that aggravates me, like giving me looks. Today, he bragged that he had a steak sandwich and cherry pie. I got sick of it. You should have seen him with cherries dripping down his face. I hope he gets a beating for ruining his shirt."

"Mark! Shame on you! That's not ..."

"Ma, listen, okay? Dad wouldn't put up with that, so why should I?"

"Don't tell me what your dad would do! We're talking about what you did!"

"Ma, I know. I promise I won't do it again. Mr. D. wants to talk to you."

Mark said he wouldn't do it again, but he made a lot of promises he never kept. Nothing was ever his fault, and fighting over aggravations became the story of his life.

"I'm trying, Ma," he'd tell me, and maybe he did.

Mark never had anybody watching his back like the twins did for each other. When JJ was four, and Mark was three, Joey told JJ to toughen up his younger brother. JJ used Mark as a punching bag. At first, Mark came to me for protection, but Joey called him a mama's boy. That was far worse than anything JJ did to him.

JJ and his father were over six feet, and the twins were six feet by the time they turned fourteen. Joey rubbed it in by nicknaming Mark "Shrimp."

I never got calls about the twins getting into fights, but they found other ways of getting into trouble. On their first day in kindergarten, the principal suspended them from the school bus for three days for teaching the other boys to play poker, which the school considered gambling.

I told Joey we should make them walk to school as a punishment. He laughed, "Why should they walk? They're chips off the old block. Don't worry, Lena. I'll talk to them. The next time, they'll be smart enough to hide the damn cards and not to admit anything. If you want to keep that fancy car I gave you, you'll drive them to school until they can ride the bus."

So I did.

They were eight when I grounded Jimmy for forgetting a chore, and they informed me they now had a punishment sharing agreement. When I told them I'd never heard of such a thing, Mikie said, "Yeah, Ma, that's because we just invented it."

"Your turn," Jimmy would say, and Mikie would take the punishment for something his brother had done. It nearly drove me crazy.

When I tried punishing both for something one of them had done, they cocked their heads, gave me their lopsided grins, and said together, "Ahh, Ma, that's not fair!" They were constantly whispering, planning, and getting smarter.

The day Mikie brought a brand-new backpack home, I said, "Where'd you get that? You didn't steal it, did you?"

They laughed hysterically, and Mikie said, "Ma, we'd be lousy thieves, but we're the best at working angles. Look at all the cool pockets. This one is much better than my old one."

The twins hid behind a flow of fast talk and excuses, Joey style. Of course, their father backed them up. "If they're smart enough to get it, they can keep it. Learning to skate on thin ice without falling in is good for them."

When they reached 7th grade, I stopped telling them to return things like a leather jacket, a signed baseball, or a camera.

Even Joey couldn't drive a wedge between them. When Mikie wrecked his bike, they made do with one, taking turns riding on the handlebars and giving me heartburn. Joey would have bought Mikie any bike he wanted, but they were happy sharing.

When the twins turned sixteen, Joey said he'd buy each of them a car. Mikie and Jimmy huddled, discussing his offer, and told Joey one car would be enough. They went to every car showroom within biking distance, spent hours studying brochures, and debated the pros and cons of every model.

When Joey offered them his advice, they said, "We got it covered, Dad, thanks anyway."

They agreed on a Shelby Mustang GT 500, and naturally, Joey got a good deal with extras thrown in. Mikie won the buck up over color, choosing dark moss green, and Jimmy picked the black leather upholstery.

They named the car Miss Clementine, and one or both were always polishing her. When Joey said Clementine was a ridiculous name for a car, they walked out the door and called, "Hey Ma, we're taking sweet Miss Clementine for a ride."

They were smart enough never to push Joey too far, and they got around me with smiles, sweet talk, and what I believed were good intentions. They explained their behavior with the most favorable interpretation, and all I could do was hope they were telling the truth.

When they gave me a dozen roses for my birthday, a purple silk scarf for Christmas, or a three-pound box of candy for Mother's Day, I asked where they got the money.

"We run errands, rake leaves, and shovel snow to help people out, Ma. You ought to be proud of how helpful we are!"

We named our firstborn Joseph John Barzetti, Jr. after Joey. Everybody called him JJ. He worshipped his dad, followed Joey around, and listened to everything his father told him. I never got calls about his behavior.

I was certain Kalayla's mama did not intend for her to run. I was never a young widow working two jobs and trying to keep track of a twelve-year-old daughter, but I knew that keeping track of kids was like chasing marbles going downhill. They kept on rolling, and you kept on running.

Somebody had to help Maureen. I didn't see anybody volunteering, which left it up to me.

HELPING THE OLD LADY

Old lady Lena was always sticking her nose in my business. That made me mad 'cause it reminded me how that jerk, Clarence, tried to butt into my life when Mama and I stayed with Grandma and Grandpa after Daddy died.

It took Grandma about fifteen seconds to enroll me in a school near them. On my second day, I was standing in the hall near my classroom when a fat-assed girl bumped into me.

"Hey, new kid," she said. "I heard your grandma told you to pass for black so you could get into a fancy private school next year. Right?"

I could've slammed my fist into her fat face, but I didn't. I could've asked her if she ate cow turds for breakfast, but I didn't. The bell rang, and I ducked into class without saying anything. I knew better than to make trouble at school, and I was used to comments from butthole kids.

When Uncle Clarence asked me how I liked the school, I made the mistake of telling him what the kid said.

He cracked up laughing. "If you ever decide to pass, Kalayla, pass for white. You'll be a beauty like your mama. A passel of dudes would pay plenty to get their hands on her creamy white skin. Your skin isn't white, but it sure is a sweet chocolate!" He was still laughing when he went out the front door.

Clarence's mouth was worse than mine, but if I told Mama that, she would've said, "Clarence is your only uncle. You should treat him with respect."

I'd rather have no uncle than a turd like him, but if I said that, Mama would make me sit in the corner facing the wall. I hated that more than I hated shutting my mouth.

I wouldn't have put up with the old lady, but she was a good cook. The first time she invited me for dinner was after I went to Mickey's for her. She said, "If you get any skinnier, you might disappear altogether."

Mama was working an extra shift, so I went. Pretty soon, I was going there all the time. I didn't bother telling her I learned to cook when I was a kid.

When Mama went to art school, she never cared how late we ate, if we ate the same thing every night, or if we ate at all. Her brain ignored her stomach, and so did Daddy's, but mine didn't.

When I complained to Daddy, he laughed and said, "That's why we have a refrigerator and stove, skinny girl. I better teach you to cook so you don't starve."

I decided I ought to get more than food for the work I was doing for the old lady. So, I said, "How come you don't pay me? Don't you have any money?"

She gave me one of her looks. "Haven't you heard of doing a good deed for the sake of helping another person?"

"I probably already earned my way into heaven. But it might be a long time before I get there, and I could use some cash now."

Lena looked out the window and tried to hide her smile.

"Well then," she grumbled, "I better put you on retainer."

"Retainer? What's that?"

"It means I pay you something now, and if your work is satisfactory, you get more later."

"Forget about later. What do I get now?"

"Twenty-five bucks."

She dug around in her purse and handed over the money. I didn't bother telling her I'd have taken ten.

Whenever I went to her place, I'd sneak a look at that photo on the beach and try to figure out why she looked so different. She reminded me of the silverware from Daddy's family that Mama made me polish for the holidays. Mama stored it in soft cloth bags, but the silver still turned dull and looked neglected.

That's how the old lady looked, but nothing would make her bright and shiny again.

CAMBRIDGE RESOURCES

When I was a kid, we lived in Watertown, and Lotta practically lived at our house. We'd beg my mother to make Dom and his friends take us when they went to Cambridge, and sometimes she did. We'd hang out near Harvard Square and get a Bartley's burger or Bailey's ice cream while the boys cruised around looking for somebody who'd buy them a six-pack or three back then.

Nowadays, boys aren't the only ones looking for trouble. Headstrong girls like Kalayla did whatever they pleased. I wore out my brain trying to think of something that would keep her off the streets and away from that damn Clean Duds. I was afraid some lowlife might see her there and decide she'd be easy pickings.

Classes at the library were free, but Kalayla was too old for Story Time and too young for films or book discussion groups. I made a few calls about the summer crafts and sports programs and discovered most of them had a fee. Maureen didn't have extra money, but I'd take care of that if Kalayla were willing to do something besides guard laundry.

The day was sunny and seventy-three degrees, so I got my coffee and was at Clean Duds before 10 a.m. Kalayla was reading a book with her feet propped up as usual.

She looked up and said, "Hey Lena, were you giving your legs a rest yesterday?"

"I was minding my own business, which you'd benefit from doing. You're turning into a couch potato with no couch. Most kids would rather play sports than lounge in a boring place like this."

Kalayla gave me a dirty look. "Sports? You mean, like, be on a team with a bunch of jerks?"

Wouldn't you know she ruled out team sports before I could give her my sales pitch? No matter, she wouldn't derail my train now that I got it going.

"You could play tennis," I said. "If you were good enough, you could play singles. Singles, as in by yourself against one other person."

"I know what singles is! Why'd I waste my time chasing a stupid ball around? Why don't you suggest something interesting? If you had a gun hidden in one of your white rooms, you could teach me how to shoot."

I took a deep breath, trying to stay calm. That girl had no idea how much she sounded like one of my twins, and she picked one thing I could teach her if I had a mind to, which I sure as hell did not.

Joey loved guns, and the twins begged to see them. A week didn't go by without Joey unlocking the footlocker, lifting out one of his precious and caressing it like a lover.

He introduced the boys to shooting the day they turned eight, the age limit for the Highland Gun Club. They started with pistols like I did. Benchrest rifles came next, and when they were strong enough, shotguns. I didn't care for the heavier guns, so I stuck with the pistol.

Joey pushed me to compete. "You can beat the ass off any of the women, Lena. We'd be the first husband and wife champions!"

I gave in, and we won both titles four years in a row. Joey was the only one I wanted to beat, and I never did.

There was no point in wasting more time in the Clean Duds oven. Kalayla vetoed sports and I was not teaching her to shoot.

When I turned and walked toward the door, Kalaya said, "Is it too hot in here today?"

The following day, I saw her across the street talking to one of the locals, Ray Ray Bingha, who was six feet five inches tall and had two hundred and fifty pounds of muscle. His dark-brown hair was in a ponytail that trailed four inches down his back, but nobody teased him about having a girly hairdo or the two gold earrings in his left ear.

You never saw Ray Ray without Thor, his enormous bullmastiff. You didn't need a "Beware of Dog" sign to warn you that Thor would rip out your throat if Ray Ray gave the signal.

Ray Ray and I were on good terms, but there was no guarantee his patience would last if Kalayla got her mouth going. I beat it across that street as fast as my legs could.

"Ray Ray!" I called as I stopped at the curb to catch my breath.

"Well, Miss Lena," he grinned. "I haven't seen you in quite some time. I thought you might've dropped dead and been buried."

"I'm not in the habit of trolling the streets like you, Ray Ray. Don't worry. You'll know when I die. My son, JJ, will hire a band and invite the whole city to celebrate! I came to warn you this girl has allergic fits when she gets close to dogs. You better keep Thor away from her."

As usual, Kalayla shifted her mouth into high gear without thinking.

"Where'd you get such a dumb idea, Lena? I love dogs!"

"Whatever," Ray Ray said, laughing. "I just explained to this little girl that Thor isn't interested in being her friend."

"I'm not a little girl, and I don't want Thor for a friend 'cause he'd probably drool all over me!"

I swear I could have slapped that girl's face!

Contrary to what she said, Kalayla reached out to pet Thor. Ray Ray's soft "Don't!" froze her hand mid-air.

"The only way Thor'd find you likable would be as an appetizer for his dinner. Don't worry, Miss Lena. He won't bother this funny little thing. She hasn't got enough meat on her to make it worthwhile."

With that, Ray Ray and Thor strolled down Mass. Ave.

Kalayla put her hands on her hips and stamped her foot. "Why'd you run over here, Lena? And why'd you tell that guy I'm allergic to dogs?"

"I must have dreamed it," I said, taking her arm like I needed something to lean on. "I want you to help sort some books in my storage bin."

I took deep breaths all the way home. That girl had no more sense than a bug, but covering her mouth with duct tape wouldn't help. Ray Ray likely had more than one gun tucked away, and if Kalayla ran into him again and the subject came up, teaching her to shoot might give him a laugh.

I needed to consult with Lotta, but first, I had research to do.

***

Cambridge was a good-sized city, but it was like a woman's handbag with different compartments of different sizes. Information about Kalayla's family was tucked in one of them, and I knew how to find it.

The members of the Ladies Knitting Club were townies who took great pride in sharing their hoard of information. Not all the members were born in Cambridge, but they grew up nearby. They knew more than a person needed to about the rivalries, tragedies, and trivia of every family in town based on a combination of facts and gossip.

The group boasted it was open to new members, which was something of a joke because you had to know somebody who knew somebody to get in. I never was a knitter and didn't plan on becoming one, but I wasn't worried about being welcomed. I'd drop a few snippets about the Manero-Barzetti clan, most of which would be pure fabrication.

The ability to tell good tales while keeping family secrets was a highly prized skill in my family. When we were kids, Nana and Mama taught us to play one note and make it sound like the whole orchestra.

While the ladies dug in their knitting, I circled the room and admired their fine handiwork. I eventually remarked that a girl named Kalayla and her mama had moved in across the hall from me, and the ladies fell all over themselves to tell me what they knew.

Maureen's husband, Jamal LeeRoyce, came from an established black family in a mixed-race Cambridge neighborhood. They were community-minded Protestants, especially Jamal's mother, Lucinda. She ran a soup kitchen for their church and occasionally took in stray kids. She was active when it came to rights for blacks. In the days of forced busing, she argued it was a lose-lose situation, and if Judge Garrity took the time to visit Roxbury and South Boston, he'd understand that.

The ladies thought the younger son, Clarence, had mental problems as a kid but was an excellent auto mechanic. The older son, Jamal, was intelligent, good in sports, and went to UMass Boston on a scholarship. He'd died while drag-racing a few years ago.

When I said Maureen's family must have helped her when her husband died, the ladies set me straight. What they told me was close to unbelievable, and I needed time to let it sink in before I went to see Lotta.

BEST FRIENDS

Carlotta Eccli had been my best friend forever. Her approach to life was straightforward, with no gray areas, and she thought my approach was incomprehensible. Lotta pointed out that I stayed married to a vicious bastard, refused to dye my hair, and insisted on wearing black, like a corpse, in search of a coffin. To top it off, I lived in a fourth-floor walk-up apartment even though I could afford a penthouse at the Ritz.

I could count on Lotta no matter what. In addition, she was a fabulous cook, so I invited myself to dinner that night. Her house was a half-mile walk from the apartment and helped me stay in shape. Even Lotta admitted I hadn't loaded on fat like so many of our high school classmates.

Lotta's house was in a Cambridge neighborhood that boasted yards with trees, shrubs, and lawns. Her neighbors were not pleased when she had a five-foot-high chain-link fence installed in her backyard. "Well," she told them, "would you prefer dogs running free and shitting all over your lawn?" That was the last she heard from them on that subject.

Lotta redecorated on the spur of the moment, but nothing had changed since my previous visit. Her kitchen was black and white, the living room and dining room pale aqua and the furniture was a Scandinavian design from Form in Teak.

We were finishing the Coq au Vin and buttery noodles when I said, "Did I tell you I went to the last meeting of the Ladies Knitting Club?"

Lotta clanked her fork on her plate. "Now, why would you do something so outrageous and act like it's normal? You do not knit, have never knitted, and will never knit. Besides, all they do is gossip."

"That's why I went. I'm trying to help a fatherless child and her hard-working, widowed mother. I needed to find out a few things. What's for dessert?"

Lotta rolled her eyes. "Mocha squares drizzled with almond sauce. What were you so hot to find out?"

"The mama told me a story that smelled like dead fish, and her daughter is wandering around Cambridge like it's her playground. You know how dangerous that can be."

"Mother, daughter, dead fish? Lena, please explain in plain English."

"Fine! Maureen is the mother, and Kalayla is her daughter. They moved into the apartment across the hall from me. When I asked Maureen about her family, she changed the subject so fast that my head spun. That seemed odd, so I asked the girl about her mama's family.

"Kalayla told me the entire family died in an explosion at a party in Brighton before she was born. I don't remember that. Do you?"

"A story like that would have been plastered on every TV station and the front page of *The Globe*, *The Herald*, and all the rags. We couldn't have missed it!"

"We didn't. Maureen was lying," I said, taking a bite of mocha square.

"That's ridiculous! Why would she?"

"I got the whole history. Maureen's grandmother and mother moved from Belfast, Ireland, to South Boston to be with family when the grandfather died. Maureen's mother moved to Brighton when she got married and that's where Maureen grew up.

"Maureen was one of four children, the family star, a straight-A student, popular and beautiful with green eyes, red hair, and a movie actress figure. She was supposed to become a nurse and marry an Irish boy named Paul O'Brien, whose father owned a law business. At least, that was her mother's plan."

"Ha! We all know how those plans work out. Did Maureen suck it up and go along like you did?"

I gave her a dirty look. "No, she didn't. She fell in love with a black boy from a Protestant family and married him!"

"Oh, my God!" Lotta's mouth dropped open. She stood up, leaned over the table, and repeated, "Oh my God!"

I had to laugh.

"Right!" I said. "Maureen's mother disowned her and hasn't met her granddaughter! Can you believe that?"

Lotta flopped down in her chair. Such a thing was as unimaginable to her as it was to me. She and I came from close-knit Italian-Catholic families. No matter what we did, our families would never turn away from us. Lotta was twice divorced, didn't want children, and had casual relationships with men, but her parents stood by her. She wasn't the critical pawn in the family's business as I had been.

"What a vicious woman!" Lotta said. "And the rest of the family went along with her! But why in hell did Maureen lie? You know as well as I do her daughter will find out, and Maureen will have hell to pay! That woman is a loony tune. Do not open the door if she comes knocking, and do not give her or her daughter another thought!"

I took a sip of coffee and set my cup down carefully. "Funny that you would say that. You never once turned your back on an abused or abandoned animal, even when it caused you a boatload of problems."

Lotta drove her parents crazy, bringing stray or hurt animals home. She now owned the most respected and best-run animal shelter in Cambridge and the surrounding towns.

Lotta sighed. "It is not the same. Animals can't help themselves. People can. You've got a burr in your side over this, and nothing I say will change your mind. How do you plan to help?"

"Maureen works at Eddie's. When one of his regular girls quit, I asked him to put her on the days and give her a raise so she wouldn't have to take cleaning jobs. Kalayla is a disaster waiting to happen, and I have no idea what to do."

We cleared the table and loaded the dishwasher. Finally, Lotta said, "I'll make fresh coffee. Tell me what you tried that didn't work."

Relief flooded me. "Kalayla refuses to play sports and has no interest in art or any crafts. She hangs out at Clean Duds or roams around alone."

"That's not good, not good at all."

While Lotta continued puttering, I settled into a living room chair. Lotta always thought about every possibility before she did anything. In the late 1940s, girls didn't leave their marriage via a back door, but Lotta did. When she caved into family pressure and married, she convinced her boyfriend they should have a civil ceremony at Watertown City Hall. She knew the Catholic Church didn't recognize marriages performed by a Justice of the Peace.

Her parents were furious and insisted that she and Stan have a proper wedding, but Lotta was already maneuvering out that back door. Stan's idea of a good time was slapping her around, and she wasn't about to put up with that. Her younger brother, Mattwo, had a heavyweight influence in her family, and Lotta went to him for help. He convinced Stan that an annulment would be his best option.

Two years later, Lotta married Jeff Procopio in a civil ceremony. In less than a month, she decided Jeff's romantic gifts and sappy notes were an irritation rather than a blessing. Mattwo again came to her rescue, and Jeff departed. No one in Lotta's family mentioned marriage to her again.

I heard the soft hum of the dishwasher. Lotta handed me a coffee mug, flopped on the sofa, and curled her legs under her.

"Maybe we'll get lucky and find out the girl has as much sense as a cat or a dog," she said.

I laughed, "So, what do you think?"

Lotta stared at me for a full minute before saying, "You won't like the idea, but I think Matty's Way is worth a try. Going there worked for your twins; no sane person would have said they were easy to control."

I came close to spilling my coffee. What was I thinking? Of course, Lotta would suggest Matty's Way.

Lotta's father started Matty's Way as a dojo for judo and karate in the 1920s. When he retired, Lotta's brother, Mattwo, took over and added aerobic and strength training classes. His son, Lotta's nephew, Rico, was next in line to run the gym.

Mikie and Jimmy loved the challenge and competition of karate. Matty's Way got them off the streets, and both earned black belts. The twins' ghosts haunted me enough without me returning to their favorite place. I never planned to go there again, but that wasn't the only reason. I didn't want to run into Mattwo.

Mattwo was in love with me in high school, but I said no to him and married Joey. I never stopped wondering what my life would have been if I'd said yes to him. I'd seen him at Eccli family parties over the years, and I still felt shy around him.

Joey must have sensed that I had feelings for Mattwo because he took every opportunity to put him down. He made fun of his name, Matthew Eccli II, which had morphed into Mattwo.

"Matt Two, get it?" Joey said. "Number two, because the only thing that comes out of him is shit."

Mattwo didn't spend his life waiting for me. He married Angi Santano, and they raised a family. Angi died four years ago, and every chance she got, Lotta told me I was a fool for not calling him.

Lotta thought getting in touch with Mattwo would be as easy as baking cookies, but it wasn't. It was a massive deal to me. Once I decided to call him, I spent the rest of the day and a sleepless night deciding what to say.

48 HOURS LATER

The walk to Matty's Way was shorter when I was younger. The closer we got, the slower my feet moved.

We were almost there when Kalayla said, "What's the matter? Do your feet hurt? We should've taken one of those taxis you love. If you weren't so cheap, you'd buy a car, and I could drive you around."

Just what I needed—a twelve-year-old chauffeur!

"Stop complaining," I said. "It's about time you did something to earn that retainer. Anyway, Matty's Way is in the next block."

Kalayla didn't need to know it wasn't my feet that hurt. It was my heart.

Memories of the twins swirled around me, sucking me into an emotional quicksand. A kaleidoscope of shifting images bombarded me. Mikie and Jimmy were in their bright white uniforms, arguing about who would graduate to the next belt, demonstrating combinations of moves, or proudly holding up trophies.

Mattwo said his son, Rico, would meet with Kalayla and me, which meant he wasn't anxious to see me himself. I was half-century too late if I was hoping to rekindle a romance with him.

The sign above Matty's Way door was dark grey with bright gold lettering. The building had undergone a facelift with a second-story addition. The exterior was painted light grey instead of dull brown.

I looked up and down the block and saw that the neighborhood had become a yuppie haven. Colors, designs, and signs were similar, a smart-looking, up-scale example of the city's neighborhood renewal program. Manzetti Properties had done the rehab, and JJ supervised the project five years ago.

The funny thing was the changes made me feel less off-balance. My memories hadn't changed, but what I saw had no relationship to that past life.

As I stopped to stare, Kalayla bumped into me.

"Cripes, Lena, what's the matter with you? This place must be freaking you out. Don't worry. I'll protect you." She darted ahead, held one of the glass doors, bowed, and waited for me to walk through.

I walked into a welcoming expanse of creamy white walls with spring-green woodwork that had replaced beige walls and dark wood. Rico waited for us at the check-in counter.

"Hi, Miss Lena. Good to see you again," he said.

My heart skipped a beat. Rico was the mirror image of Mattwo when we were in high school: six feet of muscular build, curly dark brown hair and eyes, and an open, honest face.

"I've brought Kalayla, Kalayla, this is—."

The girl was beside me, but she turned and walked away before I finished my sentence. To my horror, she began strutting like a blown-up peacock, showing off for a mate. She scattered brochures across the check-in counter, walked behind it, and stuck her head into each office.

Rico stared at her, likely wondering if she was an alien from Mars, and I didn't blame him. What had gotten into that girl?

Rico turned to me and said, "Miss Lena, this can't be the girl you mentioned to my dad. He said she was a loner who needed some structure. This kid is spoiling for a fight."

"Well, there's only one Kalayla, and you're looking at her. This behavior is way beyond her normal smart-ass routine."

And, of course, Kalayla looked like the part she was playing. She wore the usual baseball cap visor backward, red-plaid high-top Keds without laces, baggy-blue shorts covered in yellow butterflies, and a navy-blue drapery cord to hold them up. A Hawaiian-flowered shirt over a pink cami completed her outfit.

Kalayla pranced to the trophy cases and pressed her nose against the glass. When she turned to look at Rico, I saw her fingerprints and nose on the glass.

Kalayla said, "I get why the old lady dragged me here. You're going to teach me how to kick the shit out of the butthole kids at school. It's about time somebody taught me something useful."

Maybe Lotta was right. I was off my rocker to try and help Kalayla.

Rico walked over to her. I doubt he planned to slap her face, but I sure felt like doing that.

Rico looked at her, took a deep breath, and said, "Miss Lena brought you here out of the goodness of her heart, and this is how you thank her? Shame on you! The only thing anybody needs to teach you is manners. I imagine your parents tried, but they failed."

I sucked in my breath. There was no way in hell this could end well.

It didn't. Kalayla did something my boy, Mark, would have done without thinking of consequences or stopping unless somebody made him stop.

Kalayla put her head down and charged. Rico held her off with one arm, dodged her fists, and easily avoided her kicks until she wore herself out.

Slumped over and panting, she said, "Take it back, you butthole. Take it back!"

I didn't have a clue what she wanted him to take back. I'd told her she needed to learn manners at least fifty times, and she never flipped into a rage. Did she think he was criticizing her mama and her daddy?

Rico said, "Listen, Kalayla, the fact you lost control is no reason for me to take anything back. You repaid Miss Lena's kindness by acting like a jerk. I doubt your parents would be proud of what you just did. You need to apologize."

In less time than it took me to blink, Kalayla stuck her tongue at him, gave him the finger, and stomped out the door.

Kalayla was halfway down the block, and I yelled for her to wait. I thought she'd ignore me, but she didn't. She stood with her hands clenched at her sides and an expression on her face that would have frightened the neighborhood ghoul.

Neither of us said a word on the walk home. Street noise echoed around us, filling in the silence. My grand plan had backfired, but that was nothing new.

I never knew how to handle Mark when his temper exploded. He'd get into fights over something as small as how a kid looked at him. He got into four serious fights before Christmas during his first year in high school. The school administrators planned to expel him. Joey convinced them everything would be fine if Mark went to a different school where he could get a new start.

I didn't point out that attending high school was supposed to be Mark's new start. Mark transferred and managed to graduate with his class.

I hoped Mark had learned to control his temper, but there were three separate incidents of boys who an unknown assailant attacked. None of the boys could or would identify their attacker.

When I asked Mark if he knew what had happened, he said, "Nothing to know, Ma. The kid was running off at the mouth; now his jaw's wired. Good joke, huh?"

No one accused Mark, but in my heart, I wondered if he'd done what Joey likely taught him and the other boys to do: take their anger underground.

I did what I could, but they were Joey's boys. My family said I had to play the cards I'd been dealt, and Joey held all the aces.

Here I was again, trying to help a child and failing, but I couldn't; I wouldn't give up.

SELLING COOKIES

I was teaching that old lady not to mess in my life. I hadn't talked to her in more than a week and didn't plan to anytime soon. When I saw her coming my way, I went in the opposite direction. If she came into Clean Duds, I acted like she was invisible.

Then, yesterday, she almost bumped into me when she was coming out of Mickey's Market, and I was going in.

Before I could turn away, she said, "Don't you know it's impolite to ignore somebody just because you're mad at them?"

Why couldn't she have said hello instead of launching into a lecture? I'd have given her a shove, but she would've fallen over, and I'd be stuck calling 911. The old crab would tell them I pushed her, and they'd call Mama and make a big deal over nothing.

"I don't have to talk to you if I don't want to, and I don't want to."

"Nobody said you have to talk to me. All you have to do is listen. I'm sorry I didn't tell you why we went to Matty's Way. That was a mistake. I thought you'd say no like you did to everything else. I'm afraid you'll get hurt if you keep roaming around this city alone. That's why I did what I did."

Lena stopped talking, turned away from me, and walked down the street slower than usual. Her hip must've been bothering her, which served her right for going behind my back and acting like I was one of those needy kids my grandma takes in.

If the old crab told me that, I might've surprised her. I wouldn't mind learning how to kick butts.

I found out one thing by going to that gym. Lena's twins won a boat-load of trophies for karate. Why didn't she brag about them? And why'd she always wear black? That old crab was hiding something, and I was going to find out what before she did something dumb like croak on me.

***

When that jerk, Clarence, stopped on Sunday afternoon with three dozen boxes of cookies, I decided to sell them. Lena would be my first customer. She'd be so thrilled I was talking to her that she'd buy a few boxes.

I gave her my best smile when she opened her door. "Hey, Miss Lena," I said, "You know how folks support the Girl Scouts by buying their cookies? I've got four different kinds, but the chocolate-covered mints are the best. Would you like a sample?"

"You better bring them in so I can take a good look," she said. "Exactly when did you become a Girl Scout? And why are you suddenly calling me Miss Lena?"

Why'd she and Mama make a big deal out of everything? It'd be their fault if I turned into a full-time liar!

"I didn't say they were Girl Scout cookies, but they're good enough to be."

"The first thing out of your mouth was about the Girl Scouts, which makes me wonder if you're trying to con people out of their hard-earned money. Where'd you get these cookies? And don't tell me you found them on the sidewalk."

I would've thrown a box of cookies at her and stomped out the door, but I wasn't letting her cheat me out of earning money!

"Somebody gave them to Clarence," I said. "He told me with my gift for gab, I'd sell them quick as anything. I don't have to give him a percentage."

"Humph! I imagine your uncle knows a lot about selling things he somehow got for free. I also imagine he said that you'd be good at reeling in a sucker with your smart mouth. Let me try one of those samples."

I almost bit through my lip to keep from telling her my smart mouth could outsmart her.

"As long as you're here, you might as well sit and have a few," she said after buying four boxes.

I wasn't turning down a good snack, but if that old lady acted like a jerk again, I'd stop being nice to her. Then, she'd be sorry!

MAUREEN O'ROURKE LEEROYCE

JAMAL

I stared into the bathroom mirror, turning my face one way and the other. I didn't see any wrinkles or brown spots, but what would happen in October when I turned thirty? I groaned. Would I spend the rest of my life searching for signs of decay?

This birthday would be so different if Jamal were alive. He would have teased me out of feeling I was free-falling into middle age.

Jamal chose a scary adventure for his thirtieth birthday. "Come with me, sweet babe," he said. "We'll jump out of a plane, float through the clouds, and hold hands on the way down."

I couldn't resist his gorgeous brown eyes and gentle coaxing. Besides, jumping out of a plane wasn't nearly as terrifying as how I felt when I met him at the beginning of my senior year in high school. My best friend, Katie, was dating a high jumper, and on the last Saturday in September, we went to a five-town meet to watch him compete.

There was a ceremony to induct previous graduates into the district-wide Athletic Hall of Fame, and Jamal was that year's honoree. All four years at Cambridge Rindge and Latin, Jamal had won every event he entered, from sprints to long-distance runs. Katie and I got seats in the front row, and Jamal sat on the platform near the podium. I couldn't stop glancing at him, and he was staring at me, too.

I felt the heat on my face and knew I was blushing. The athletic director called Jamal's name. I'd never met anyone named Jamal. The muscles in his brown arms rippled, and his movement to the podium was smooth and graceful. If he'd been a white boy, I would have nudged Katie and whispered that he was sexy.

When the program was over, Jamal pushed through the crowd and stood in front of me, not closer than was proper but nowhere near close enough.

"Hey," he said, his voice low, a magnet drawing me in, "What would a guy like me have to do if he wanted to get to know a girl like you?"

My heart was a kettle drum pounding the way romance novels said it would when you met your true love. I longed to reach out and touch him. I told myself to turn and walk away like my mother would expect me to.

I grew up in an Irish Catholic neighborhood in Brighton. My mother volunteered at our church, helped run programs at the town library, chaired the garden club's Brighton Beautification Committee, and was active in the Parents/Teachers Association. We were the perfect family without any warts or wrinkles.

My two older sisters and brother were content playing their good-doobie roles. I wasn't. I didn't plan to be a carbon copy. But inviting a black boy into our lives was more provocative than saying I intended to be an artist. My mother would say I was purposely setting off an incendiary device in our living room.

My parents never mentioned race, and neither did their friends, but when a house near us sold, everyone knew the new residents would be white. My mother didn't care about skin color, but she cared mightily about what the neighbors thought.

Katie went to find Johnny while Jamal, patient and relaxed, waited for my answer. I willed myself to tell him there was nothing he could do because there was no way he would ever get to know me.

But the words wouldn't come. The invitation in his eyes spellbound me, and I didn't see why I should turn it down. Our parish priests and nuns taught that Jesus loved everyone and we should treat others the way we wanted them to treat us.

The crowd thinned, and a guy from the clean-up crew stacked the chairs on the podium, occasionally glancing in our direction.

We couldn't stand there forever.

I reached deep inside, pulling out the words, "He'd have to ask."

Jamal's laugh was deep, and he slapped his hand on his thigh. "That's all? I wouldn't have to slay a dragon, find a treasure, or fight off the thundering hoards to prove I was worthy of you? I might do that if you asked me to, especially if your smile was my reward."

I blushed and giggled, charmed by his boldness.

"I'm Jamal LeeRoyce," he said. "How about going for a coffee? A couple of friends of mine went to Boston University. We used to meet at a little coffee place near here."

I imagined the excitement I'd feel walking off the field with him, getting into his car, sitting next to him. I imagined my mother's reaction.

"It's okay," he said. "I won't take you anywhere you don't want to go."

Jamal didn't move closer or touch my arm as I thought he might. He simply stood, patiently waiting. If I said no, I was sure he would say, "Okay, then," and walk away without looking back.

The risk of saying yes was irresistible. I couldn't be the clone my mother wanted.

I took a deep breath. "I'm Maureen O'Rourke."

Jamal waited near the stands while I found Katie. She and Johnny were joking around with a group of friends. When I told her, she grabbed my arm, pulled me away from the others, and whispered, "How are you getting home?"

When I didn't answer, she sucked in her breath, squeezed my arm so hard it hurt. "You're not going with that black kid, are you?"

I didn't answer.

"Holy shit, Maureen! That'll be around the neighborhood in thirty seconds!"

"Katie, please, I'm not doing anything wrong. All you need to tell my mother is that I got a ride home with somebody else. Don't turn it into a big deal."

Katie dropped my arm and said, "It is a big deal, Maureen. You're sticking your hand in a hornet's nest. Call me when you change your mind, and I'll come get you."

I didn't change my mind.

Neither Jamal nor I talked much on the way to the Coffee Grinds. Knowing I'd crossed the line into unknown territory was scary and intoxicating.

The lighting in the Grinds was low, and artwork was visible on every wall. Geometric mobiles hung from the ceiling. High tables with stools faced the windows that looked onto Huntington Ave., with round tables for two or four scattered around the room. The side wall had a counter with a glass snack case filled with brownies, muffins, and scones, with coffee choices on the wall behind it.

Jamal smiled. "This is a haven for the arty types. You can hang a painting on the back wall with the owner's permission. My friends say that's a big honor."

I told Jamal how much I loved art and was applying to the Rhode Island School of Design even though my mother wanted me to attend Boston University's nursing school.

No one paid attention to us when we sat near the window. We wandered from one subject to another like old friends catching up. I lost track of time until Jamal cocked his head and said, "Is there a particular time when you need to be home?"

I glanced at my watch and flinched. "Oh my gosh, it's 8:00!" I grabbed my jacket. "I have to go! Is there a bus to Brighton from here?"

Jamal shook his head. "Not that I know of, but I can take you home."

I wanted to say okay, but Katie was right. My family would be the headline for the neighbor's gossip page. My mother thought black people should fight for their rights the way the Irish nationalists were, but she wouldn't take on the neighbors no matter what the cause.

I said, "I don't think that would be a good idea. I mean, I need to talk to my mother first."

Jamal grimaced. "I get it, but I hope this doesn't mean I won't see you again. I can drive you to Newton Corner, and you can catch a bus on Waverly or call someone to pick you up there. Will that work?"

I nodded. I wanted to see Jamal again, but I needed time to think. "I'll call you," I said.

"That's fair enough, but call no matter what you decide, so I'm not left wondering."

My mother met me at the door with questions I wasn't ready to answer. I clutched my stomach, groaned, and went upstairs to bed. The next day, I played sick, hiding in my room to avoid Katie at church and the family at meals. I couldn't stop imagining Jamal's warm smile, the way he cocked his head when he was thinking, his strong hands holding the coffee cup.

Jamal graduated from UMass and was a researcher at a respected tech company that invented medical devices. Both his parents were college graduates. But the neighbors would only care that his family wasn't white, and the fallout would freak my mother out.

All of us kids had seen our mother seesaw between depression and hyper-spirits. If I went out with Jamal and decided he wasn't for me, I'd have gotten her and everyone else upset for nothing. I decided not to say anything until I was sure how I felt.

Sneaking out to see Jamal turned into an irresistible game. I'd take the bus and meet him for a late lunch or coffee at Faneuil Hall. We'd walk around Boston Common, visit a museum, or stroll down Newbury Street to explore art exhibits.

Instead of wanting to see less of Jamal, I longed for more time with him. I wanted Katie and Johnny to get to know him, but she said, "You can lie to your parents all you want, but I won't be part of it."

Katie's words ate at me. I hadn't lied, but I let my mother assume I was with Katie when I wasn't.

We were at the Grinds when Jamal mentioned that his parents were active in their Protestant church. I didn't know what to say or do. I felt like I'd been punched in the stomach.

My mother told us Ireland was divided into two sections in the early 1920s. My mother's family was part of the Catholic minority in Northern Ireland, which was primarily Protestant and remained part of Great Britain. The rest of the country, the Irish Free State, had a larger Catholic population and was independent of Britain.

When I told my mother dividing the country didn't solve anything because Catholics and Protestants were still killing each other, she was furious.

"That shows how ignorant you are, Maureen! You have no idea how complicated it is. You have no idea what it's like to be constantly terrified!"

"Is that why you and grandma left? Why didn't Grandpa come with you?"

My mother gritted her teeth as if she resented uttering each word. "My father died. My mother and I left because we had to."

"Why?" I said.

"Because we had to! That's all you need to know! Don't ask me any more questions!"

Jamal and his family had nothing to do with protestants in Ireland. I hoped my mother would see what a good person he was. But my mother ran into Katie and Johnny the following Saturday afternoon at the mall. When she asked them where I was, Johnny said, "Not with us, that's for sure. Maureen doesn't have time for Katie anymore."

When I came into the house that night, my mother lost it. She screamed, "Katie tried to hush Johnny up, but she admitted she hadn't seen you for a month. She said you'd been spending time with a black boy! Everyone in the neighborhood knew what you were doing except your family, didn't they? Can you imagine how mortified I was?"

By then, I was crying and feeling so guilty that I'd kept Jamal a secret that I blurted out he was Protestant.

My mother reacted hysterically, "Everyone knew that, too, didn't they? They'll shun us or worse. Don't you know that?"

When I tried to explain to Daddy, he said, "You've always been a rebel, Maureen. But you should have respected your mother enough to tell her what you were doing. You could have come to me. You better think very carefully about what you do next and what the consequences will be."

I had been inching away from being the daughter my mother wanted long before Jamal came into my life. I didn't want to be a nurse. I didn't intend to marry the O'Brien boy. And no matter how much I hurt and disappointed my parents, I couldn't stop seeing Jamal.

My mother's rage was unrelenting. "We used to be safe, but now we won't know who's waiting to hurt us. You're just like your grandfather! You only care about yourself!"

I had no idea why she said I was like my grandfather and had no way of finding out. My mother's rage turned to cold silence when I was home. I stayed out of the house as much as possible, and the chasm between us got deeper and broader.

***

My senior year was a roller coaster of joy with Jamal and despair at home. Katie and I lost touch, and I skipped the usual senior activities at school. I studied or spent time with Jamal. My father came to my graduation but left after I gave the valedictorian address.

Jamal opened his heart to me but didn't sugar-coat what would happen if we stayed together.

"You'll see sides of people you never imagined existed."

My graduation present to myself was to marry him, and my mother cut me off like a gangrenous limb. My mother's fear for her family was more important to her than my happiness.

I moved into Jamal's apartment, started classes at RISD, and sometimes we saw his family. I was shy about making new friends because I didn't know how they'd react to a mixed-race couple. I buried myself in art projects. And, to my shock, I became a fumbling, ill-prepared mother. Jamal teased me into laughing at my mistakes; most of all, he loved me.

My life fell apart when he died.

I knew I'd miss Jamal forever, but thought I'd stop missing my family. My mother would have thrown an enormous party for my thirtieth birthday and baked her orange crunch cake, the very best cake in the world. We'd take turns telling outrageous stories or jokes, interrupting each other like a fabulous jazz improvisation. Uncle Sean would play tunes on the Uilleann pipes to make us cry and urge us to dance.

I glanced at my watch. I was filling in on the early shift at Eddie's and had a cleaning job. My mother would never get over that, even though she taught me to clean. She'd assign me a room, and when I finished, she'd put on white gloves and wipe every surface, searching for dust or dirt.

"There's a proper way to do things, Maureen," she said. "Someday, you'll own a large house and hold your staff to this standard."

My father might laugh at the irony. But I couldn't let myself think about him.

Kalayla was my priority now. I would love her no matter what she did or who she wanted to marry.

MAUREEN'S STORY AND RICO'S CALL

After the fiasco at the gym, I sat at the kitchen table, consoling myself with a hunk of Lotta's chocolate raspberry cake when the phone rang.

"Miss Lena," Rico said, "I'm sorry about what happened this morning. Kalayla's got a chip on her shoulder, and I bumped into it."

"I was as shocked at her reaction as you were, Rico. But she's had a hard time. She lost her father, her mother works two jobs, and she doesn't have any friends."

"The thing is, Miss Lena, when a kid comes to the gym to learn a martial art, we've got to find out how they'll react under stress. When we push kids physically or emotionally, sometimes they turn to mush and blubber. Sometimes, they shove you back or taunt you. It's rare to find a kid who charges full throttle without giving any warning like Kalayla did. She's got acceleration but no brakes, which means somebody's left doing damage control."

Damage control. I had plenty of experience with that. Maybe that first day on the landing, I should have walked up the stairs without saying boo to Kalayla. I didn't, and I was in the middle of an alphabet soup filled with letters I couldn't turn into words.

"Your dad told me you offer more than martial arts now," I said. "Kalayla said no to everything I suggested, and I hoped she'd find something at the gym she liked."

"There might be, Miss Lena, but the thing is, she didn't want to find out what we offer."

What Rico said was true. Kalayla could bury the truth in a maze of lies when it suited her, but her reactions were as transparent as a newly washed window.

"Kalayla aimed to make a statement, and she didn't like how I responded. Some kids storm out but come back after they calm down. Some hang around out front, waiting for us to notice. Some bring a friend. A few are gone for good. Matty's Way isn't the place for Kalayla unless she decides it is."

"Rico, you've been saying the thing is this or the thing is that, but the most important thing is I've run out of ideas, and I was hoping you'd give me some."

"I wish I could. Kalayla needs to think before she reacts. Or, she'll get into more trouble than she can handle."

I do wish Rico hadn't said that. It's what I'd been thinking while stuffing my face with cake.

I'd tried many things in my time, but eating my way out of feeling helpless wasn't one of them. Good as that cake was, Lotta hadn't baked any solutions into it. I shoved it away.

I didn't see who'd help Kalayla if I gave up. All I could do was hope I'd succeed more with her than with my four boys.

I had high hopes for all my boys, especially my firstborn, JJ. He listened to me before he started working after school with his father.

I bought JJ a tennis racket when he turned ten. He went to the city courts and found people who showed him strokes and discussed strategy with him. He loved that sport more than he'd ever loved anything, and I encouraged him as much as I could. But I never heard him talking about tennis with his dad, and I never saw his tennis racket in the front hallway with his baseball glove and football.

The summer before JJ went to high school, the tennis coach came to the house one afternoon to talk with him. That's when everything changed.

"Ma," JJ said after the coach left, "Coach says I'll make varsity, and there's a chance I can play singles. He says colleges will be after me if I keep at it. Is that cool, or what?"

Joey sat at the kitchen table that night, having a scotch while I prepared dinner. JJ was glowing like a giant firefly lighting the room when he told his dad.

Joey listened silently, but his scowl was deafening. The light from JJ's fire dimmed bit by bit until every spark died.

"Your mother put the tennis bug in your ear, didn't she?" Joey said, then looked at me. "Didn't you, Lena? No son of mine is going to turn into a sissy who plays tennis. You'll play football, just like I did."

"But Dad," JJ said halfheartedly, "football practice has already started. It's too late."

I could hear the tears in JJ's voice, and I prayed he wouldn't cry in front of Joey.

"Don't worry," Joey told him. "I'll talk to Coach tomorrow."

I don't know how Joey made it happen, but JJ joined the team. He was the star quarterback in his junior and senior years, just like his dad.

More than a year later, I got the cleaning bug. I found a plastic bag in the back of JJ's bedroom closet hidden behind shoes, boots, and an accumulation of junk. I stared at the destruction inside the bag and realized I was looking at the remains of his tennis racket.

What would make a boy smash something he loved so much? If I were telling you about the JJ I tried to raise, I'd say he trashed his racquet along with his dream, but he didn't have the heart to throw it in the garbage. And I'd have cried. If I were telling you about the JJ that Joey raised, I'd say he was keeping it to remind himself he wasn't a mama's boy. And I'd have cried.

I hadn't been strong enough to buck Joey, but dealing with him taught me you can't succeed if you stop trying.

***

I decided talking to Kalayla's mama was a good place to hit the restart button. It was a typical mid-August day with high heat and humidity that caused a person to sweat. The forecaster predicted a thunderstorm and possible lightning. If I believed in weather as an omen, I'd have shelved the idea of solving problems that were none of my business. But I didn't.

I invited Maureen to my place for a neighborly chat. After she got comfortable on the sofa, I said, "I want to talk with you about Kalayla."

Maureen had a lot bottled up inside, and my remark popped the cork. She spewed words like a contestant in a speed-talking contest who was getting in as many words as possible before the buzzer sounded.

"Oh, Lena, I'm so glad. I always worry about whether I'm taking care of Kalayla like I should. I don't have much time for her. I had to get a job so we could move back to our apartment after my breakdown."

Maureen stopped for half a second. "Oh, I forgot you didn't know. I mean, how could you know? I haven't told anyone. I had a breakdown after Jamal died, and we had to live with my in-laws, and it was awful. Oh dear, I don't mean Lucinda and Harmon were awful, but it was awful because I felt paralyzed and couldn't do anything but—."

"Whoa, girl!" I said. "Slow down so this old brain can catch up."

"Oh, sorry." Maureen paused for five seconds and then charged on. "I had a breakdown, and Jamal's mother said we could live with them, and I wouldn't have to go to a hospital or a sanitarium.

"She enrolled Kalayla in a school near them. Kalayla hated that school, but she hated every school. Lucinda was good to us, but she is a terrifying person. If she ever came face to face with the devil, he'd turn and run."

I couldn't help laughing, and Maureen laughed, too. I decided to keep my mouth shut and listen.

"We lived there for three months. I spent most of the time curled up under the covers until Lucinda scared me into pulling myself together. She marched into the bedroom and said, 'Maureen, I have been patient with you because I know this has been a terrible shock. But you are not the only one who lost Jamal. Your daughter did, too. Have you forgotten about her? Harmon and I will raise Kalayla permanently if you don't assume your responsibility as her mother.'

"Can you imagine? I didn't dare say a word. Jamal said his mother never used threats. She told him or Clarence the consequences if their behavior continued, and she kept her word. When Lucinda walked out of the bedroom and closed the door, I was afraid she might be closing the door on me for good.

"I couldn't let them take Kalayla. You're a mother, Lena. You know I couldn't do that. I lost my family and Jamal, and I couldn't lose her, too."

I nodded. I didn't envy Lucinda for being the one who had to point out the obvious to Maureen.

"I got cleaned up and dressed as fast as possible. I went into the living room, and Clarence was sprawled on the sofa like he had nothing to do.

"When I asked him where Kalayla was, he snorted and said, 'Since when do you care?'

"I almost broke down because they thought I was a terrible mother, but I didn't. I had to prove they were wrong. I told Clarence I was going to take Kalayla home.

"He smirked. 'Kalayla is in school. My dear mother saw to that the day they brought you here. You haven't figured out how things work in this family, have you, Maureen? I'm the only one who gets to take up space and not give back. My mother gave you idleness credits when you moved here, but I'd guess your sudden interest in Kalayla is because she informed you you've used them up, right?'"

I shook my head. Maureen's description of Clarence confirmed my feeling that he wasn't trying to earn points as the uncle of the year.

"I went to Kalayla's school, picked her up, and took her back to our apartment. I froze when I opened the door. I felt lonely and frightened without Jamal, but Kalayla darted around me and ran to her room, so I had to go in, too. I realized how uprooted she'd been living in a new place, going to a new school with her father suddenly gone. Lucinda was right. I'd been preoccupied with my grief and hadn't thought about her."

"Was that when you got a job and moved?"

"I got the job immediately, but we didn't move until the apartment here became vacant. Eddie told me about it."

It was time for me to stop ignoring the elephant in Maureen's story. Otherwise, it might come strolling across the hall and move in with me.

"What about your family?"

Maureen pulled her knees close to her chest and buried her face in them without saying a word.

So, I asked again, "What about your family?"

Her voice was muffled, and my old ears strained to catch her words.

Maureen paused. "My mother said I'd betrayed the family. She'd always been paranoid about the neighbors, and I never understood why she was afraid of them. I assumed she was punishing me for not obeying her but would get over it and forgive me. She didn't. My mother disowned me when I married Jamal."

"When I found out I was pregnant, I was sure she'd want to know about her grandchild. Jamal warned me not to get my hopes up, and he was right. I was too scared to go to the house, so I called. When my mother answered, I blurted out the news. At first, she didn't say anything. Then, she said, 'I don't have a daughter named Maureen,' and she hung up."

I'd heard the story from the knitters, but listening to them was easier than listening to that girl's heartbreak. Maureen was older than Kalayla but just as much in need of a mama.

When I put my arm around her, she started crying, and so did I. The two of us must have been a real sight.

After our tears dried up, I said, "Why does Kalayla think your family is dead?"

Maureen groaned. "Because that's what I told her. I knew I'd have to tell her the truth, but I didn't know what to say. How could I tell her my mother disowned me and refused to acknowledge her granddaughter?

"When Kalayla was little, she didn't ask. She wasn't a chatterbox, and she took in everything around her. When she was four, we'd just returned home from Christmas breakfast at Jamal's parents. I unhooked her seat belt, and she squirmed out of the car without help. She looked adorable in a bright red snowsuit and red and green plaid snow boots.

"She stood beside me while I gathered presents from the trunk, her eyes intense and focused as she said, 'Do you have a mama and daddy?'

"Her question sucked the air out of my lungs. When I didn't answer, she tugged my arm and said, 'Mama!'

"Well, of course I do, Layla. Everybody does."

"She said, 'I'm going to build a snowman before we go to their house, okay?'

"She jumped up and down, kicked snow with her new boots, laughing, impatient to be off. 'Okay?' she said again.

"I didn't think about what to say. The words came out of nowhere as if they had a will of their own. It was like I'd pressed start on a recording and didn't know how to pause or stop it.

"We can't go to their house, Layla. My mother and father are dead. My parents were giving your daddy and me a wedding party, but your daddy and I were caught in traffic and were late. There was an explosion in the reception hall, and my whole family died."

"'Okay, I'm going to build my snowman,' Kalayla said as she stomped off, scattering snow with each step.

"Jamal walked past me into the house, and I followed him. He was in the living room, pacing slowly. He was always strong and capable, but at that moment, he looked defeated. He said quietly, 'Why would you tell our precious daughter such an outrageous lie?'

"I felt guilty and stupid and couldn't bear to see the disappointment in Jamal's face. I told him Kalayla only wanted to build her snowman and probably didn't hear me.

"Jamal stared at me in disbelief. 'Kalayla hears everything! You've had five years to think about what to say. Kalayla will believe anything you tell her. I get that you never understood how your parents could disown you, and I get that you are obsessed with the idea that they will change. But at some point, Kalayla will ask more questions, and you'll have to explain what your parents did and why you lied.'

"Jamal went out the door, and hours went by with no word from him. I was afraid to call his parents or Clarence. I was frantic. That night at dinner, when Kalayla asked where Daddy was, I told her he'd be home soon and would kiss her goodnight even if she was asleep. Jamal came home the next morning looking haggard and unbearably sad. He didn't take my hand or call me his sweet babe.

"We sat at the kitchen table, and Jamal said, 'I fell in love with you the first time I saw you. I never pushed you because I knew you'd have to be sure. I thought that if our love was deep enough, we could deal with all the shit that would come our way. I never imagined we'd have to face anything like this. Kalayla didn't ask to be bi-racial, but she'll be dealing with the fact she is all her life. This situation is different. You can't explain that your mother hasn't forgiven you for marrying me, so you made up a story about why we never see your family.'"

Maureen paused, her arms still wrapped around her legs. "Jamal was right, but I couldn't do it, and he didn't force the issue. We went on knowing my lie lurked in the background like a low-grade fever."

Maureen's green eyes, the mirror image of Kalayla's, pleaded for understanding. I finally said, "You're showing Kalayla every day that you're doing your best to care for her. When the time comes, that should count for something."

"My mother did her best, too, Lena. Look how that worked out. What if Kalayla is like me? What if she turns out to be the opposite of what I hope? What if I lose her?"

I understood why Maureen was afraid.

When I was a girl, my parents took us kids to the beach in the summer, and we'd build sand castles and forts. If the tide came in, the water smoothed out the angles, ate the walls, or washed away any sign of what we'd built.

I realized then that nothing was forever. Everything changed, and our control over our lives was limited to personal decisions. We could choose to rebuild the sand castles and forts, but their fate wasn't up to us.

Lotta used to ask me why I refused to see what kind of man Joey was.

The truth was, I saw him more clearly than she did. But, I was as stubborn and naïve as Maureen.

Maureen staked everything on the hope that her parents would change. She and I believed everything would work out how we wanted if we held tight to that belief. I learned that we can't force people to change any more than we can force them to stay the same. Maureen would learn that, too.

I thought filling Kalayla's time would keep her off Cambridge streets and out of harm's way. I didn't know Maureen planted a time bomb in their lives that could explode any second. All I could do was be there, do my best to help, and pray that would be enough.

FALL 1999

WAITING AND THINKING

Darkness squeezed out daylight on both ends now, but the days felt longer because I wasn't guarding Kalayla while she was guarding Clean Duds. The girl was back in school, so you'd think I'd have stopped worrying.

It wasn't like I had nothing to do. When I turned seventy, I reduced my official time at Manzetti Properties to one day a week plus Board meetings. I wasn't eager to close the door completely, but I was too busy worrying to fit in much of anything else.

The only thing that staring out the window and drinking coffee did was exercise my plumbing, which nobody my age needed. But facts are facts. When you let a child into your life, there's no limit to fretting over them. Kalayla was as unreliable as fireworks on the 4th of July. Every year, I read about faulty batches that exploded. Kalayla had the same self-igniting fuse that might blow up in your face without warning.

Imagining future disasters wasn't any more helpful than thinking about past mistakes. I ought to know. I'd done enough of that in my time.

If I'd been like Lotta, I'd have been in divorce court as soon as my naïve illusions about Joey crumbled. But I did what my family expected. Joey and I exchanged sacred vows in a wedding mass and celebrated with two hundred and seventy-six guests at a dinner/dance reception. It didn't take me long to find out what a fool I'd been.

When we first got married, to explain the bruises on my arms and legs, Joey joked that marriage had turned me into a hopeless klutz. I loved wearing shorts and halters but traded them for long sleeves and slacks even when the temperature hit the nineties. I hated the ugly, discolored skin.

When Lotta saw me sweating in the sweltering heat, she said, "What the hell, Lena? Is this your version of a cheap sauna?"

I shrugged it off. "My doctor said the sun might cause bruising, so I should cover up. Weird, huh?"

Lotta looked at me like I had three heads, and I knew I hadn't heard the last of it. She was dating a cop then, and he said that was bull. No wife turned into a klutz when she got married, and anybody who blamed the sun instead of the husband was full of shit.

Lotta didn't waste a second getting to my house. "I know you're lying, Lena! Don't let that bastard hurt you!"

I shrugged that off, too.

When I told Joey what Lotta said, he laughed. "Don't worry, I know how to make us both happy. You'll be able to wear shorts, and I'll—well, you'll see, won't you?" He slapped my butt and laughed again.

That night was my first experience with pressure points. Joey could hurt me without leaving any tell-tale evidence and loved finding the places that caused me the most pain. "You're my guinea wife, Lena, like the guinea pigs they use in labs."

That was fifty years ago, but the memory still made me shudder.

We'd been married a month when Joey said it was time he took me to his favorite hangout in Somerville. It was mid-July and smelled fresh, as if rain was on the way. We parked on a street with ordinary brick office buildings, a few upscale restaurants, and a pizza joint. Nothing hinted at the depravity that was coming.

Joey put his arm around my waist, ran his fingers over my hip, and pulled me close. The streetlight lit up a discreet sign that said UG in tasteful white letters on a black background.

"That's a funny name. What does it stand for, Joey?"

Joey laughed and hugged me. "UG stands for Underground, which means what we do here is private. You'll see!"

A tall, muscular doorman in jeans and a black polo shirt grinned and winked as he said, "Hey Joey."

The entrance foyer was dimly lit, and eerie lighting engulfed us as we passed through a second door into a room with strobe lights slowly circling the dark space. Undulating dancers hugged poles on a runway in the center of the room and paced their languid movements to sensual music.

"Joey," I gasped, "those girls are almost naked."

He steered me to a horseshoe-shaped booth with velvet curtains. We sank into deep cushions, enclosed in a private, erotic world. A waitress

in tight shorts and a bra brought a margarita special for me and a double
scotch for Joey.

Joey pulled me onto his lap and turned me to face the dancers. The
alcohol dissolved my resistance as we watched them, and I felt myself
move with them. Joey massaged my breast and twisted the tip. "You're
not a mama's girl anymore, Lena. You belong to me." He breathed into
my ear and circled my pelvis with his other hand.

"People can see us, Joey."

"I'm willing to share you," he said.

I could feel his hardness as he slid a hand inside my panties and whispered in my ear, "Yeah, Lena, turn yourself inside out."

One of the dancers mimicked Joey's hand movements, slid her hand
over her breasts into her mouth, and licked her fingers.

I was horrified and shamed. I sat up and tried to push away.

Joey yanked me around to face him. "Don't fight me, Lena."

"Let me go," I said, struggling to get away.

He slapped my face, grabbed my arm, and dragged me out of UG's.

When we got home, Joey said, "You embarrassed me, Lena."

Joey took off his belt. When I tried to run, he tripped me and used his
foot to hold me down. He aimed the belt with slow precision, hitting
me everywhere except my face. He wanted me to look in the mirror and
see the price of my resistance.

I told him I didn't care what he did, but I wouldn't go to UGs.

"Have you forgotten the obey part of your marriage vows, Lena? You're
going, and you'll watch me with women who'll let me do what I want."

Joey invited business associates to join him in a private room at UG's.
Joey owned every man who joined him. They didn't know three hidden
cameras recorded their secret pleasures.

"Leverage in case I ever need it," Joey told me.

***

That was ancient history, but nothing could erase Joey's brand of ownership or wipe out the memory of my helplessness.

I reached the breaking point when JJ was a year and a half, and I was
pregnant with Mark. I told my mother everything and asked her to help
me get away.

She wiped my tears and sat me down next to her.

"Oh, Lena," she said, "my poor baby. I thought you understood your marriage cemented our business partnership with blood ties. You can't leave."

"I can if you and Dad help me."

"This isn't about you, Lena. It's about what's best for the family. I can't help you leave your marriage, but I can help you survive. Come back when you understand that's how it must be."

I went home, called Lotta, and told her Joey was abusing me.

We were sure we could hide from Joey and be safe at a Holiday Inn near Greenfield while we planned our next steps. We didn't realize how easy it would be to trace a toddler and two women, one of whom was pregnant.

Joey found us in less than twelve hours. He sent Lotta home with a warning, but he gave me a lesson in obedience that went on for days. The only thing that saved my life was that I was pregnant. No matter how much Joey wanted to hurt me, he had no intention of hurting a potential heir.

The week after that, I saw Lotta when Joey was at work.

As if it were a foregone conclusion, Lotta said, "We have to kill him."

"I can't, Lotta. He's the father of my children."

"You may be a fool, but I'm not. I'll kill him."

"Lotta, please, don't say that." She didn't realize what Joey could and would do to her and me if she tried and failed.

"Mattwo will help me," she said. "He knows what an ass Joey is. Besides, he's still in love with you."

"Dear God, Lotta! If Mattwo went after Joey, one or both of them would end up dead. You know what that would do to our families. Please, don't do anything!"

Lotta scowled. What I said was true, and she hated it. "Am I supposed to forget what he does to you?"

"If I can live with it, you can, too. Be my friend the way you always have."

Lotta did what I asked.

I didn't have to tell my mother why I'd come to see her. We crossed into uncharted territory when she closed the door to her sitting room.

My father ruled that the doors should stay open, and his word was the law. None of us kids dared disobey him. When he closed his study door, we knew a business deal needed his immediate attention. The routine family business was conducted at a nondescript two-story building in Allston we called home base. The offices and boardroom were furnished simply to convey fiscal responsibility and competence. As you whizzed by on the Massachusetts Turnpike, you might see the small sign that read Manzetti Properties.

My mother said, "I knew you'd come eventually. I have a plan, but you must decide if the risk is worth it."

"Joey said he'd bury me in one of our building sites if I ran away again."

My mother shrugged. "He wouldn't be the first to do that. Running away was the most obvious thing you could do and the least likely to succeed. He'll never expect you to take over the business."

When I gasped, my mother said, "Oh, not overnight. You'll need time to make yourself indispensable. The board will assume your interest is a passing lark until you show them it isn't. You'll build your power base shrewdly and quietly. They'll respect you, and more importantly, they'll fear you. Think of yourself as a gardener waiting for plants to take root and grow. You'll share Dom's office, and he'll teach you about the finances. Study sites outside of Boston and think about how we can expand. Encourage Joey to tell you how he's solved construction challenges. His innocuous comments about clients could give you future leverage."

I cringed. "Joey taught me about leverage."

My mother frowned. "Not his type of crude leverage, Lena! You'll discover subtle ways to influence competitors, clients, or business associates. People who flaunt power are revealing weakness. You simply have to discover what their weakness is."

I never asked my mother if my father was like Joey. I watched her anticipate my father's wishes and maneuver around his moods. She spent a lifetime perfecting the art of survival and was now teaching it to me.

I became the public face of Manzetti Properties, fundraising for city park benches, sponsoring the local blood drive, and fielding volunteers for the Earth Day clean-up. I opened the office every morning and attended to details that eased the burden for others. My suggestions, posed as questions, were adopted and solved problems I purposely created. Four years after Joey's death, I sat at the head of the boardroom table. My only regret was Joey wasn't there to see it. But my mother was.

***

If I'd married Lotta's brother, Mattwo, instead of Joey, my life would have been so different.

Joey and I were the hotshot seniors in high school, and Mattwo was a junior. Joey was polished and smooth like Michelangelo's David; Mattwo was rough and earthy like Marlon Brando in *On the Waterfront*.

I loved being in the center of Joey's spotlight. He was every girl's dream: star quarterback, senior class president, handsome and charming. I was flattered when he bragged that he was going steady with the most beautiful Homecoming Queen and May Queen.

In the fall of our senior year, Mattwo made the varsity football team as a tight end. As the head cheerleader, I went to all the games and practices. Joey didn't stay after them because he was shadowing his dad at work. But Mattwo and I did. I'd known Mattwo forever, and hanging around with him was natural.

When Lotta saw how much time Mattwo and I spent together, she said, "Don't lead my brother on, Lena. He cares about you."

"He knows I'm Joey's girl. We're just friends," I said.

"Yeah, right," she said. "How dimwitted are you, Lena?"

Things between Mattwo and Joey boiled over after the last game of the season when we won the city championship for the third time. The guys in the locker room said the two went at each other so viciously they had to drag them apart. The kids assumed the fight was over something that happened in the game.

It was the fourth quarter with a minute to go, and the game tied 14-14. Kids in the bleachers were jumping up and down screaming as we watched Mattwo zig and zag around every defender until he was wide-open, waiting for the pass. He'd proved he could catch anything, and everyone was sure we'd win the game.

Instead of making the pass to Mattwo, Joey threw a nearly impossible pass through blockers to a wide receiver who was tackled two yards from the goal line. We scored on the next play.

Joey told everyone he hadn't seen Mattwo and had to take the chance on a difficult pass. Mattwo called him a liar, and that's what started the fight. The kids thought Mattwo was jealous because Joey was the game's hero.

They were wrong. Mattwo came over later in the weekend to explain what happened. He tried to warn me about Joey, but I didn't listen.

The porch at my parents' house wrapped around the house. Mattwo and I sat on the giant swing in the back where I'd sat countless times with Joey.

I pulled Joey's letter sweater around me to fend off the November wind, and Mattwo's words added to the chilliness. He was like Lotta and said things without sugar-coating them.

"The fight didn't have anything to do with the game. It was because Joey is an asshole. You shouldn't put up with him."

"Mattwo, come on. You're saying that because you're mad now."

"I'm not. Joey told the guys you were pretty with your clothes on and twice as hot with them off. He told the guys you'd let him do anything he wanted and beg for more. He couldn't keep his mouth shut, so I slugged him!"

I felt sick to my stomach. Mattwo made it sound like Joey thought I was a trophy instead of the girl he loved. Joey had seen me in my panties and bra. He said he was entitled to a preview before we got married.

The swing moved as the wind picked up, a cardinal flew by, and Bailey, the neighbor's dog, barked when a car door slammed, everyday simple things.

For a split second, I leaned toward Mattwo. If I slid my hand into his hand, I knew my life would change instantly.

I couldn't. My future was settled. I sat back on the swing and said, "Joey and I are getting engaged at Christmas and married after graduation in June. Our families are merging their businesses into Manzetti Properties."

Mattwo's face turned into a blank mask. I saw him swallow before he said, "Okay."

He got up, squared his shoulders, and walked to his car. He pulled out of the driveway slowly, and I watched until he was out of sight.

That was a turning point that determined the rest of my life. Mattwo had given me a way out. I refused to take it, and I paid the price.

After the twins died in Vietnam, I turned into a drunk and tried out gutter life. When Lotta found me passed out in a bar for the third time, she confiscated my car keys and donated the car to the local Veterans' Association.

"Kill yourself if you want," she said, "but I'm not letting you kill anyone else!"

Lotta still enjoyed reminding me how much I aggravated Dom and her.

The only one I was aggravating now was myself. When Kalayla found out about Maureen's family, we'd need to take cover inside a shit shelter. Instead of wasting time on the past, I better figure out how to con Dom into building one on the apartment house roof!

MY GREAT IDEA

Mama acted like the world was ending when she had a birthday, but she always wanted to have a party for me. I hated birthday parties, and I told her I didn't want one every year. But Mama loved parties, and she was turning thirty in October. Throwing a party at Eddie's would keep her from getting depressed thinking about Daddy's thirtieth. He talked Mama into jumping out of an airplane.

We had photos of Daddy, Mama, Grandpa, Grandma and me. If I had to, I could get one of Clarence. But I'd never even seen one of Mama's family. She acted like a big hole swallowed them and everything about them. I knew her family was Irish, and the library had a lot of information about Ireland. We could decorate Eddie's with balloons and streamers in green, white, and orange, the Irish flag colors.

I hoped the old lady could help with my next idea. I was pretty sure not even a whacko would toss family photos in the garbage, and I bet anything Mama still had some. I could get them blown up, and we could decorate Eddie's walls. It'd be like her family was celebrating with us. Lena had a way of getting information you didn't want to give, and she could trick Mama into telling where she hid the photos.

Lena was eating a cookie when I started explaining my idea about the photos. She doubled over and started hacking like she was going to throw up her guts.

I jumped up, knocked over the lemonade pitcher, and yelled, "I'll call 911!"

Lena waved her arms and shook her head but kept coughing. I had to do something so she didn't croak on me. When I was a little kid, I got a potato chip stuck in my throat, and Mama gave me a whack on the back. Lena might've gotten a cookie stuck in her throat, so I whacked her back.

That old lady shoved me away so hard I nearly fell on my butt! That pissed me off 'cause she hadn't stopped coughing. Anybody with half a brain could tell she needed a good whack!

"Leave—me—alone," she gasped. "Let me—catch my breath!"

I wasn't in the habit of doing what she told me, but I stood beside her and waited about a year for her face to go from bright red to its usual pasty old white. She finally quit coughing.

I stood there patient and cooperative and thought about the shove she gave me. Her weak old lady routine was nothing but an act. I bet I wasn't the only one she fooled!

When she seemed about back to normal, I said, "You want anything?"

"I want you to keep your mouth shut and give me time to get my brain in gear. And clean up that lemonade mess you made."

The old crab could've at least thanked me for saving her life! Next time, I won't bother!

By the time I cleaned the table and floor, Lena's brain was working, and she started talking.

DEFLECTING PARTY IDEAS

I swear Kalayla could take the slightest whiff of a breeze and turn it into a tornado! Irish colors and family photos! If this didn't prove Maureen better tell Kalayla the truth, I didn't know what did. That girl was about to bust open a door that her mama barricaded shut and drag me smack dab into the middle of a mess.

If Kalayla had warned me about her party idea, I might've switched her train onto a different track. But she was going at such a high speed that all I could do was try to stop her from crashing.

"It's good you want to do something for your mama's birthday. The thing is—," I paused when I realized I sounded like Rico. Why is it that when you don't know what to say, you sound so foolish?

"Well, the thing is," I said again, "a good idea can turn into a bad one if you don't think it through beforehand."

For the first time since I'd known Kalayla, she kept her mouth shut and leaned forward like she expected to hear words of great wisdom. Seeing her so serious and hopeful made my heart sore.

"The thing is, Kalayla, you wouldn't want to make your mama sad on her birthday, now would you?"

Kalayla frowned. "Don't you think she'll be happy if I give her a party?"

"I do believe she will. But having pictures of your daddy and her family could make her sad."

"Oh, I didn't think of that. It'd be a real bummer if she turned her tear faucet on."

"What about things other than the photos?"

"Mama loves flowers, bright colors, animals, and dancing. We danced around the living room when Daddy was alive, and Daddy sang. Mama said he had the best bass voice she ever heard. Grandma LeeRoyce made him sing in the church choir."

"Well, then," I said, "let's do something with flowers and dancing to show your mama you're thinking about her."

"We'll invite Grandma and Grandpa and everyone working at Eddie's. Do you think your brother Dominic might want to come?"

Back in the days when I had parties, I invited family, friends, friends of friends, and anybody else I felt like sticking in the pot. But Kalayla could get a case of brain strain thinking about who to invite besides the people from Eddie's and Maureen's in-laws. Uncle Clarence was so far down on Kalayla's hit parade she might skip him, and if Maureen had any friends, I wasn't aware of them.

I said, "Dom loves parties; knowing him, he'll bring family. Don't worry. Eddie will help, and my friend Lotta practically has a Ph.D. in throwing parties. We'll handle the guest list."

Kalayla's eyes got big, and she had the nerve to say, "You got a friend?"

She acted as if my having a friend was the most unbelievable thing she ever heard! I gave that girl a look she won't forget anytime soon!

BEFORE AND DURING THE PARTY

It turned out to be true. The old lady did have a friend. When I asked Lena why she hung around with somebody so young, she gave me a vicious stare and said, "For your information, Lotta and I were in the same high school class, and we were both cheerleaders!"

Yeah, right, in her dreams.

When the old lady said she and Lotta would help, she meant they'd take over. They spent most of their time ordering me around! If I asked about food, they said, "Put it on the list." If I asked about decorations, they said, "Put it on the list."

I finally said, "What list?"

"What do you mean, what list?" Lotta said. "Making the list and crossing off things is your job."

What a pisser!

I didn't see how they could be best friends. They argued about everything until one of them said, "Fine! If we don't do it your way, you'll never shut up." The weird thing was the next minute, they'd be laughing like they were having a great time.

I decorated a pole with flowers and streamers that Eddie would put in the middle of the Eatery so everybody could dance around it.

When Lotta offered to have a good friend set up the music, Lena snorted and said, "I bet that's not the only thing this good friend does!"

Lotta gave her a dirty look and said, "Watch your mouth, Lena Manero. An impressionable child is listening to you!"

If Lotta thought I was an impressionable child, she was as dense as the old lady.

Lena said I had to get Mama to dress up and deliver her to the Eatery without making her a nervous wreck. I told her Mama wouldn't dress up unless I told her why.

Lotta said. "When have you ever had trouble making up reasons for doing anything?"

Eddie called the night before the party and told Mama he had a family emergency and the Eatery would be closed the next day. Then Lena called to say she was sick and needed Mama to fill in at the Women's Shelter. That proved I wasn't the only one who lied whenever they wanted to.

We spent the afternoon of the party decorating, and Lotta was so bossy I was ready to tell her off. The old lady went bug-eyed and almost turned blue when I opened my mouth, so I didn't.

I told Mama that Lena was taking us someplace special for her birthday, and she got all duded up in her green chiffon dress, gold necklace, and dangle earrings Daddy gave her one Christmas.

When Mama saw the Closed for Private Party sign on Eddie's and all the windows covered, her face lit up. After we went inside, Mama said, "Oh, Layla, remember the Maypole you decorated at school? I'm so glad you used an idea you learned there."

Mama would've freaked out if I told her all the fabulous things I learned in the girls' bathroom at school!

Lena and Lotta must've invited everybody they knew, and Mama was happier than she'd been since Daddy died. Everybody said she looked beautiful, and she did.

Lena and Lotta helped me make a black-eyed Susan costume 'cause that was Mama's favorite flower. Lotta had a couple of yards of green material that covered my body for the stem. We dyed a mop yellow for the petals, and Lena painted my nose dark brown for the button in the middle.

While Mama was greeting the guests, I changed in the Ladies' Room. I looked pretty dumb, but when Mama saw me, she smothered me with a hug.

I thought my costume would be the party's hit until Lena took off her black cape and put on a wide-brimmed hat. The belt on her dress was covered with green flowers, and her wide-brim black hat had green flowers around it!

I figured she might've gone color blind or had a spell like she did when she dragged me to Matty's Way.

When Mama got upset, Daddy said, "Don't worry, skinny girl. Your mama just needs a hug."

I wasn't about to hug the old lady, but as soon as I got the chance, I went over and said, "Are you feeling okay, Lena? Do you need to go to the hospital?"

She looked puzzled. "Why would I need to go to a hospital?"

"To have them fix what's wrong with you."

"Nothing is wrong with me, girl! Where did you get such a ridiculous idea?"

"You're wearing green, so your brain must be screwed up."

"My brain is most certainly not screwed up! I am wearing green because the guest of honor is Irish!"

Then she started laughing! "I didn't mean to scare you. I wanted to surprise you."

If that was her idea of a good surprise, I was thinking up a few to try on her and see how she liked them!

"I wasn't worrying about you! I didn't want you to take a fit and ruin Mama's party!"

I could tell the old crab was about to hug me, but I wasn't letting her squash my petals! I shoved my way to the food table and decided to stay there for the rest of my life. Lotta's calligraphy signs said cheese & pesto stuffed shells, shrimp scampi, Italian sausage & peppers, garlic roasted potatoes, spinach, and feta ricotta pie. I gave up reading and started tasting. I planned to sample every dish.

For once, Lena was right. I had never tasted anything as good as Lotta's desserts. I tried about ten different cookies, a cannolo with chocolate and vanilla cream, and the birthday cake with eight layers of chocolate cake with vanilla and raspberry cream in between. I decided I might as well keep eating until my stomach exploded.

When Lotta came by, I asked if she bought the zucchini and sausage ravioli at Mickey's. She got all bent out of shape as if I insulted her.

"This is an Italian feast. Everybody cooks in Italian families regardless of their gender! Every dish was made by someone in my family or Lena's."

Well, pooh, pooh to her! I almost said I bet she didn't make the butter or olive oil, but I didn't want to make her mad.

Things were going great until I looked across the room and saw that turd from the gym. I ducked down so he wouldn't notice me. I bet anything Lena invited him to piss me off! I kept an eye on him until Lena came to the food table. By then, he'd worked his way over to Mama and was talking to her!

"What's that turd doing here?" I said. "I'm going to kick his butt out of my party!"

The old lady shoveled a hunk of cake on a plate and said, "This is your Mama's party, not yours. She's having a fine time talking to one of the guests, whose name is Rico. He is Lotta's nephew, and I imagine she invited him. Why don't you stuff your mouth with food instead of spoiling your Mama's good time?"

Lena turned and went in Lotta's direction, but before she got there, some old guy stopped her and started yakking in her ear. He was probably asking where he could take a piss!

Mama stood beside the dancing pole, blushing like when Daddy teased her. That turd, Rico, was making her laugh! I wanted to punch him, but the old lady was right for once.

I decided to have another slice of Lotta's cake.

DURING THE PARTY

I had suddenly crossed the Atlantic and landed on the Emerald Isle, my mother's birthplace. Gigantic posters of the Irish countryside covered the windows and walls, orange, green, and white balloons floated on the ceiling, streamers and flowers in similar colors decorated a pole in the middle of the room.

People I knew and didn't know surrounded me, wishing me a happy birthday punctuated with hugs and kisses! What an absolutely wonderful surprise!

Kalayla introduced me to Lena's best friend, saying, "This is the old lady's bossy friend Carlotta, a.k.a. Lotta." Kalayla was lucky Lena didn't insist they tape her mouth as part of the costume!

I was tapping my foot to Irish tunes from groups like The Frames and The Divine Comedy when I felt a hand on my shoulder. I turned and saw a man wearing a short-sleeved blue polo shirt. He looked like a weightlifter and had a swarthy, rugged demeanor. I'd never seen him before, but Lena said she and Lotta invited family.

"Green Greetings, my lady. I'm Rico." His eyes darted to my left hand.

"I'm Maureen," I laughed, "the birthday girl. I guess I should say the birthday woman, now that I'm 30. It's such a milestone, don't you think? Did you do something special for your thirtieth? Oh dear, please don't be offended. I didn't mean to imply you look old."

"No need to apologize," Rico said. "Thirty-three is much older than thirty, but I hope I don't look decrepit."

"No, you don't." I stammered and felt myself blushing. "You look healthy and strong."

Rico laughed, "I plead guilty to healthy and strong. My Aunt Carlotta invited me. She gave me the time, the place and told me to show up. She neglected to say the guest of honor was such a beautiful woman."

A man I'd just met called me beautiful! I was a widow with a daughter but was exhilarated and shy as if I were young and single. I swallowed and said, "That is so funny! I just met your aunt. My daughter said she was Lena's bossy friend."

"That she is! Once, I called her, and she said, 'Give me a minute, will you, Rico? I'm in the middle of shagging my boyfriend.' I think she gets a kick out of keeping me off balance."

"She sounds like a character! My Uncle Seamus thought mooning the neighbors was funny. My aunt swore she'd tie him to a lamp post the next time and invite everybody in Brighton to see what he had to show."

Rico laughed, "Can you imagine if your uncle and my aunt got together? The families would run for the hills!"

The families. How stupid of me to tell him about Uncle Seamus. The last thing I wanted was to talk about my family on such a lovely day.

"How'd you get the name Rico?" I said. "I'm Irish, and Maureen is an Irish name. Rico doesn't sound Italian. At least, I don't think it does. Is it?" Oh dear, I sounded like a total airhead!

Rico leaned a little closer, which made me nervous because he was attractive and sensual.

"That's another story," Rico said. "My Grandpa's name was Matthew Eccli, and my grandparents named my dad Matthew Eccli II." He gestured toward the front windows. "He's talking to Eddie. Anyway, everyone calls him Mattwo. When my parents named me Matthew Eccli, III, they called me Matthree. I hated that name! When I started kindergarten, I told the teacher my name was Rico.

"At dinner that night, I told the family I wasn't talking to anybody unless they called me Rico. And I didn't. My dad flipped out and gave me at least fifty lectures about carrying on the family name. My mom spent most of her time trying to calm him down. I wouldn't say anything to him or anyone else, which drove them all crazy. After two weeks, my dad gave up and gave in. I admit I was a little prick."

"What a hoot! How did you choose that name?"

"I blamed my older sister for the idea. She was doing research for school, and I saw the name Ricardo in her notebook with the meaning next to it. Ricardo meant great and powerful leader, and Rico was the nickname. I liked that."

I smiled, "And are you a great and powerful leader?"

"My dad thinks I'm a great and powerful pain in the butt. I'm taking over the management of our gym, and we argue about every suggestion I make. I usually convince him, so we're offering yoga and Tai Chi. So, ah, Maureen, I don't see a wedding ring. Is there a boyfriend lurking around in this crowd?"

My stomach flip-flopped. What if he asked me for a date? I wasn't sure I was ready. But he was relaxed and friendly, and flirting with him was fun.

"I don't have a husband. I mean, not now. I'm a widow. I don't have a boyfriend, but I do have a daughter. She's guarding the food table. This party was her idea."

Rico looked in Kalayla's direction and muttered, "Ah." I was surprised when he said, "If the black-eyed Susan is your daughter, I have met her. Miss Lena brought her to Matty's Way, our gym. If she has a favorite people list, I imagine I'm at the bottom of it."

"But you're so outgoing and friendly, and so is Kalayla. She's always telling me about conversations with people walking their dogs."

"Yeah, well, she was outgoing but not so friendly. We had a bit of a misunderstanding, and I haven't seen her since. How about if I tell you what happened over coffee sometime? That's a more serious conversation; now is a time for dancing. If I'm not mistaken, that song is Neil Hannon's National Express. I heard The Divine Comedy in Ireland, and they're great."

"That's just who it is! And you saw them! My family is Irish, and I'd love to go there!"

Rico took my hand and twirled me around. He was muscular but as light-footed and agile as Jamal. Not that it mattered. I'd have coffee with him and find out why he thought Kalayla didn't like him. But that was all. Well, maybe I'd ask him about Ireland.

I looked toward the dessert table and saw Kalayla staring at us. I didn't think a black-eyed Susan could scowl, but this one was. Oh dear!

BEFORE AND DURING THE PARTY

The birthday party showed me a new side of Kalayla. Every time she went to the library, she came home with a new idea. I spent a fortune on taxis chauffeuring us from one store to another in Cambridge or Boston.

The Harvard Coop had posters of the Connemara ponies, the Cliffs of Moher, castles in every state of repair, and the Irish countryside. According to Kalayla, all of these were indispensable items. To her credit, the first time we went shopping, Kalayla said, "I don't have enough money for all this, but I'll work for you free 'til I get it paid off."

I looked at the total on the sales slip. "You might be working for me until you turn twenty-one."

"I don't care. Working for you isn't the worst job I ever had."

That wasn't saying much. Unless you counted peddling cookies and guarding laundry, working for me was the only job Kalayla ever had!

Kalayla sneaked over to Eddie's every chance she got and drove him crazy. She suggested removing the booths next to the back wall and the wall between the counter and the kitchen.

Lotta, the general, assigned every cook in her family and mine a recipe with instructions on where to purchase the ingredients and a timeline for completion as if we were inexperienced assistants!

I finally had enough and said, "Lotta, you remember we've all been cooking since we were five years old, don't you?"

She said, "Of course I do. I think I'll make chocolate and vanilla cream for the cannoli filling. What do you think?"

That was how it went until Lotta came to inspect what I was wearing to the party.

"Well, it's about time!" Lotta said when she saw me. "My best friend, who has worn nothing but black for the last thirty years, is plastered in green flowers."

"I am not plastered in them. They're tastefully and appropriately placed!"

Lotta looked me up and down. "Cover that dress, and don't put on the hat until we get there. I don't want people fainting in the street!"

Everybody Lotta and I knew was already there or followed us through the door. Kalayla's grandparents were running a church fundraiser that night. She didn't mention why Clarence wasn't there, and I didn't ask.

Kalayla made a perfect black-eyed Susan, and if she managed to keep her mouth shut, guests would think she was as sweet as could be. HA!

Rico was smart enough to make a beeline for Maureen, but he wasn't the only one waiting to dance with that beauty. Lotta and I invited the younger generation and told them to bring friends.

Lotta smugly informed me she invited her brother, and it wasn't long before Mattwo came to say hello.

"You look good, Lena," Mattwo said. "You added a little green for the celebration, eh? Did you and Lotta plan this?"

"We got it organized, but Kalayla supplied grand ideas, such as tearing down the building and putting up something bigger!"

"Rico said she's a handful."

"That's one way to describe her."

"If you need help, call me," Mattwo said, touching my arm.

I needed help, but I wasn't about to tell Mattwo he was the cause of my seesawing emotions!

"Rico did as much as he could, given how Kalayla acted. Once you meet her, you'll understand what I mean. She's appointed herself guard at the food table, but I'm not sure she'll let us eat anything."

Mattwo laughed. "Sounds like a typical kid to me."

Ha! Wait until he met her.

Kalayla was surveying the desserts when I said, "Kalayla, I'd like you to meet an old friend. Mattwo, this is Kalayla."

She looked at Mattwo, frowned, scanned the crowd, and zeroed in on Rico. Mattwo's partially bald head and bit of roundness at the gut didn't fool her. He and Rico were related. Her eyes narrowed, but instead of insulting Mattwo, she bit her lip.

I almost fell over when she shook his hand and said, "Pleased to meet you. You might get sick if you eat the cake, but one cookie won't upset your stomach too much."

I smothered a laugh.

Mattwo smiled. "Lotta's my sister, so I know about her desserts. I like her Tiramisu better than the cake, but maybe you've eaten all that. The Florentines are my all-time favorite cookie."

Kalayla pointed at Mattwo's stomach. "If she was my sister, I'd be fat, too."

Mattwo laughed. "Listen, kid, I'm in damn good shape for a guy my age."

She shrugged, "If you want to stay that way, have the spinach-feta pie instead of dessert. It tastes healthy."

Lotta smirked at Mattwo and me from across the room. I'd be hearing about green flowers and my chat with her brother for the rest of my life.

That didn't bother me. I was with the man I should have married, and I knew one thing for sure. There was life left in this old woman!

BEING A GOOD MOTHER

"I'm making angels for Grandma, so she'll give me a few extra fudge balls," Kalayla said.

"Layla, Lucinda always gives you plenty of fudge balls! You don't have to bribe her!"

Kalayla muttered, "That's what you think," under her breath, but I didn't have the energy to call her on it.

I wanted to spend time with Kalayla, but finding something she was willing to do wasn't easy. I was younger than Kalayla when my mother taught me to monogram handkerchiefs, knit scarves, and embroider dish towels, but I was a willing, eager learner.

Kalayla was neither willing nor eager. When I tried to teach her to embroider, she stuck herself twice with the needle, dripped blood on the white dish towel, threw it on the floor, and stomped on it.

"This sucks blood," she yelled and ran out of the house.

I hoped crocheting or knitting might be more successful. At least there wouldn't be any spilled blood. According to Kalayla, the only thing needles were good for was "to stick up the butt of a kid I don't like."

I sighed. This was our first attempt at making cookies and was a thank you to the people who helped her with my birthday party. The kitchen table was covered with ingredients: flour, sugar, butter, cinnamon, ginger, eggs, and sprinkles for decorating. So far, Kalayla hadn't burned herself, ruined a cookie sheet, or set the kitchen on fire.

"Mama! Look how good this looks!"

She was applying decorations haphazardly. That was a small price to pay because she was enjoying herself.

"You know what we should do, Mama? Let's talk Grandma and Lotta into throwing a party. It'd be fun to see her and Grandma fight over who the big boss was. I bet Lotta would win." Kalayla giggled her way through, cutting out several angels.

I admit it was a funny idea, but I never laughed when I thought about Lucinda. When Jamal and I discussed getting married, I asked him when I'd meet his parents.

He shrugged off the idea. "Trust me, sweet babe. She'll welcome you after we're married. If I introduce you before then, she'll tell you to find a white guy and spare yourself pain. My mother is the most realistic person you will ever meet."

I didn't need to hear that from Lucinda or anyone else. My mother showed me how painful it would be, but she wasn't the only one.

Jamal and I thought it would be fun to live in Boston, and I was excited when I began searching for apartments. I found two I liked, but when Jamal went with me to see them, the owners said they were rented. They didn't say that when I called to confirm our appointment.

We broadened our search to Cambridge, but this time, we both went. We found a large apartment on the first floor of a two-family house with a yard along one side of the house. The light was perfect for my studio.

I almost cried when the owner said, "If your money is green, it's good enough for me." She told the Asian couple on the second floor the same thing.

A couple of weeks after we married, Jamal said, "Okay, sweet babe, brace yourself. It's time for you to meet my parents and my brother."

I understand what Jamal meant when we went there for Sunday dinner. "Well, daughter-in-law," Lucinda said, "now that my son stopped hiding you, I trust we'll get to know you. I hope you're not as fragile as you appear. Being a mixed couple will require strength. Jamal knew that, and you're about to find it out."

Jamal's father, Harmon, stood next to her and nodded.

Clarence, Jamal's brother, swaggered into the living room, saw me and said, "Hot damn! What a beauty!" His stare was so intense I was embarrassed. He circled me, whistled, and said, "Whoa, Bro, those hips must be giving you some kind of ride."

Jamal grabbed the front of Clarence's shirt and said, "Shut your mouth, Clarence. She's my wife!"

I was shocked because Jamal was gentle and soft-spoken. I couldn't imagine him hurting anyone.

Clarence gave Jamal a military salute. "Chill, Bro. It's cool you got such a prize. No disrespect meant."

I wasn't sure how to react to any of them. Lucinda was intimidating. Harmon seemed nice but very quiet. When I asked Jamal about Clarence, he told me what happened when they were kids. For the first time, I truly understood that Jamal and I had grown up in different worlds.

JAMAL'S WORDS

Well, sweet babe, welcome to the LeeRoyce family. Neither of my parents is the warm-fuzzy type, but if you need help, they'll be there for you. Clarence is their soft spot.

Clarence is a year younger than I am, and no matter where I went, he begged me to go, too. Maybe all little brothers are like that, but he never let up. It drove me crazy. If Mom wouldn't let him go someplace alone, I had to take him.

Clarence wanted to be a fireman, but the fire station was five blocks from our house. Mom said that was too far for him to go alone, so he begged me to take him. The firefighters liked Clarence because he was curious and wanted to know what every piece of equipment was for and how it worked. On his birthday, one of the firefighters jumped down the fire pole with Clarence on his back. That must have been against the rules, but the other guys laughed and said they wouldn't squeal.

When Clarence learned to ride a bike, there was no way I could get away from him. The summer before I went into third grade, I wanted to prove I could do something bigger kids could. I decided to ride to Fresh Pond even though I had no idea how far that was. Later, my dad told me it was three miles each way, but I don't think knowing that would have made a difference. I was cocky enough to think riding a block, a mile, or three miles was the same.

I made the mistake of telling Clarence. Of course, he wanted to go and was positive he could keep up. We stopped every couple of blocks so Clarence could rest. Both of us were thirsty, and I promised him we'd get ice cream and water at Friendly's when we got to Fresh Pond.

We came out of Friendly's and walked our bikes toward the theatre when I saw a car cruising the parking lot. White kids were hanging out the windows, shouting at anyone they saw.

I knew we were in trouble when they pulled in front of us. Five of them got out of the car. One of them said, "Hey, look what we got here. A couple of strays from a baby coon litter!"

Another one said, "Yeah, and the runt of the litter is gonna cry! I never saw black tears!"

They all laughed. One of them grabbed me, and two others circled Clarence, poked him in the arms, chest, and back, and called him a crybaby and a sissy.

I did my best to help him, but the guy holding me was two feet taller and weighed at least twice as much as I did.

One of them said, "Maybe he's bawling because he's got a honey pot instead of a dick, and he's scared we're gonna stick him!"

They pulled down Clarence's pants, pointed, and hooted at how small he was.

One of them waved a knife and said, "Okay, let's vote. Should I cut off the kid's dick, cut out his black tongue, or do both?"

"Hey!" the guy holding me yelled. "He'll bleed like a pig! You're not getting my car covered in coon blood. Here!" He tossed over what looked like a gun. "Stick this down his throat and pull the trigger."

When they tried to force open Clarence's mouth, he shit and peed all over himself. They jumped away, and somebody yelled, "Let's get out of here before we catch cooties from coon shit!"

They chanted, "Cooties from coon shit," as they piled into the car and burned rubber.

Clarence was curled in a ball next to the curb, whimpering. I was afraid to leave him, and two white women going to the movie theatre asked what was wrong. They called our parents.

Clarence wasn't the same after that. He was afraid to leave the house. When my mom finally got him back to school, he'd shit in the hallways and wipe it on the walls. The school put him in a special class, but that didn't help. Mom had to quit her second-grade teaching job and homeschool him.

All of that was my fault. I never should have let Clarence go with me.

✳ ✳ ✳

"Mama!" Kalayla waved a hand in my face. "I'm going to Mickey's for more sprinkles!"

Oh, dear! I was daydreaming while she was decorating. Three empty packages of sprinkles littered the table.

Kalayla was halfway to the door when I said, "I'll go with you. We can pick up something for your lunch, too."

She rolled her eyes, "I got it covered, Mama. Go back to fantasy land."

I wouldn't have blamed her if she had slammed the door, but she didn't. How could I get A's on every assignment, test, or project in school and be such an incompetent mother?

When I had coffee with Rico a couple of weeks ago, he said I shouldn't be so hard on myself. He gave his parents a hard time, which wasn't their fault. He worked through college even though his dad wanted to pay his tuition. After graduation, he cycled around Europe for a year instead of going to work at the gym the way his dad wanted.

When he did start work, he rode his bike, so whenever he suggested a new class or activity for the gym, his dad said, "You get that highfalutin idea riding around town on that damn bike? Why don't you get a car?"

Rico laughed, "My dad jabs at me, but he's always there for me. Before Mom passed away, I lived in an apartment a couple of blocks from them. When I went for dinner one night, my dad and grandpa were having a beer in the living room. I don't like beer, and I always brought wine.

"After the usual chitchat, Dad said, 'Papa and I want you to move here. The third-floor apartment is empty; you can renovate it to suit yourself. You can decide how and when to tell the rest of the family. Your mother will want to give a party to welcome you home.'

"I almost gagged on my wine. Anybody else in the family would consider that an honor not to be refused. But I wasn't willing to live in a fishbowl with Dad and Mom on the second floor and Papa on the first. I spent a couple of days thinking about how to avoid a family crisis and then set up a time to talk.

"I went into Dad's living room and saw Papa wasn't there. When I asked why, my dad said, 'It's better with just the two of us. Tell me what you came to say.'

"My dad knew my answer, but he was waiting to hear it from me. I said, 'I appreciate you asking me to move here, but I have to say no. I love you and Mom and Papa, but I can't live in the same house with you again. I'm too old to explain what I'm doing, where I'm going, or who I'm going with.'

"My dad looked briefly at the ceiling once, sighed, and said, 'Okay. If that's how you feel, that's how you feel.'

"That was that. I never loved or respected my dad more than I did then. When I put a down payment on a house in a different section of Watertown, he said, 'You need any help with the move?'"

I told Rico how lucky he was to have such a wonderful family and couldn't stop myself from blurting out everything about my mother disowning me and the lie I told Kalayla.

Rico said, "No matter how she reacts when you tell her, at least she'll know you're sorry you lied to her."

That's what Lena said, too.

If Kalayla had been a blank canvas, I'd have known what to do. Art projects didn't talk back or stomp out of the room in a huff the way Kalayla might. But even if she did, I had to tell her.

I was taking a batch of cookies out of the oven when Kalayla opened the door and said, "Wow, Mama! It smells like a bakery in here!"

She put the grocery bag on the table. "I got M&M's, sprinkles, and Red Hots. I'm putting horns and a tail on the cookie for Clarence and sticking Red Hots all over it. I hope he burns his tongue!"

WINTER 1999/2000

USING THE INTERNET

The weather forecasters and snow plow guys were all jacked up. They thought piling up new snow records was better than the invention of ice cream. Normal people like me knew this winter was a real pisser. The streets were narrow, and snow buried the curbs. Sidewalks were non-existent except around schools. I was sick of slogging through snow or finding a way around it.

My fingers would've frozen if the old lady hadn't given me waterproof down mittens for Christmas. I looked like a mummy buried in layers. I wrapped a scarf around my head and left slits for my eyes like a knight wearing a vizor. Mama could've walked by me without knowing who I was.

Clean Duds turned into a smelly steam bath with dirty, wet floors. The cleanup crew showed up every night, but by the time I got there after school, it was a yucky mess. Weekends were the worst, and I cut back my time there.

Mama filled in a lot at Eddie's for staff who couldn't get to work. The old lady should've stayed at home, but she had Ray Ray drive her around. He brought a step stool so the old lady could get into his truck more easily. I asked her if I could get a ride, but she said Thor needed the back seat.

When I got tired of being alone, I headed to the library. It was on the corner of a main street where the sidewalks were clear. The new section had windows with open spaces for tables, but the old section had awesome nooks where you could hide out. I asked the librarian if I could reserve my favorite nook. She said that was against library policy, so I moved the alcove chair to one of the tables when I left. Anybody who wanted to sit there could drag it back, but nobody ever did.

My social studies teacher assigned a research project that required using old newspaper records and doing internet searches. I decided to interview Lotta about her animal shelter. While I was at it, I'd tell her she ought to invite a poor, starving kid and her hard-working mama to dinner. I hoped she'd get a laugh out of that, and we'd get an awesome meal.

The librarian showed me how to find newspaper articles. I found a good one about Lotta opening the shelter and decided to look up Daddy's car crash. Grandma wouldn't let me see the newspaper stories. She might've been afraid I'd go whacko like Mama, but she was wrong. Daddy said he and I were strong as steel.

The article said it was Daddy's first time drag racing, and the photos of the smashed car were creepy. I was glad I didn't see them when I was little.

The obituary said Daddy was survived by Mama, me, his parents, and his brother, which was a dumb way of saying he was dead and we were alive.

Being alone gave me time to think about Mama's family, and one Sunday afternoon, I started researching to find out more about how they died. I keyed in stuff like whole family killed in an explosion and the Brighton gas explosion, but I didn't find anything.

When I asked the librarian for help, she tried a bunch of different topics but found nothing. The strange thing was that she didn't remember reading about the explosion, and she was like a newspaper addict and read everything.

Finally, the librarian said, "Kalayla, what makes you think there was an explosion?"

I almost told her 'cause my mama said there was. I could've, and I would've, but something didn't feel right, like in a puzzle when you're sure you have a piece in the right place, but it doesn't fit.

So, I said, "I don't know, but it doesn't matter. I'll research something else. Thanks for the help."

* * *

After I went home, the librarian's question kept buzzing in my head like a wicked giant mosquito. It followed me into my bedroom. When I went to Lena's, it beat me through her door. I opened my locker at school, and it smacked me in the face. I rolled myself into a tight ball, hoping it wouldn't find me.

But it did. Why did I think there was an explosion?

86

I thought about saying something to Lena, but she always told me to get my brain in gear before I opened my mouth, and my gears were stuck. I didn't know what to say, and pretty soon, I wasn't saying much of anything.

Mama didn't notice, but that sharp-eyed old lady did. She stared at me and said, "What's wrong with you, girl? Did something happen?"

I stopped going over to Lena's.

I woke up feeling worse every morning, so I stopped going to sleep. The mosquito kept biting, and I scratched until I asked myself, "What if there wasn't an explosion? What if Mama was lying?"

Was that why Daddy told me to ask Mama when I asked questions about her family? If he knew Mama was lying, why didn't he say, "Liar, liar pants on fire," like he did when I said I wasn't the one who decorated Clarence's hair with chewing gum while he was asleep on our sofa?

The following Saturday, I returned to the library but wasn't sure how to start. I was killing time and picked up *The Chronicle*. The sports headline read, "O'Rourke Does It Again!" The article said Sean O'Rourke played basketball for Brighton High School and scored twenty points against Cambridge.

I stopped reading. My grandfather's name was Kevin Sean O'Rourke.

My mama used to live in Brighton.

I could've put down the paper and walked away. But I'm no sissy. I asked the librarian if Brighton had a local paper. It did, and the sports page headline read, "O'Rourke Courted by Colleges." The photo showed the kid after one of the games with his grandparents, Colleen and Kevin O'Rourke.

Colleen and Kevin O'Rourke. My dead grandmother was Colleen O'Rourke. My dead Grandfather was Kevin O'Rourke.

I stared at the photo for a long time. It was easy to see that Sean resembled his grandparents, and my mama looked like Colleen.

I was hot and dizzy and felt like I might throw up. I went to the bathroom, splashed cold water on my face, and washed my hands three times. But I couldn't wash the thoughts out of my head. I had to find out if they were my dead grandparents. I had to find out if Colleen and Kevin had children. I had to find out if Mama was their daughter.

I went to the nook and searched the internet. I found out that Colleen and Kevin O'Rourke had three children: Colin, Leah, and Kate.

Mama had two sisters, Leah and Kate, and one brother, Colin. They had to be Mama's siblings. Why wasn't Mama's name with her sisters and her brother? Why did she think they were dead? It didn't make any sense.

I twisted my brain into contortions, trying to come up with answers. I finally gave up. Any dumb-ass kid at school could figure it out. Mama knew her family was alive. Daddy knew it, too. They belong in the Guinness Book of World Records for being the World's Biggest Liars.

Mama said she trusted me, but she would've told me the truth if she did. I stared at the computer until the librarian came by and said, "We'll be closing in ten minutes, Kalayla. You should get your things together."

It was freezing outside and dark except for the streetlights and head-lights. Snowflakes pelted my face, and it was hard to see. Nothing looked familiar, and I wasn't sure I could find my way home.

A CHILD IN MY HOUSE AGAIN

The knock on my door was so soft I wasn't sure I heard anything until it came a second time. Kalayla stood in the hallway with her head down like she was fascinated with something on the floor. I looked down, but nothing was there. Kalayla didn't say a word, and I was afraid she'd mouthed off to the wrong person. I didn't see bruises, scratches, or torn clothes, which I took as a good sign.

I put my arm around her and led her through the door. Whatever upset her must be worse than bad, or she'd never let me do such a thing.

"You come in here and tell old Lena what's going on," I said, guiding her to the sofa. She curled into a fetal position without saying a word. My old brain knew too much about too much that could happen to people without warning. My imagination ran wild, wondering if Maureen had been mugged or had heart failure.

I rubbed Kalayla's back and shoulders while I worried about what else I could do. I always told that girl to keep her mouth shut, and now I wished she'd open it. But she didn't.

It was past dinner time, and I knew Kalayla must be hungry; once she had eaten, she might decide to talk. I was about to go to the kitchen when she looked at me and said, "Lena, has anybody ever told you such a big lie you were sure it was true?"

So, somebody had shone a spotlight on the elephant living with Kalayla and her mama. Even if I could have, I wouldn't have chased it back into the shadows. The time to face it was long past due.

I felt like crying for Kalayla and crying for Maureen.

"Not that I know of," I said. "But once, a long time ago, I told a big lie, and everybody believed it."

Her eyes opened wide like she was stretching to make room for a part of me she hadn't known was there. "You did? But why? It's not right."

"Right doesn't always enter into it when you're trying to protect people you love, Kalayla. Maybe your mama thought she was protecting you."

To my last breath, I will not forget how sad and hurt that girl looked.

"You knew," she said. "You knew, and you didn't tell me."

"Yes. I did know, but your mama didn't tell me. I found out on my own, and it wasn't my place to tell you. That was up to your mama. I guess she finally worked up the courage to do it."

Kalayla's eyes got fierce, and she exploded. "No, she didn't! I found out on the computer. Mama should've told me. She doesn't care about me! I hate her, and I hate my daddy, too. He should've told me."

"Ah, Kalayla, this has been a terrible shock, but your mama and daddy would never hurt you on purpose. You need to give her a chance to explain."

She sat up ramrod straight, as tight as a coiled spring, ready to let fly. Those green eyes came close to burning a hole through me.

"I'm not listening to any of her lies! I hate her, and I'm going to tell her so!"

Before I could move, Kalayla bolted out my door and down the stairs. She ran across the street and almost knocked down two customers leaving the Eatery.

Later, Maureen told me Kalayla stood in the middle of the restaurant and screamed, "I hate you, Maureen LeeRoyce! You should've told me my family was alive. You should've told me the truth! You're a liar, and I hate you."

Maureen dropped a tray of dishes and stumbled after Kalayla, but the girl barreled out of Eddie's and down the street.

By the time I got there, Maureen was leaning against the building, bawling her eyes out, while Eddie and some customers did their best to get Maureen inside out of the cold and snow.

Eddie and I dragged Maureen to my place, with her sobbing, "I should have told her," over and over.

I wanted to say, "Yes, you should have," but there was no point in pouring oil on the fire. Maureen hadn't realized her lie would take over their lives, and now, she had to face the consequences.

As soon as we got her into my apartment, Maureen started pacing the living room, wringing her hands, switching from bawling to whimpering. Eddie had to return to the Eatery, so I was left dealing with her. I told her Kalayla would stomp up the stairs any minute, but I didn't convince her any more than I convinced myself.

As the time passed, I got more worried. The temperature kept falling. By nine o'clock, it was twenty-eight degrees and going down. By ten o'clock, Maureen was slumped on the sofa, and I was pacing.

"No more waiting," I said. "We have to search for Kalayla. I'll get people in the building organized. Eddie can roust folks he knows. You call the LeeRoyce clan and get them over here."

Maureen's face turned ghostly white. "No! We can't tell Jamal's family that Kalayla ran away. Please, Lena, we can't."

"Maureen! Jamal's family will be here in a flash to help find her!"

Maureen started sobbing again, and I had a devil of a time making out her mumbled words.

"Lucinda—will take her away from me—because I'm not a good mother."

What Maureen said could be true. Lucinda might not be willing to give her another pass.

"All right," I said, hoping Maureen would turn off the water fountain. "We won't call them now. You call Eddie. I'll recruit people from the apartment building and call Dom. He'll get my family over here."

Thirty people split into teams headed in different directions in less than half an hour. The stores were closed, and traffic had disappeared. Maureen and I took a neighborhood with houses and a few apartment buildings adjacent to Mass. Ave.

There were plenty of places a kid Kalayla's size could hide. I shined my flashlight under cars, behind trash barrels, around garages and sheds, any place that might provide shelter from the cold and wind.

Having Maureen hang on me was no help at all. The later it got, the more she carried on, and her wailing got on my nerves. Half the time, we had to walk in the street. Between guiding her and keeping myself upright, I was working overtime.

My patience evaporated when she flopped on a curbstone and nearly pulled me over. "You listen here, Maureen! We're out here to find Kalayla, but I'm spending more time on you than searching for her. Stop sniveling and start helping, or go home now!"

No doubt she thought I sounded like Lucinda, but she shut up, and we kept looking. One of the corner houses had a big yard, and I thought Kalayla might be hiding there, so I opened the gate to go in.

The yard lit up with floodlights, a dog inside the house went crazy barking, and a man opened the front door and yelled, "Hey! What are you doing in my yard?"

I was afraid he might shoot us for being on his property, so I yelled, "We're searching for a runaway girl!"

The man yelled back, "I don't see any girl. If she's buried under one of those snow piles, I'll find her when the snow melts. Get the hell off my property!"

I dragged Maureen back to the street. Guys like that wouldn't help us, but they weren't the ones worrying me. Some of the searchers were afraid Kalayla would freeze to death, but I wasn't one of them. I was scared she'd find the wrong place to get warm. Being alone on the street at night made her easy prey for perverts. I wasn't sure that girl would smell danger if it stank like a dead mouse.

It was almost eleven o'clock when I told Maureen we had to call the police. She looked terrified. "But Lena, if the police come, it will be on the news, and Lucinda will find out."

The only thing that kept me from dialing 911 was I understood how frightened she was. After Joey found Lotta, JJ, and me, I knew if I left him again, he'd kill me or do something a lot worse. He'd make sure I never saw my boys again.

We could wait a little longer before getting the police, but we needed reinforcements. Mattwo could gather the Eccli clan on a frigid winter night, so I dialed his number for the second time because of Kalayla.

Mattwo guessed what was wrong when I said, "Matty, I'm sorry to be calling at this time of night."

"It's the girl, isn't it?" he said.

"She took off a few hours ago, and we're out searching."

"She picked a cold night to run. Where'll we meet you?"

Mattwo arrived with Lotta and Rico; my stomach lurched when I saw how strong and capable he looked. He walked over without saying a word and hugged me. I could have stayed in his arms forever.

I gave myself thirty seconds to breathe in that safe feeling.

"We'll find her," Mattwo said. "I brought the cavalry." Three additional cars filled with the Eccli family pulled over to the curb.

I never was one to rave about cell phones, but that night, I thanked whoever invented them for saving us from backtracking or duplicating efforts.

Mattwo and Rico went off together, and I hoped Rico wouldn't be the one to find Kalayla. Who knew what she'd do if she saw him before he saw her?

Maureen and I met them a couple of times to check in. While Mattwo and I decided where to head next, Rico huddled with Maureen, talking to her quietly and calming her down.

Just after three, Rico called to say they found Kalayla wedged behind a dumpster about eight blocks from Eddie's. I could hear her screaming in the background, probably waking up everybody for blocks around. Maureen took off running, and I beat it after her as fast as my legs could manage.

By the time I arrived, Kalayla had Maureen on her radar along with Rico. The variety of swears that girl knew was appalling, but maybe all that screaming was keeping her warm.

By that point, Rico was at the same place on the patience scale as I was. When he tried reaching in and grabbing her, Kalayla bit his hand and unloaded more swears. A snowball had better odds of surviving in hell than Rico or Maureen did of getting her to come out. That left it to me.

Once I knew she was safe, I wasn't in the mood for sweet-talking or cajoling, but I did try that. "Kalayla, you can't spend the rest of your life wedged behind a dumpster. You may as well come on out now."

"I'll stay here as long as I want. Maybe for a year."

"What a fine idea! You'll end up skin and bones and smelling like a dead skunk."

"Won't either! I'll come out during the day. Lots of people will give a homeless kid like me a meal and a shower."

Homeless kid, my ass! I'd had enough of that girl and her mother for one night! "I spent this whole damn night looking for you, Kalayla! My bones are icicles. My fingers barely move. My back hurts, and I'm hungry. I am too old to put up with any more of your crap! Get out here now!"

"Well, since you asked so nicely," she said. She crawled out at the speed of an inchworm to make sure I knew she was coming out of her own free will and not because I told her to. She stood up, brushed herself off, turned her back on Maureen, and stuck her tongue out at Rico.

Her teeth were chattering, and she was shivering, but when Rico offered his coat to her, she said, "I'd rather freeze than wear any turdy coat of yours!"

Mattwo took off his jacket and handed it to her. "Here," he said, "No turds on this one."

"Thanks," she said, pulling it tight. Five of her might have fit in it, but it was better than nothing on such a night.

Yawning searchers straggled in. The temperature was fifteen degrees, and daylight was coming. They needed to climb into warm beds, which was precisely what I had in mind for myself.

Kalayla read my mind. "I'm not going anywhere with her," she said, pointing at Maureen. "And you can't make me!"

I was too cold to spend another second listening to her. Maureen was teetering on the edge, and there was no point giving Kalayla a chance to shove her over. I did the only thing I could. I took the girl home with me.

***

Naturally, the first thing Kalayla wanted was food. I sat her down at the kitchen table and fried up a three-egg omelet with cheese, onions, and frozen broccoli I keep on hand for emergencies. She shoveled that in with four slices of toast slathered with butter and jam and washed it down with orange juice.

When she'd finished, I said, "You stink like you crawled inside that dumpster and rooted around looking for treasure. Put those clothes in a pile with Mattwo's jacket. We'll have to get that washed or cleaned, or he'll never be able to wear it again."

"I got money from my cookie sales," Kalayla snapped. "I can pay for it myself!"

"Get into that shower while I go and get some clean clothes for you. You used up your quota for dumb behavior for the next twenty-five years, and you better be clean by the time I come back here!"

It was a good thing I was immune to her nasty looks.

Rico opened Maureen's door and given that she was dangling from such a thin thread, it probably wasn't a bad idea for him to hang around. Maureen mentioned they had coffee after the birthday party but hadn't said anything about him since. I thought maybe they hadn't hit it off, but I might have been wrong.

Maureen rushed at me, "Is Kalayla okay? Did she eat? Is she coming home? Oh, Lena, I've made such a mess of things."

I didn't want to listen to one second more of her mea culpa recording, but Rico seemed to be managing okay. He was rummaging in the fridge when Maureen and I came out of the bedroom with Kalayla's clean clothes. Rico must've offered to cook breakfast because he asked if she wanted bacon with her French toast.

When I got home, Kalayla was stretched out on the sofa, wrapped in my fleece throw, as talkative as a speck of dirt.

I hoped the sound of my sweet voice would put her to sleep, so I made up stories about all the creatures I had to fight off with a flashlight while looking for her. I was having a fine time amusing myself, so after I ran out of make-believe creatures, I told her true stories, like when Lotta asked Mikie and Jimmy to pass out flyers for one of her shelter fundraisers. The twins made up anything they thought would encourage people to show up, like saying Evel Knievel would give free rides on his motorcycle.

Lotta spat nails when she found out, but that woman never turned her back on a challenge. She convinced an ex-boyfriend who owned a Harley it would be fun to pass himself off as Evel's cousin. Mikie and Jimmy drove the guy crazy, begging for rides, but the fundraiser was a huge success.

Even though I was talking about my twins, Kalayla didn't raise an eyebrow, smile, or bombard me with questions. I doubt she heard one word I said, so I gave up storytelling.

By then, it was late morning. When I mentioned food, Kalayla grunted, and that empty pit she called a stomach led her to the table. She chowed down two turkey sandwiches with tomato, onion, cheese, lettuce, pickle, and mustard. That would have been beyond imagining if I hadn't raised four boys who could do the same.

I ran out of turkey and was about to open a can of tuna fish when she decided she hadn't given up talking altogether. "If you wanted to be nice for a change, you could give me one of Lotta's desserts." I cut her a hunk of chocolate pie.

I figured it was time to shut up and let her be, but not before I did one more thing. I dug into the back of my storage closet and pulled out an old cardboard box tied with plain string. No one would have guessed it contained something I couldn't give or throw away.

Cody was a four-foot-high stuffed brown bear. His fur was rubbed off in a few spots, and one ear was sewn back on with big, uneven red stitches. I'd wrapped him in layers of tissue paper. I folded each one carefully and put all of them back in the box. I held him close and let images of my boys holding, sharing, and loving him flood me.

I carried Cody into the living room and put him beside Kalayla. "This is Cody," I said, "He belonged to my four boys."

Kalayla pulled Cody close and buried her face in his fur like my boys did when they needed comfort. That was more than I could take. I marched into the kitchen and set about cleaning things that didn't need cleaning. I could hear Kalayla crying, and there wasn't a single part of me that wasn't crying with her.

I was glad it got dark early. Kalayla was fading long before the shadows came, which was no surprise since she just lived through the worst twenty-four hours of her life.

I thought I'd try one more thing, so I said, "Going to sleep angry interferes with digestion, and given all you ate, you could develop a gigantic stomach ache. You might prevent that if you went home and talked to your mama."

"She'd be the only one talking, and all she does is lie!" Her words were angry, but her face was forlorn enough to make a stone heart weep. She held onto Cody like she was never planning to let go.

I sat down in the chair near her and waited a minute. Then I took a deep breath and said, "So, exactly where did you plan to spend the night?"

Her voice cracked when she said, "I was hoping you'd let me stay here."

I knew that was as close to pleading as she would ever come. I struggled to keep myself from wrapping my arms around her, pulling her close, and crooning to her the way I had when my boys were little and hurting. Even Mark, who picked fights with anybody in sight, and JJ, who wanted to be cool and tough like his dad, even those two would let me pull them close when they were her age.

But right then, it seemed Kalayla needed time and space to work through the mess her mama and daddy handed her. And that was something I could give her. "What do you plan on doing if I say no?"

She squared her shoulders and pulled herself upright. "I'd go find another dumpster."

"Then I'll have some cop dragging me out in the cold in the middle of the night so I can identify your frozen body. At least if you stay here, my old bones will be warm, and I might get some sleep."

She almost smiled. "Can I sleep in the white room and keep Cody with me?"

All of a sudden, my boys were shoving at each other, all of them wanting to claim Cody for the night. JJ turned to me, asserting his privilege as the oldest. Mark grabbed Cody and ran for his life. The twins used their secret sign language to divide up the night, equal shares of Cody. Then they tore after Mark.

Mark, furious and knowing the two of them would overpower him, hurled Cody by the ear, shouting how they were unfair assholes, too chicken to face him one on one. All four boys froze mid-step, stunned, and focused on the ear in Mark's hand. JJ screamed, "You're the asshole for hurting Cody," and launched into Mark. And I remembered JJ, sitting on the sofa using that red thread on Cody's ear, determined to sew it back without my help.

A voice broke through the memory, calling me back.

"Can I, Lena?" Kalayla stared at me, waiting for my answer, not realizing I was listening to my boys' voices fade away.

"Of course, you can," I said, taking a deep breath and holding back exhaustion for a few more minutes. "Cody has to sleep someplace, and he likes kids. If you want to, you can sleep on that sofa you've been hogging. The only bed in the spare room is the floor."

"I don't care," she said, sticking her chin out, stubborn as always. "It's quiet there. And it's empty. I like it."

***

Quiet and empty, reminding me of the big house that had been Joey's showpiece, where, bit by bit, the sounds had faded into silence, and all the life was gone.

JJ was the first to leave, moving to an apartment with friends after graduation. Joey wanted him in the business full-time, so he went nights to Lowell Tech.

Mark was the next to leave, going to Boston, New York City, and then out West. At first, he sent postcards, but the last one was years ago. I wondered if his broken body was buried in an anonymous grave. When I asked JJ if he knew where Mark was, he shrugged and didn't answer.

Joey's death didn't leave a hole in my life, but I was lost when the twins died. Despite all the protests against the Vietnam War, they were determined to enlist.

I didn't tell them Joey thought the war was for ignorant schmucks too stupid to figure a way out of going. He was thrilled that World War II ended before he was old enough to be drafted.

When I asked Mikie and Jimmy why they wanted to go, they said, "Look, Ma, those guys running away to Canada are cowards. The Marines need guys like us who'll fight for what's right." They enlisted and were shipped home in body bags.

After their funeral, I wandered around Joey's house, poked in the boys' rooms, and straightened this or that. I'd go down the basement to the game room, stare at the pool table, or go up to the attic and pick through toys, report cards, or prized possessions like the twins' first stripe on their karate belts, the first dollar JJ earned shoveling snow, or the dog-eared playing cards Mark bragged taught him how to cheat and not get caught.

Lotta meant well when she said, "Face the facts, Lena. Mikie and Jimmy are dead. Mark jumped into a black hole, and JJ is making his own life. He'll never come home."

But Lotta had no idea how I felt. What happened to my boys was my doing. They might have had a chance if I had gotten them away from Joey. I left that empty house and fell into the gutter, drinking my way from one dive to another.

Three months later, Dom came looking for me.

"Clean yourself up," he ordered. "Mother asked to see you. You're not fit to see anybody, especially not her!"

He drove me back to Joey's house to shower and change out of clothes that reeked. I longed to drown myself in scotch, but Dom followed me up to the bedroom and waited outside the bathroom door. I swear that man would have come in with me if he thought I'd hidden a bottle underneath the sink. I wished I had.

My mother, the family matriarch and my mentor, pressed her fingers into my arm. "Don't you dare let the vultures get you, Lena! We bury them. They don't bury us. You're a survivor, just like me. Don't you ever forget that!"

I nodded. The family would never tolerate a drunk in a high position. I pulled myself together and used the skills she taught me to do what she expected.

After I dried out, I stripped the house where I'd raised my boys and gave away everything connected to life with Joey. I sold the house, moved into the apartment building, and bought what I needed. I could imagine someone walking into my apartment and wondering if I hadn't finished moving in or out. After almost thirty years of living here, I still wouldn't know what to tell them.

Nothing except the photos, and Cody carried memories, and Cody had been buried in the back of that closet until Kalayla gave me a reason to take him out.

My spare room might be a haven where Kalayla could begin to heal. I spent days exposed and defenseless in that room, staring out the windows and seeing nothing, enduring a self-styled flagellation without a whip. Kalayla was young and innocent. Maybe she'd find answers I hadn't.

I pulled out some blankets and sheets. The floor would have to do for tonight, but I'd buy a blow-up mattress tomorrow. It looked like Kalayla would be a long-term guest.

The next morning came too soon for me. To my surprise, Kalayla said nothing about the hard or uncomfortable floor. After breakfast, I marched her to the door and reminded her there were laws requiring kids her age to attend school.

She resembled a zombie, but that didn't stop her from taking the stairs two at a time and yelling, "What does somebody as old as you know about school? It wasn't invented when you were a kid."

The minute she was gone, I plopped down on the sofa. My bones and muscles were aching for a lullaby, but my thoughts were jumping beans. If Kalayla got to school and stayed until the end of the day, what would I do when she got home?

Was I a fool to offer a hurting child shelter in my house?

My mother told me a complicated question never had a perfect or permanent answer, and searching for one was a waste of time and energy. "Make a decision, Lena. Choose a direction, put one foot in front of the other, and move toward it."

I guess that's what I was doing.

DINNER AT LENA'S

I came home from work every day, stood in the apartment doorway, and held my breath, hoping Kalayla would be home. Speakers blared the silence when I called her name. I covered my ears, trying to shut it out. I knocked on Lena's door, but when she opened it and shook her head, I went home to an empty apartment.

On the eighth night, I said, "She has to talk to me tonight, Lena. She has to."

"She doesn't have to, but I sure hope she will. You have to keep trying regardless of what she does. She's in the spare room doing homework. At least, that's what she said. For all I know, she could be standing on her head."

"What will I do if she won't ever come home?"

"Now, Maureen, don't make it worse by exaggerating. Stay here for dinner. I'll finish getting things ready and make coffee. If anything can get Kalayla out here, it's food, but don't get your hopes up. Nothing is going to make her civil."

I didn't care if Kalayla was silent, scowling, or insulting. I needed to see that she was all right, and anything would be better than hearing her shout through the door, "Go away, I hate you."

"What if she won't come out?" I said.

"Well then, we will have a good meal without her. It's high time we gave her a shove. Otherwise, we might be waiting forever."

I sat on the sofa, fidgeting. I could have made a whole meal in a quarter of the time it took Lena to brew coffee. My life was a mess, and I was waiting for coffee. A songwriter could have turned that line into a solid gold recording.

Lena finally called, "Dinner is ready. Come and put this food on the table while I prod that girl of yours."

Lena went to the spare room door. "Dinner is ready, Kalayla. Run a brush through your hair. We've got a guest."

I heard shuffling, and Kalayla said, "Maybe I'll come out, and maybe I won't. Who's the guest?"

"If you don't come out, maybe I'll toss your share of fried chicken, green beans, mashed potatoes, gravy, and Lotta's lemon meringue pie in the garbage. A polite response would be: 'Thank you for going to the trouble of cooking my favorite dinner, Miss Lena.'"

"If I'd known what the menu was, I would've said thank you on my own. Who's the guest?"

"It's your mama."

"Eating with her would make the food taste like cow turds. I'll bring my plate in here."

"You will eat with us at the table, or your next meal will be a long time coming."

Silence from the room.

"Fine!" Kalayla said. "But I'm not talking to her, and you can't make me."

"Suit yourself. It's a free country."

Kalayla muttered, "Fat chance with you around, you old crab," but Lena didn't respond.

By the time Kalayla stomped to the table, we'd already served ourselves. She sat as far from me as she could.

I hadn't seen her in over a week. That's not long compared to six months or a year, but Kalayla seemed more grown-up and serious. It was hard to imagine her sitting at the kitchen table, singing under her breath and giggling while she stuck Red Hots on Clarence's cookie.

Kalayla helped herself to a chicken breast, mashed potatoes, and gravy and said, "At least she's a pretty good cook."

When I asked Kalayla how school was going, what she'd been doing, and if she needed anything, she acted like I was invisible. My appetite drained away. I pushed beans around my plate, wishing I knew what to say or do. I hoped Lena would help, but she didn't. When I asked how her day had been, Lena said, "Just fine, thanks," and kept eating. Staying for dinner was another mistake. Making mistakes seemed to be the only thing I was good at.

And then, out of the blue, Lena said, "I haven't seen that Clarence fellow lately. He must be working or something, more likely or something."

Kalayla's head snapped up, and she stared at Lena.

"Clarence?" I said. "Funny you should ask. He called to say he might be stopping by this weekend. He does work, Lena. He's an expert mechanic and a freelance car location agent. I'm not quite sure what that means. He was curious whether you'd be at home, Kalayla, so he must want to see you. I told him you might not be around this weekend."

Kalayla stared at Lena and said, "Clarence never wanted to see me before! Why does he want to know if I'll be home? Ask her that, Lena!"

I thought Lena would yell at Kalayla for being rude. She frowned but didn't say a word. I didn't care. At least Kalayla acknowledged I was in the room. Besides, I wondered the same thing but I didn't want to sound like I didn't trust Clarence.

Then, Lena said something even more surprising. "I've been thinking about how decent it was of him to give you those cookies he happened to acquire. I'd like to meet him and add myself to his cookie list. I didn't realize Clarence had a car location business. I'm aware of the skills that line of work requires. I'll see if he can relocate one of those cute little Mercedes convertibles into my garage. Wouldn't that be fun, Kalayla? We could ride with the top down all summer."

I was utterly astonished. I opened my mouth, but the words jumbled together, and all that came out was, "Agg."

Unlike me, Kalayla was not tongue-tied. She slammed her fork down on the table and said, "Don't say anything like that to him, Lena! Clarence won't like it if you act like you think he steals cars!"

I was shocked when Kalayla looked at me and said, "Mama, tell her! Tell Lena to stay away from Clarence!"

I was so happy, I almost jumped out of my chair. Kalayla had talked to me! Lena smirked, clearly pleased with herself.

Before I could gather my wits, Lena turned to Kalayla and said, "Don't talk with your mouth full. I'm not taking a trip to the emergency room on account of you choking on food. And I will thank you not to tell me what I should or should not do. You'd be surprised what I'm willing to do at my age that I wouldn't have dared do when I was your mama's age. Back then, I was just as scared as she is."

I gasped.

Kalayla sat bolt upright, pointed a finger at Lena, and said, "My mama isn't scared! You don't know anything!"

"Well, girl, my eyes may be old, but they see better than yours. Your mama is terrified she's going to lose you!" Lena's gaze narrowed as if she were gauging Kalayla's reaction.

Kalayla scowled and glanced sideways at me. "The only reason she wants me around is to tell me big fat lies!"

Lena threw her napkin on the table. "You don't understand your mama at all! She does stupid things just like you, me, and everybody else! You're the one who put her on the Perfect Mama Pedestal. She never belonged there. Nobody does."

Kalayla stared at her plate. She squinched her face like she was about to spew rotten food.

Lena kept talking, "It's about time you gave your mama a chance to explain why she lied to you."

I held my breath. Kalayla blinked a few times. Lena helped herself to potatoes and gravy. For some ridiculous reason, the words from that old gambler's song popped into my head: Know when to hold them; know when to fold them; know when to walk away, and know when to run.

Lena laid her cards face up on the table, and I prayed Kalayla wouldn't bolt for the door.

Time passed in slow motion. Kalayla stared at her plate. Lena spread gravy around the top and sides of her mashed potatoes. I watched.

Finally, Kalayla looked up, speared a drumstick with her fork, and said, "At least I was smart enough not to put you on a pedestal!"

Lena shoveled potato onto her fork and gave a good chew before saying, "Well, Miss Smarty Pants, that remark earned you your walking papers! After you finish stuffing your face, clean up the room where you've been squatting, go home, and practice acting decent!"

Mustering the dirtiest look she could, Kalayla said, "Fine!" And then, under her breath, "Turdy old crab!"

Lena twirled her fork around the potato pile, then turned to me. "I expect you to let me know when I should come and meet Clarence."

I nodded. I was afraid anything I said might make my chance to make things right disappear.

When Kalayla came out dragging her canvas bag, Lena handed her a hunk of Carlotta's lemon meringue pie on a paper plate. After Kalayla left, Lena hugged me and whispered, "Telling her you love her is enough for now. That and this."

She handed me another plate of pie.

LOOSE ENDS

When Mama said Clarence was coming, I knew I had to declare a temporary truce with her. I couldn't take the chance of not being there if he showed up. What a pisser!

Anybody could see Clarence was sniffing around Mama, and I wasn't giving him a chance to do more than sniff. The old lady would say I didn't know what I was talking about, but she'd be wrong. I saw Daddy slap Mama on the butt and ask how his honey pot was plenty of times. She'd snuggle up close, laugh, and tease him about being in heat.

Lena thought she knew everything, but she didn't know a thing about Clarence. If I told her what he was like, she would've flipped into a tirade, and who knows what else she might've done.

Once, Clarence brought a sack of gold bracelets and necklaces a friend gave him. He told Mama to take whatever she liked, and he'd come by for payment some other time. Luckily, Mama said she wasn't interested.

Another time, when Mama thought he was taking me to the park, we went to his favorite bar. He said I could order any drink I wanted, and it'd be our secret. I got a large coke. The place had a pool table. Clarence said I had a natural talent for the game, and my innocent face would be a fine enticement if I wanted to make a little money.

When Lena saw how Clarence acted around Mama, she'd stick her nose in full-time. Mama didn't understand that and insisted on telling Lena that Clarence said he'd come on Sunday morning.

***

Wouldn't you know that old lady knocked on our door at nine a.m. with a stack of magazines prepared to stay as long as was necessary? We were lucky she didn't come Saturday night! Mama made caramel-covered brownies for the occasion.

Mama and Lena were so busy yakking that I answered the door when Clarence knocked. Seeing his face drop when he saw me was the best thing that happened to me in six months! He was probably hoping I fell into a sewer and drowned.

"Kalayla!" he said, "I didn't think you'd be home! Your Mama said you were staying with a friend for a few days."

There wasn't snow on his leather jacket or shiny bald head, and he wore a silk shirt, tight blue jeans, and new loafers. I bet he wouldn't've dressed that way if he knew I'd be there.

I gave him my sweetest smile and said, "Hey, Uncle, aren't you happy nobody kidnapped me?"

Before he could answer, Lena grabbed his hand and shook it like a bottle of salad dressing.

"I'm Lena Barzetti from across the hall," she said. "Maureen and I were making plans for our next Neighborhood Watch meeting. She probably told you we keep a close eye out for each other here."

Neighborhood Watch?

I don't know who was more shocked: Mama, me, or Clarence. I knew the old lady would pull something out of her hat, but cow turds, a Neighborhood Watch?

Clarence got over being stunned and said hello but didn't put down the shopping bag. I pointed at it and said, "Oh, Uncle, did you bring goodies?"

He looked daggers at me, so I gave him another big smile. This was turning into the best day ever.

Clarence shifted from one foot to the other. "Ah, I went shopping and bought some clothes I didn't want to leave in the car."

"I know just what you mean," Lena said quickly. "It's best to be careful. If a thief decided to relocate your car, I imagine he'd be happy to discover fine clothes in the backseat!"

If my smile got any wider, it would split my lips! "Oh, Uncle Clarence, please give us a fashion show! We love fashion shows, don't we, Miss Lena?"

Lena said, "Clarence—you don't mind me calling you Clarence, do you? I told Maureen it was high time I met her kind-hearted brother-in-law. Everyone in our Neighborhood Watch notices how you check on Kalayla and her mama. While we're having a snack, I want to hear about you and your business deals. I so enjoyed the cookies your sweet little niece sold me!"

I almost wet my pants! That old lady's mouth must've tasted like sour lemons and vinegar. Her nose would wrap around the world twice for telling that big a lie. You can bet I wouldn't let her forget she said I was sweet!

Mama said, "Why don't we have coffee and a sweet? Clarence's fashion show can wait until later."

Clarence knew when to retreat. He said, "Sorry, Maureen, I can't stay. I just stopped by to make sure you're okay. I'll catch you when there's less going on." He was out the door and down the stairs in a flash.

Lena called after him, "I look forward to chatting with you, Clarence, dear."

The three of us burst out laughing and feasted on caramel brownies.

***

Being home was as fun as playing in cement. Mama tip-toed around like she was scared I'd explode if she breathed too loud, and I wasn't my cheerful self.

That didn't mean I was hot to go back to Lena's. If I stayed at her place again, I'd buy a pair of earplugs to block out her lectures.

Being in all that white fired up my brain, and I couldn't turn it off once I got home. I wondered when Mama would take me to meet the O'Rourkes. I wondered what my grandparents were like and if the other cousins were like Kieran or the butthole kids at school.

I wondered about other stuff, too. Why didn't Mama's family come to Daddy's funeral? And afterward, why didn't they help the way Daddy's family did?

I stopped by Lena's every day to make sure she hadn't dropped dead without me looking after her. When I told her I'd been thinking about Mama's family, she said, "People don't always turn out to be what we hope, Kalayla. Remember that if you meet your O'Rourke grandparents."

Why'd Lena have to say something like that? I wasn't scared of meeting them if that's what she thought. I wasn't afraid of anything and had scars to prove it. When I was five, a neighbor kid said I was too chicken to jump out a second-floor window of his house. I cut my hands and knees when I landed on broken glass. I didn't care. He never called me chicken again.

As if having the O'Rourkes on my mind wasn't enough, I got tired of being polite to Mama when I said goodbye or hello, while we were eating, and when I said goodnight.

By the fifth day, I couldn't stand it any longer. I was sitting on the sofa munching an apple and surfing channels when Mama came in from work. She said she was happy I was home now.

So, I said, "Yeah, and now you can introduce me to my O'Rourke family, right?"

Mama turned white as Lena's walls. She started to say something but stopped. She took a deep breath and said very slowly, "I will call my mother, and she will hang up on me."

That pissed me off. "She's mad 'cause you never took me to meet your family, right? I'd be mad, too!"

Mama's face twisted like I'd sliced her open, and her guts spilled out.

I would've heard what she whispered even if my ears were stuffed with cotton.

"That's not the way it happened, Kalayla. My mother wanted me to marry an Irish Catholic boy who lived in our neighborhood and planned to be a lawyer. She disowned me when I married your father. She said what I did could hurt the family. It had nothing to do with you."

Was that why the newspaper didn't have Mama's name as one of Kevin's and Colleen's children? Colin, Leah, and Kate, but no Maureen.

Mama went on in the same soft voice. "You were my mother's first granddaughter, and I was sure she'd forgive me and want to see you. When I called her, she said, 'I don't have a daughter named Maureen,' and hung up."

Mama looked at me, and I looked at her. Neither of us said anything.

I stood up, walked to the apartment door, opened it, walked across the hallway, and knocked on Lena's door.

I walked past Lena into the spare room, closed the door, and stared out the window. Families couldn't disown you, could they? What if they did?

I wanted to know the truth, and now I did. I wasn't mad, glad, or sad. I wasn't anything at all. My brain was numb.

FACING THE ELEPHANT

Kalayla walked past me like I wasn't there, went into the spare room, and closed the door. Maureen was standing in their doorway. Sometimes, Maureen hovered a foot off the ground like she was about to float into outer space. But at that moment, she was an oak with roots planted deep. Whatever caused that likely was what propelled my squatter into the spare room.

Maureen said, "I told her the truth, Lena. And you know what? It was like I was throwing garbage in the trash."

Maureen's smile was so peaceful I heaved a sigh of relief and hugged her.

"Kalayla walked out without saying a word. Do you think I should have stopped her?"

"I sincerely doubt you could have. The fact that Kalayla said nothing means she's got nothing to say. Give her time to let what you told her sink in. Your worrying won't help or hurry her."

Maureen smiled and went back to their apartment. I brewed a cup of lemon ginger tea and settled on the sofa. The confident face I put on for Maureen sure didn't reflect how I felt. Kalayla knew the O'Rourkes had shunned her mama and daddy and acted like she didn't exist. Would knowing that turn Kalayla's good-natured feistiness into close-hearted hatred and anger?

I had to do something. Kalayla could walk out of this apartment without asking my permission as quickly as she walked into it. I went over and knocked on the spare room door.

Silence. I waited and then knocked again. Silence. I might be dead and buried before that girl was ready to talk. I pulled a folding chair out of the closet and went into the spare room without knocking.

Kalayla was slumped in the chair by the windows, with her face hidden in her hands. She didn't move when I put my chair next to hers. I didn't go in there to look out the window. I rested my hand on Kalayla's back, and she did something that broke my heart open. She nestled her head on my shoulder and came as close to curling up in my lap as she could. Her soft crying built to a crescendo, with every bit of her body joining in.

"It's okay, girl," I whispered. "Your mama loves you. I love you. We'll find a way out of this."

I thought Kalayla's tears would never stop, and when they did, I got worried about what she was thinking.

I burst out laughing when she said, "Is there anything to eat in this house?"

A geyser of relief gushed through me. "There is always something to eat in this house. Let's go see what I've got." I grilled two tuna and cheese sandwiches and got a bag of sea salt and vinegar potato chips.

Kalayla ate every bit, then looked at me and said, "Families can't kick you out even if you're a real jerk, can they, Lena?"

I was grateful Kalayla didn't know some parents could sell their kids like chattel or a husband could disfigure his wife while her family watched. She didn't know my family insisted I stay married to Joey no matter what he did to me. I prayed she never learned the things families could do.

"Some families take care of you and love you no matter what. Other families don't. Your mama's family is one of those that don't. I don't understand why they did what they did. But that's their loss, Kalayla. If they were willing to get to know you, they'd love you as much as I do. They'd be proud to have you as their grandchild."

Kalayla's beautiful green eyes were wide open. She cocked her head to the side like she wasn't sure she understood what I said.

"You said if they got to know me, they'd love me like you do, right?"

I nodded.

"They'd be proud I was their granddaughter, like you are, right?"

I wouldn't have believed it if I hadn't heard her say it! Kalayla granted me grandmother status! If that didn't beat all!

I nodded, and when that girl smiled, my heart bloomed with spring flowers.

My son, JJ, hoarded my flesh and blood granddaughters, his gold-plated kids. He disapproved of where and how I lived. "Look, Ma, I don't want my daughters thinking how you live is normal. If Dad were alive, you'd live in Weston near us and always see Juliana and Ronnie."

When the two girls were young, JJ brought them to my apartment for an annual visit on Halloween. I have no doubt Joey reached out from Hell and whispered into JJ's ear: "Halloween is the perfect day to visit that bitchy old witch." Juliana dressed up as a princess or a kidnapped damsel in distress. Ronnie was a cowgirl or an astronaut.

JJ invited me to Weston for Thanksgiving, Christmas, and Easter. Every few months, I asked his family to dinner at a restaurant that met with JJ's approval. His distaste for my lifestyle never interfered with our business relationship.

The lovable pain-in-the-ass girl sitting next to me didn't realize what a precious gift she'd given me. If life were a fairy tale, we'd live happily ever after. Kalayla would make friends and control her mouth. Maureen would marry a prince. And I would be a grandmother in more than name.

"Miss Lena," Kalayla said, interrupting my daydreams. "Would it be okay for me to stay here tonight?"

I got stuck buying cookies the last time Kalayla called me Miss Lena. This time, I'd better get to Mickey's and stock up like I would have for my boys.

"Yes, but first go home and show your mama you're among the living. Cody will be waiting when you come back."

"I'll go, but I'm not talking to her. She should've told me her parents are buttholes!"

"Did I say a word about having a chat? Show her you're breathing and tell her you'll be here tonight. I imagine you plan to hog the shower, so bring clean clothes, too."

"Fine!" she said in an oppressed martyr tone so I'd know seeing her mama was as much fun as being stung by a swarm of yellow jackets.

So much for Miss Lena and fairy tale endings!

WHAT'S NEXT?

I twirled around the apartment, gleefully singing and laughing. It was finally over, fini, finito, terminado! I'd never again worry about how, when, or where to tell Kalayla!

I'd tell her how sorry I was when she decided to speak to me. But I couldn't explain what my mother did because I didn't understand then, and I still don't.

My mother moved from Belfast to South Boston when she was nine and hated both places. The best thing that ever happened to her was meeting my father at a St. Paddy's party in Boston and moving to an Irish Catholic neighborhood in Brighton where the neighbors shared their background, religion, and values.

My mother wanted me to live in the same rigid world with clearly defined boundaries. But I couldn't. I lived in a world of nuance and shading and did the opposite of what she wanted.

Kalayla might not do the things I wanted her to, but there would always be a place for her in my life. Rico's family let him carve a separate path inside his family, and he might give me advice. The afternoon we had coffee, he gave me his cell number and said I could call anytime. I punched his number in quickly before I could change my mind.

He answered on the second ring, said, "Maureen?" and sounded pleased to hear from me. I was so startled I almost hung up.

"Rico, hi," I said in a rush, "I'm calling because you found Kalayla, and I wanted you to know I did it. It took me a long time, but I did it."

Rico's voice was soft, low-key, and friendly. "You did it? The only thing I can imagine that would make you so happy is that you told Kalayla about your family. Right?"

"Yes, and I wanted you to know. Can you believe it?"

"I can, and that is news worth celebrating! How about meeting me for a bite to eat?"

"I'd love that. Kalayla is at Lena's, so this is a good time."

"Great! Let's do a twofer. The Connemara is a pub across from Matty's Way. We can have a bite to eat there, and I'll give you a tour of the gym."

I threw on black wool slacks, an orange, long-sleeve wool sweater, a gold chain, dangle earrings, and a warm jacket.

Parking in Cambridge was awful in winter, and people marked their shoveled spots so no one else would take them. Rico was standing in the middle of a newly cleared parking space, holding a shovel like a warrior ready for battle. He looked swarthy and warm in a pea coat, turtleneck, cords, and boots.

"Hey," he said as he opened my car door. "This is the gym." He pointed at the building in front of me. "When Dad's friend, Larry, retired from the appliance business, we bought the two lots next to us and put on an addition that tripled our space. We convinced every business owner on the block to rehab."

I looked up and down the block. The sidewalks were clear, with periodic openings so people could enter the street without walking to the nearest driveway. Rico was rightfully proud of what they'd done. The buildings and signage were tasteful and attractive. "It's great that you didn't tear everything down and build bigger and higher."

"I'll tell you more, but let's get inside before we freeze, or I die of hunger."

Rico took my arm as we crossed the street. The lighting inside the Connemara was low, and a crowd stood around the bar chatting with friends or new acquaintances. We worked our way to the back, where the hostess sat us in a booth.

We ordered Merlot and snacked on popcorn before wolfing down cheeseburgers and the house specialty, broccoli slaw. After the waitress cleared our dishes, Rico said, "I've thought about calling you, but it seemed like you had to work out things with Kalayla first. Dating somebody with kids adds complications. A while back, I was seeing a divorced woman who had two terrific little boys. I ended up liking them better than I liked their mother. When we stopped dating, I missed seeing them. So, I'm glad you told Kalayla because it cleared away a hurdle."

Oh! My jittery stomach came back with a vengeance. I wasn't sure what to say, so I nodded. Rico sounded like we were negotiating a business deal with no frills, just straightforward facts, and I had to smile.

"Besides that," Rico said, "I got off to the worst possible start with Kalayla. Before we take on a new martial arts student, we want to determine their trigger points. When I pushed Kalayla, she exploded, and it was not pretty."

I groaned inside.

Rico said, "But I saw a different side of her at your birthday party. Kalayla planned that because she loves you. When I found her at the dumpster, despite her foul mouth, it was obvious that she was scared and hurting."

I nodded again.

"The thing is," he said, "I'd like to spend time with you. That means I have to make peace with Kalayla. The Irish step-dancing group *Riverdance* is coming to town, and I thought I could get tickets for the three of us. It's at the end of May, so Kalayla will have plenty of time to get over being angry at me. But first, I need to know what you think."

I'd be going on a date with my daughter as the chaperone. What a hoot! "I'd like that, Rico, but I don't know if Kalayla will."

"I'll ask her. Does this sound like a plan?"

I was delighted and excited, but I told myself to stay calm. May was almost two months away. Anything could happen between now and then, especially with a daughter like Kalayla.

"It sounds like a good plan," I said.

"Okay then. If I get the go-ahead from Kalayla, I'll get tickets. Now, how about dessert? Connemara's bread pudding is the best!"

SPRING 2000

WHAT'S NEW?

The bubble bath temperature was perfect. I eased my old bones into the tub, slid down to my neck, and sighed. Kalayla was back where she belonged, and my apartment was peaceful and quiet again.

I thought raising girls would be easier than raising boys, but I sure was wrong. If my boys had run off the way Kalayla was prone to do, Joey would have installed revolving doors, and the men in white coats would have hauled me off to the nuthouse.

The bubbles tickled my nose, and shifting my butt from side to side felt good. I added hot water, leaned against the back of the tub, and let my mind wander.

I giggled when I thought of the expression on Clarence's face when Kalayla opened the door. We let the air out of his tires, but slowing him down wouldn't stop him and his flashy shirt and tight jeans. His brash manner of staring at Maureen left no doubt that he was on the hunt. The fact he hightailed it proved he wasn't stupid enough to go through Kalayla and me to get to Maureen. He'd wait until she was alone.

I was glad Eddie gave Maureen enough hours so she could stop cleaning houses. No doubt Joey's ghost was coaching Clarence on how to get Maureen cornered, and following her to a cleaning job would be one way of doing that. Well, Joey, I will make sure Clarence won't have an easy time of it. And I was still working on finding a way to flush your ghost down the toilet.

***

After volunteering at Helping Hands Shelter the next day, I stopped to see Lotta at work. She was at the front desk, multi-tasking as usual.

"I see you're busy, Lotta, but you've got to hear how Kalayla and I put the skids on a slippery creep who has his eye on Maureen. You'll be downright proud of us."

Lotta flipped through the index cards and made a few notes before looking up to say, "Let Maureen save herself. Why don't you help me save some animals by changing the no-pets policy in your apartment building?"

"You bring that up every time we talk, Lotta. I told you I'm thinking about it."

"You've been thinking about it since you and Joey bought your first building!"

"Come on, Lotta, you have to hear this. I'll spring for take-out."

"Well," she said, "seeing that you're willing to open your deep pockets!"

We were at Lotta's an hour later, munching on chips and roast beef sandwiches with horseradish. Lotta slapped her legs, laughing over Clarence's visit. "I wish I'd been a spider on the wall and seen you outsmart that man!" Lotta laughed. "A victory like that deserves a reward! Why don't we go shopping?"

"Now that you mention it, I suppose I could buy a new dress."

"That's an understatement! You're supposed to be enticing my brother, not auditioning for a dowdy old woman magazine."

"Stop that, Lotta! I admit I could use new skirts, blouses, and dresses."

Lotta's eyes widened. "Well, hot damn! It is about time!"

I had to agree. When I looked in the mirror that morning, I saw the extreme to which I let myself go. I resembled an old-fashioned cast-iron pot with dings and scratches buried under a ton of rubble.

It was time I made changes! Whatever had opened inside me might have started on a small scale, but it had grown exponentially. I was clawing out of that tomb and seeing sunlight for the first time in years. I didn't know if something might slither after me, but I didn't care. I wasn't crawling back.

LENA'S FAMILY

I was making a list of people who lied to me. I didn't put Daddy on it 'cause he was dead, and he didn't exactly lie. He told me to ask Mama instead of telling me the truth himself. Mama lied better than anyone 'cause she had so much practice. She'd be on my list forever.

I wasn't sure what to do with the old lady. She was like Daddy. She didn't lie, but there was plenty of stuff she didn't tell me, like why her kids and grandkids never came to visit. What if she told them not to come over 'cause they did something she didn't like? I didn't think she'd do that, but I wasn't sure of anything. I decided the only way to find out was to ask.

Lena opened the door and said, "I figured it was time for your afternoon snack. Oatmeal raisin cookies and milk. Take it or leave it."

"I'll take it," I said. The cookie plate and milk were on the table, and I didn't waste time digging in.

"For goodness sake, Kalayla! If you keep gulping that milk, you'll choke! And why are you stuffing your pockets with cookies? Is hoarding food your new hobby?"

"No, I wanted the cookies before I asked you a question."

She shrugged her shoulders like that was no big deal.

"You know that photo of you and those little boys on your bookcase? Did you kick them out of your family? Is that why they never come here?"

Lena didn't yell or throw me out like I thought she might. She frowned, rubbed one of her bony fingers after another, got up, and walked to the bookcase slower than she walked the day we went to the gym. She took down the photo. If my life depended on how fast Lena came back to the table, Mama would've been picking out my coffin.

"It's not a secret, Kalayla. It's that telling about my boys makes me sad."

Lena held the photo so I could see it and pointed to the tallest boy. "This is JJ, my oldest. He lives in Weston, maybe half an hour from here. He has two daughters. When they were little, he brought them over on Halloween. Now, one is a senior in high school, and the other is in college. They'd be welcome here anytime. I go to their house for most holidays."

She pointed to the next boy. "This is Mark, my second born. He moved to Boston after high school, then to New York City, and then out West. The last postcard I got from him was fifteen years ago from Chicago.

"These are my twins, Mikie and Jimmy. You saw their trophies at Matty's Way. They joined the Marines after high school and were killed in Vietnam. I wish I had kids and grandkids coming over, Kalayla. They'd be welcome no matter what they did or said or how much trouble they got into."

I shoved the milk and cookies away. The old lady looked so sad my stomach turned sour. I wished I hadn't asked. Lena's kids looked like any kid I see on the street.

"If I got to know them, I would've liked them," I said. "Leastways, if they were like you, I would've."

Tears rolled down the old lady's face, and I didn't know what to do.

She wiped away the tears and said, "You better get home so your mama doesn't start worrying."

"Okay," I said. "Would you mind saving a few cookies for me?"

I pushed my chair under the table and then did something pretty dumb. I patted the old lady on the head.

Later on, Mama asked why I was so quiet. I didn't feel like telling her I was thinking about Lena's kids. So, I said, "I must've caught pneumonia or the flu. There's lots of that at school, plus AIDS and hepatitis. I better stay home for a few days."

I should've known better. Mama ran to the medicine cabinet to get a thermometer.

"I'll call Lena," she said. "She knows the symptoms for everything."

I grabbed the thermometer. "I was joking! I'm not talking because I don't feel like talking. Stop bugging me!"

"Oh," she said. "I was trying to take care of you."

She looked so deflated I felt like a jerk.

"Mama, you don't need to take care of me! Please, leave me alone."

"Okay," she said, but I knew she wouldn't.

My brain was so jammed with thoughts there wasn't room for weather updates, which was all Mama and I could discuss without one of us getting upset. For once, I was glad to go to school and learn useless stuff about pyramids in Egypt. If Cambridge had mountains, I would've climbed one and found a cave bears or mountain lions hadn't claimed.

I dropped in on Lena every day, and about a week after telling me about her kids, she was wearing a red blouse when I stopped by. I closed my eyes, but the blouse was still red when I opened them.

Cow turds!

"Well," Lena said, "are you planning to stand there with your mouth gaping and open and close your eyes all day? I hope some poor fly doesn't mistake your mouth for a new home."

I clamped my mouth shut. "In the Stone Age, when you grew up, flies were dumb. Now they're smart enough to know what a mouth is!"

"Humph! I should think instead of talking about flies, you'd tell me how much you admire my new blouse!"

"Did you go batty and forget you only wear black?"

"I haven't gone around the bend yet. I went shopping with Lotta and bought colors I'm partial to, like red. I forgot to ask your permission! I suppose you're dying of hunger."

Nobody asked my permission, even if they screwed up my life. Mama lied to me. Her parents kicked her out of the family. Daddy died. And now the old lady stopped wearing black.

None of those things would change if I went on a hunger strike. So I didn't.

KALAYLA'S QUESTION

I'd seen Kalayla shoveling in cookies plenty of times, but never like this. She gobbled one after another, with a gulp of milk in between like Carlotta's starving strays that wouldn't stop eating until you took the food away. If I didn't step on the brake, she'd be vomiting all over my floor.

There was no point in asking her what was wrong. The list stretched halfway around the world.

Kalayla gave me a dirty look and said, "Why aren't you wearing black?"

"My slacks are black, and I'm wearing a red blouse because that's what I feel like doing. That probably shocks me more than it does you. I started wearing black after my twins died, but now I feel like wearing colors. Something changed, and I don't know what or why. But it did, so I'm wearing red."

Kalayla looked disgusted, "If I said I was doing something forever, I wouldn't stop just 'cause all of a sudden, I felt like doing something else!"

"Kalayla, I never said I'd wear black forever. Sometimes things change when we don't expect them to."

I was used to Kalayla's sudden silence but knew better than to think nothing was happening inside her head. Something was gnawing at her. I took the plate with the last cookie and her empty glass to the kitchen.

When I sat down again, she said, "Do you think my butthole grandparents might wake up some morning and decide to let Mama back in their family?"

I should have known! Kalayla's world was blown to bits when she learned about her grandparents. She thought if they changed their minds, she might be able to put a few pieces back together.

"Now listen here, Kalayla, the fact I'm old doesn't mean I can answer impossible questions. And that is an impossible question."

"But you're older than anybody, and you changed your mind about something big without a reason. If somebody told Mama's parents what stupid buttholes they are, they'd have a reason to change. Right?"

Life hadn't been fair to that girl. I couldn't bear to shatter her hope, no matter how unlikely it was to come true.

"I suppose that's not impossible. But being able to change and wanting to change are two different things, Kalayla. There's no way to predict what your mama's parents might do today, tomorrow, or next year, any more than I can predict what I'll do or you'll do."

"But they ought to, right?"

What could I say? Kalayla made complicated things sound simple, just like Lotta did. In my experience, life was many things, but simple was not one of them. If I understood correctly, Kalayla's grandmother cut off Maureen because she thought her relationship with Jamal threatened her family. I doubt she'd welcome a mixed-race grandchild.

Redemption was possible. At least, that's what I learned in church. The fact I hadn't seen much of it didn't change that. I said, "To my way of thinking, yes, they ought to. But they're the only ones who can decide if they want to, Kalayla."

Kalayla nodded. "Since you're out of cookies, I'll go home."

I'm glad she didn't ask what I thought would convince her grandparents to change. I sure didn't know.

MAUREEN

A CALL FROM THE SCHOOL

Eddie's was quiet after the morning breakfast rush, and I automatically glanced up at the apartment window. Kalayla was at school, but I wasn't looking forward to seeing her later. I'd have to talk with her about the call from her teacher. It threw me into such a tizzy that I gave Dave the hot chocolate with double whipped cream his wife, Ellie, ordered and gave Ellie his black coffee.

It wasn't as if Kalayla had sworn at a teacher or hit another kid. But I'd never gotten a call before. And, of all things, Mrs. Spencer asked why Kalayla hadn't turned in her roommate choices for the mountain trip at the end of May.

How could I answer that? Kalayla hadn't told me about a mountain trip, permission slip, or roommate list.

Mrs. Spencer continued, "You remember the information we sent home with students a month ago? The trip isn't until the end of May. We require students to choose three buddies, and we make sure they're with at least one of their friends. Most kids turn in their choices immediately.

"I double-checked yesterday and saw that Kalayla didn't turn in a permission slip or bunkmate choices. She shrugged when I asked who she wanted on her buddy list. It's an opportunity for the kids to bond in a different setting, and we encourage all of them to participate."

How embarrassing! I couldn't tell Mrs. Spencer I didn't know about the trip. So, I said, "I will certainly remind Kalayla and encourage her to go."

I was about to hang up, but Mrs. Spencer kept talking.

"There's another reason for my call, Mrs. LeeRoyce. We have weekly team meetings, and the teachers noticed a change in Kalayla. She's been a solid B/B+ student, does her homework, and completes all her assignments. But her grades have dropped to C's. She doesn't finish her homework, turns it in late, or not at all in all her major subjects. The third term ends soon."

I gulped. Third term? I had no idea when the third term began or ended. Or when the first or second term did. Jamal kept track of Kalayla's schoolwork, showed me her report cards, and told me about conferences. That was my job now, and I wasn't as conscientious about it as Jamal. "Thank you so much for calling," I said. "Please tell the other teachers how much I appreciate their work. I'll talk with Kalayla tonight."

I felt like crying, but I couldn't do that at work. I could count on some things not changing, and good advice from Lena was one of them. I'd talk to her later.

***

Lena brewed coffee and set out a plate of brownies.

"Lotta's best," she said.

"Lena, thank you, but I'm too upset to eat. The most awful thing happened. I got a call from Kalayla's teacher, and her grades have fallen."

Lena didn't look surprised. "Well, it sounds like this winter's turmoil has come home to roost."

I nodded. "It's not just that. The kids in her class go on a mountain trip, and she hasn't picked bunkmates."

"Bunkmates? You mean they'll stay overnight in one of those mountain huts with bunkbeds and an outhouse?"

"Yes, and kids do day hikes, cook meals, and clean up."

Lena laughed. "My twins loved that type of thing, but I suspect Kalayla would hate it. Is she required to go?"

"I didn't ask that. But when the teacher said she didn't put down buddy choices, Kalayla never mentioned any friends, and she's never been to a sleepover. Maybe kids don't do that anymore. But all girls have friends, even if they gossip and say mean things to each other. I had lots of friends until I started dating Jamal. I haven't been a good model for her."

Lena shook her head. "There's no point in blaming yourself. Some people are loners. She might be one of them. I wouldn't push her to go on this trip, but I wouldn't let her off the hook for her schoolwork."

"You're so smart about kids, Lena. Kalayla's schoolwork is the most important thing. She can always make friends if she wants to, can't she?"

THAT JERK RICO

The snow piles were gone. I could go outside without wearing five layers, and the last few nights, I didn't dream my O'Rourke non-grandparents were monster flies I killed with a giant fly swatter. So, I thought it would be a good weekend, but it turned out to be a real pisser.

Mama started in about school when I walked through the door on Friday. Why wasn't I doing my homework? Was I having trouble with the kids? Did I have a problem with a teacher? Was I depressed?

Cow turds! Turdy Mrs. Spencer wouldn't have called if I'd followed the rule I made on my first day in kindergarten. Screaming kids were hanging onto their mama's legs when they tried to leave, but not me. I couldn't wait for Daddy to go to work.

It didn't take me long to see that the teacher paid particular attention to kids who cried or who didn't do what she wanted them to. I decided I'd never give any teacher a reason to pay attention to me. When I got older, if some kid pissed me off and I wanted to punch him in the face, I ignored him. I could get even after everybody except me forgot about it.

I forgot that, so Mrs. Spencer called, and Mama freaked out.

The teachers are whackos if they think I'm staying in a crummy hut with no heat or electricity and using a hole in the ground to pee and poop. I wasn't asking Mama to buy a sleeping bag or a backpack that I had to stuff with toilet paper, bug spray, snacks, and extra socks. No way was I going.

I told Mama I wasn't going, and she said, "But Kalayla, honey, you might make some good friends. It could be a real bonding experience."

Yeah, right, if our shit bonded in the outhouse! I told her I'd improve my grades if she stopped bugging me.

Lena cracked up when I told her what I thought of the mountain trip. I asked what was so funny. "The image of you in the outhouse being dive-bombed by flies!"

***

I spent Saturday in the library working on homework, finishing assignments, and reviewing notes for my two tests on Monday. I could've aced both tests, but Mrs. Spencer would've called Mama to tell her how wonderful that was!

I showed Mama every assignment and figured the rest of my weekend would be good. It was until the buzzer rang around noon on Sunday. We didn't expect anybody, but sometimes Clarence dropped by to see if I got hit by a truck.

It was that jerk Rico from the gym. Of course, Mama heard his voice on the intercom, so I had to buzz him in. He smiled when he saw me. "Hey, Kalayla. How are you doing?"

Cow turds!

Mama held the door like she thought I might slam it in his face. She didn't need to worry. I would've politely explained that turds weren't allowed in our apartment before I slammed the door in his face.

Naturally, Mama offered him coffee, but he said, "No, thanks, Maureen. I came to talk to Kalayla."

Double cow turds! Why'd he want to talk to me?

"Okay," Mama said. "I'll be in the kitchen."

Rico said, "Would you be willing to talk with me for a few minutes, Kalayla?"

What a pisser! I would've told him to stuff it up his butt, but Mama, Daddy, and the old lady programmed me to be polite. So, I said, "I guess," in a tone that let him know I'd prefer a caterpillar sandwich.

Rico sat on the sofa, and I sat in the chair opposite him. I wished there was a twelve-foot-high wall instead of a coffee table between us. He leaned forward, and I leaned as far back as I could.

"I want to apologize to you, Kalayla," he said. "I've thought about what happened when Miss Lena brought you to the gym. I'm sorry what I said upset you. I hope you'll give me a chance to make up for that."

A normal adult would be telling me why he was right and why what I did was wrong. So, why wasn't he?

I didn't want to give him another chance, but the old lady would say, "Don't spend your life being mad, Kalayla. Rico did apologize."

So, I said, "I might. If you don't act like a jerk again."

Instead of telling me I was a spoiled brat, Rico reached into his pocket and took out an envelope. "I have a peace offering. I'd like to take you and your mama to see *Riverdance*. It's an Irish step-dancing group that's gotten great reviews."

"I have a lot of stuff to do. I'm probably busy that day."

"I'll leave the flyer; you can look at it when you have time and let me know. It's on Saturday afternoon, the last weekend in May. How does that sound?"

I thought that sounded as peachy keen as the outhouse did.

"Okay," I said.

I thought Rico would hang around to see Mama, but he didn't. "Thanks for talking with me, Kalayla."

"Hey, Maureen," he called from the door. "I'm taking off. I'll talk to you soon."

Mama looked puzzled when she came out of the kitchen. "That was a short visit."

I snorted, "Yeah, just long enough to mess up my weekend!"

BEING A GRANDMOTHER

I came out of the bedroom when I heard pounding on my door. When I opened it, Kalayla said, "I've been here three times, and you weren't home!"

"Well, if it's any of your business, I was shopping with Lotta. What put you in such a fine mood?"

"I hope you didn't buy another blouse. You already have every color there is. What've you got to eat?"

"I have mint-chocolate-chip ice cream, but I see no reason to give it to anyone as rude as you are."

"Okay, I'll stop being rude. I hope you have chocolate syrup and almonds."

"It so happens I do."

"I'm glad you're finally getting some decent stuff."

It was becoming abundantly clear that Kalayla's idea was that a grandmother was the equivalent of a quartermaster in charge of supplies while the granddaughter was the Chief of Staff.

I put the bowl of designated ingredients in front of her and said, "For your information, I am not your maid. Next time, get the food yourself."

"If I went into your cupboards or refrigerator, you'd throw a fit and tell Mama to teach me manners."

"I would not, as long as you put things where you found them, cleaned up after yourself, and told me when supplies were low."

"That's too long a list to remember."

There was no dealing with that girl. What a shame she wasn't Lotta's daughter; they deserved each other!

Kalayla shoveled ice cream, nuts, and chocolate syrup into her mouth. "Not bad," she said. "Did you ever hear of the Irish step-dancers?"

Ah, she was in such a charming state because Rico had talked with her. I saw *Riverdance* with Dom and his family a couple of years ago, but Kalayla didn't want my opinion as a dance critic. She'd likely looked them up on the internet and knew more about them than I did.

"Why do you care? Did tickets float down from the sky and land on Clarence's doorstep, and he asked you to peddle them? Am I your first mark?"

Kalayla scowled and handed me the flyer. "No! HE invited me. I haven't decided if I'll go."

"HE? Do you mean Santa Claus? No? The Easter Bunny? No? Humm."

Kalayla was getting more agitated by the second. I could see this wasn't the time for teasing her, but I wasn't letting her off scot-free.

"Well then, I guess HE must be Rico, Lotta's nephew, the person you attacked at Matty's Way. To answer your question, yes, I have seen the Irish Step Dancers and would go again in a minute if you don't plan to use the ticket Rico got for you. I have no doubt you told him how nice he was to ask you despite all the names you called him."

Let her stuff that in her mouth along with the ice cream!

To my surprise, Kalayla finished her ice cream, said "Thank you," and went home.

My, oh my, the times they were a-changing!

MAGIC ONSTAGE

The old lady once told me I put her between a rock and a hard place. That's where Mama's wannabe boyfriend put me. He was afraid she'd say no if he asked her to go to *Riverdance* alone, so he was sucking up to me.

If I didn't go, Mama would feel guilty, and she'd go anyway. I'd be at home wondering what they were doing. I could sit between them if I went, but I'd have to talk to him. If somebody buys you an ice cream, you can't ignore them while you're eating it.

Cow turds if I went and cow turds if I didn't.

When I told Mama what Rico wanted, she said, "Now, wasn't that nice of him!"

Yeah right!

Mama didn't mention the step dancers again. She never let things go, so Lena must've told her not to bug me about it.

I finally told Rico I wasn't dumb enough to pass up a free ticket.

***

Our seats were in the first row of the balcony. Rico said a dancer friend explained that we could see the dance patterns better from there, but I bet he was too cheap to get good seats near the stage.

I could see everything from our seats. The theatre walls were decorated with giant paintings, and the high, fancy ceiling was awesome. The house lights blinked out one by one until the theatre was dark, silent, and a little scary.

The curtain opened to a magic world.

The music, wailing and eerie,
Rolled over me.
A voice in the wind called:
Come dance, Kalayla.
Surrounded by fog,
Standing straight as a flagpole,
Arms tight at my sides,
My feet moved slowly
Then, faster and faster
Mimicking the sound of the drum.
Deep inside, something stirred,
Stretched upward.
A flower emerged from winter cold and wind
Reached for the sun's caress
Welcoming spring.

***

The next day, everything was back to normal. Mama asked for the hundredth time, "Did you change your mind about the mountain trip?"

I didn't bother saying no. I said that every time, but Mama didn't listen.

I hoped I could stay at home, but Mrs. Spencer said I had to be supervised and do assignments in the Guidance Office. Yeah, like I needed a babysitter. I told Mama I could earn money at Clean Duds if I skipped school, but she took a fit. Another kid didn't go, but he stayed home sick. I would've played sick, too, but the secretary in Guidance had a stash of candy in her drawer and let me help myself to Snickers bars.

Being there was okay 'cause it gave me time to plan. Lena asked why I was so quiet, and I told her even a genius needed time to think. She speared me with her hawk eye but didn't bug me. That was one good thing about her.

The weather was warm, and the trees stopped looking like skeletons. That was funny 'cause I was stripping down, and they were layering up. I picked a sunny day to walk to Matty's Way and tried not to think about the things Rico did to piss me off, like calling Mama, or dropping by Eddie's, or asking how I was doing. I decided to use the same approach on him that I used on the old lady when I wanted something.

I waited at the desk while hot babes in workout clothes chatted with the receptionist. I was glad Mama wasn't the exercise type. I said I wanted to talk to Rico, and the receptionist pointed toward his office as if a kid wanting to speak to him was no big deal.

Rico was stuffing his face with a sandwich and shuffling through papers. I thought maybe seeing me would make him choke, but it didn't.

"Mr. Rico," I said, "Is it okay if I talk to you?"

He looked up from a paper but didn't say anything. He was probably calculating the odds of me dumping the papers on the floor or throwing the desk lamp at him.

I didn't want to get him nervous, so I repeated, "Mr. Rico. Is it okay if I talk to you?"

"The only Mr. around here is my dad, Mr. Matty, and he's not in today."

"Don't kids call you Mr. out of respect?"

Rico's eyes narrowed, and I was afraid I was laying it on too thick. Lena would've told me to cut the crap, but he wasn't as smart as she was.

"Nope. Kids call me Rico. So, what brings you here?"

"I want to take lessons."

Rico looked puzzled, but I was tired of repeating myself. I waited, and finally, he said, "What kind of lessons did you have in mind?"

"I want to learn to dance like the Irish step-dancers."

And what does he say to that? Nothing. He was worse than the old lady. Maybe he forgot we went to see step-dancing. I said, "You know, like they did in *Riverdance*?"

"Yeah, I know what you mean. The thing is, we don't teach step-dancing here. The dance studio in the next block does. The owner gave me the *Riverdance* flyer and told me to get balcony tickets. I can call her to find out about lessons if you'd like me to."

If I'd like him to? Why'd he think I walked over here? No matter how dumb he was, I wasn't cutting off my nose to spite my face.

"Thank you, Mr. Rico," I said. "That'd be great. There's some stuff I have to figure out before I can start. The lessons cost money, right?"

"Right."

"So, I'll need a job. I don't earn enough at Clean Duds. I work for Lena, but I never know when I'll get paid or how much. I need a regular job. Can I work for you?"

Rico tapped a pencil on his desk. A bunch of babes walked by his office, laughing and talking. He looked at them and waved. "Aerobics class just finished," he said, as if I cared. "So, the thing is, you're too late for shoveling and too early for raking."

"I didn't mean doing stuff outside. I meant in the gym."

"Oh." He thought that over for about three years and said, "Now that I think of it, you could do a few things. But I doubt you'd like it."

I squared my shoulders, "I don't care what they are. I need a job."

He smiled. "I could use somebody to check the women's locker room, pick up towels or coffee cups, check supplies, and check none of the toilets are plugged. The cleaning crew comes every night, but we could use a pickup during the day."

"The girls at school are slobs, too. When can I start?"

I didn't know why he thought that was funny, but he practically fell off his chair laughing.

"You can start right now. Let me call the dance studio and see what we can set up for you."

Dance lessons probably weren't cheap, and picking up cups and towels would take me about five minutes. I had to find other stuff to do. While Rico was on the phone, I checked out the classrooms, exercise equipment room, and storage rooms and got plenty of ideas.

When I went back to see Rico, he told me I could have my first lesson after school on Monday.

"Monday? Are they too lazy to work tomorrow?"

Rico laughed, "Tomorrow is Sunday, Kalayla. The Dance studio is closed."

Well, that was a pisser!

SUMMER 2000

FUR AND FAVORS

Monday night, around 8:00, Kalayla banged on my door. That was normal for her, but she hadn't acted normal since the night she went to *Riverdance*. Sometimes, she was so quiet I almost forgot she was on my sofa or sitting across from me at the table. Her body was in front of me, but her brain was somewhere else. My attempts at conversation were nothing but a bothersome interruption to her. I was getting fed up with that.

I could understand she might need a breather from her mother's nervous chitchat and questions. If somebody invented a technique for pausing the brain, Maureen would have benefited from it. Rico was dropping by frequently, but that'd be a reason for Kalayla to shoot her mouth off, not muzzle it.

Kalayla whirled past me into the living room when I opened the door!

"Well, now!" I said. "Something turned your light bulb bright! Did that shifty uncle teach you a new way of fleecing people out of their hard-earned money?" Instead of giving me a flip answer, she ignored what I said.

"Oh, Lena, I had my first lesson today, and I love it! And I have a job! I didn't tell you 'cause I wasn't sure it would work out. But it did!"

"What job and what lessons you're talking about?" I said. "If you're doing something shady, I am telling you right now, I am not bailing you out of jail!"

Kalayla poured out the story in one long breath without periods or commas. It turned out Rico worked a deal for her. She got a step-dancing lesson for every two hours she logged working at the gym.

"But not for free," she explained. "Rico said it was bartering. He doesn't pay me to work at the gym. I get paid in dance lessons."

That was the oddest bartering arrangement I ever heard of. Rico evidently worked out a deal at the dance studio, but somebody had to pay for those lessons, so he must be financing the transaction.

"So, Miss Lena," Kalayla said and then paused a minute.

Here we go again. If that girl called me Miss Lena, she was planning to suck me into something.

"So, Miss Lena," she repeated, "you know I'm good at carrying laundry, picking up coffee, running to the drugstore, and—."

"Stop right there, Kalayla. Skip the convince-the-old lady speech. Tell me why you're being so polite and how your self-praise connects to what you want me to do."

Kalayla frowned but didn't object. "I need money to buy two pairs of dancing shoes. Mama taught me everything she knew about cleaning. I could clean your apartment and order taxis, so you wouldn't have to bother."

I could hardly believe my ears. Not only did Kalayla discover something she was interested in doing, but she was also working out how to pay for it! I could have spent the rest of my life thinking and never come up with Irish step-dancing.

Relief swished from my white hair to my gnarly toes. Summer vacation was coming, and I was already worried about Kalayla wandering around looking like a girl instead of a skinny kid. Now, she wouldn't have time.

I suddenly got a better idea that gave me a big chuckle. "I just thought of a way you could make money doing something you'd like more than cleaning my apartment or calling taxis. Give me a couple of days to work it out, okay?"

"Okay."

My, oh my, Kalayla didn't ask what I'd be working out. How do you like that?

* * *

I counted on early morning being a slow time at Animal Friends, and the next day, the taxi dropped me off at 7:45. Greg was at the front desk sipping coffee brewed with the gleaming espresso machine on the counter. Lotta insisted her staff pass a proficiency test before brewing coffee because the reviews warned that you could clog the machine if you didn't handle it properly!

138

I walked into her office without knocking. "Hi dear, isn't this a beautiful day?"

Lotta scowled. "Crap, Lena. If you got up this early to tell me it's a beautiful day, it means you want something!"

"Now, don't be an old grouch! I wanted to hear the cheerful voice of my dearest friend. You work so hard you deserve a break."

"What flavor of bull are you peddling today, Lena Manero? It's too early for a coffee break. What do you want?"

"It's not a question of what I want, Lotta. It's what you need."

"I have everything I need. I take good care of myself, which is much more than you have sometimes done. Now, cut the crap."

Why did I think dealing with Lotta today would be different from any other day?

"Imagine the good publicity you'd get if you started a work-study program for kids here." I paused so that idea could sink in. "You could introduce them to what's involved in running a business, and they could clean cages, stock the supply room, and help out in general. You could test it out with one kid, and naturally, you'd only pay minimum wage."

Lotta frowned. Why was she so suspicious of my good intentions?

"Why would I pay anything? You're the one with bags of money. Why don't you finance it?"

"I can't just give her money, Lotta. It has to be a legitimate job. If the Shelter is hard-pressed for cash, I'll cover it. But, you'll have to be the one to write her paycheck."

"Ah, now you've changed anonymous kid to her. I'm sure I know the name of the kid we're discussing. I must be turning into a psychic."

"Think of it as a family project. If Rico and Maureen get married, Kalayla will be part of your family. Besides, by doing this good deed, you'll earn points for getting into heaven, which you sorely need."

"I earned enough points to get me and three other big-time sinners into heaven by putting up with you all these years!" Lotta looked daggers at me, but she didn't say no. I took that as a good sign.

By the time I finished explaining why Kalayla needed money and the independent way she'd gone about getting it, Lotta was laughing.

"I might enjoy helping a young woman who knows her mind and has enough gumption to go after what she wants. But you won't get my help for free. If I do a favor for you, you owe me one in return."

I could tell from Lotta's smug expression she knew what the return favor would be the minute I started my sales pitch. She helped me plenty, and she never asked for anything in return. I had the feeling my I.O.U. just came due, and I'd repay the principal with hefty interest.

"I know that," I snapped. "I can take out a full-page ad about the Shelter in the *Chronicle* and the papers in surrounding towns."

"I can do that myself. I operate in the electronic age, whereas you don't know how to text on your cell unless my brother recently gave you a crash course. I don't need your cash. However, there is something you can do that I can't. You can institute a pets-permitted policy in your building. Crap, Lena, don't look like you're in life-threatening pain. I didn't say all of your buildings. We'll start with the one where you live. Don't worry. I'll screen any tenant who comes with a pet or wants to get one after they move in and veto boa constrictors and tarantulas."

I always knew I'd eventually cave in. When Lotta went on a crusade, she never ended it. I nodded, glad to be off the hook until she pushed for the policy in all our rental units.

"Now," she continued, "You realize I will be creating an internship for Kalayla and paying her, so you owe me double. The second thing you can do is to adopt two adorable kittens."

The smirk on Lotta's face made it clear she knew she had me. She knew I loved cats and dogs. I never let the boys have animals because I was afraid Joey might hurl a cat across the room or kick a dog down the stairs. How could I allow pets in the rental units if the boys couldn't have any at home?

The only way not to get crushed was to give in, but I didn't have to go down quickly. "Lotta, you know I don't have the time to litter train kittens and scratch-proof the furniture."

"Oh, stop making a fuss. I said two kittens to aggravate you. The cats you're adopting are two gorgeous, well-mannered Siamese. One is a chocolate point; the other is a blue point. You remember Becky Foster, don't you? She has end-stage cancer, and her daughter can't take the cats. I promised I'd find a good home for them. Napoleon and Petunia are brother and sister, four years old, and perfectly trained indoor cats. I'll bring them over after work with everything you need, including scratch posts, beds, and litter boxes."

So, this is what happened in old age. Life as you knew it disappeared. The next thing I knew, I'd be getting a boyfriend!

"Fine!" I said. "But call before you come. I want to be home so you don't drop off a dog and ten guinea pigs."

"Now, Lena, don't be a spoilsport. You know I'd never dream of doing such a thing."

EVERYTHING COMING UP ROSES?

The winter had been so long and traumatic that I was afraid spring would never come. But it did. Daylight didn't disappear in a blink, and the budding trees and flowers were coming to life. Best of all, Kalayla was captivated by step dancing and bubbling over with cheerful energy!

And then this morning, Rico called to ask if we could meet for coffee. He didn't sound upbeat, which made me wish the song said tulips instead of roses because they didn't have thorns. Rico didn't imply Kalayla had done anything outrageous at the gym, but I had to be ready if things turned prickly.

Parking in Harvard Square was hopeless unless you could afford a parking garage, which I couldn't. I decided to walk but had to jog because I was late. I hoped I wouldn't be sweaty and smelly when I got to Starbucks. Rico was near the front of the line, his smile as warm as usual.

"Hey, Maureen, how are you doing? Your usual latte? Why don't we take our coffee and walk to the Common?"

We found a sunny bench, and Rico told me what had happened.

RICO

It started when I got this text from Jennifer at the front desk that said, HELP! That made me laugh because Jen could force a full-grown grizzly to beg for mercy. Her second text said: ABOVE MY PAY GRADE, which made me think it was probably a client asking for a discount.

The guy standing at the desk didn't look ferocious, impatient, or demanding. He was on the small side, about five feet eight, and carried himself like he was, or had been, fast on his feet. His nose had probably been broken more than once, so he wasn't a guy who'd knuckle under without a fight. I put him somewhere in his sixties. Despite the pot belly, bald head, and age, this guy knew his way around.

"Hi," I said, "I'm Rico. What can I do for you?"

"I'm Kevin. Nothing for me. For my grandson."

I looked around. No stray kid in sight.

"I left him in the car. This is private."

Private—just the type of meeting I hated. Parents or grandparents who came in without the kid had an agenda. Most of the time, they wanted me to do a makeover, fix the kid up, and turn him into something he wasn't. They'd discover that no gym could give a kid a new personality.

"Okay, let's go talk in my office." I led the way. If the guy wanted complete privacy, he wouldn't find it in my office. The corridor wall was solid on the bottom, and the top half was glass, open to public view. I sat behind my desk and gestured Kevin to a chair. "Tell me what's on your mind."

"I want you to teach my grandson to defend himself. I asked around, and they told me this place was the best. We don't live in Cambridge, but I'll see he gets here."

"And your grandson needs to defend himself because—?"

"He gets picked on at school and in the neighborhood. He doesn't fight back."

"Some kids don't."

"My grandsons do. And he will. He needs to toughen up and prove he can handle himself. You know what I mean?"

Yep, fix them up, make them over.

"I do know what you mean. Let me talk with your grandson, and we'll go from there. Is that okay?"

"Yeah, I guess. I'll send Kieran in and wait for him in the car."

Five minutes later, I heard a soft knock. The boy standing in the open door could have been the model for a 'Fair Game for Bullies' poster. Red hair with cowlicks, pale white skin, freckles covering his face, and arms so skinny you wondered if any muscle was attached to his bones. But I think his grandpa brought him to Matty's Way because of the hint of softness—his mother might have called it sweetness—in the boy's demeanor. His grandfather sniffed it out, interpreted it negatively, and was determined to eradicate it.

"Hi. I'm Rico."

"I'm Kieran."

Kieran's gaze wandered from the floor to the ceiling before returning to me. "Grandpa wants you to teach me to defend myself. He thinks I'm a wuss because I won't fight. He owns three garages and wants me to learn about cars. I won't do that, either. And I don't like ice cream."

I've got to tell you, Maureen, I stifled a laugh. He looked like a pushover, but he'd use his brain instead of his fists to avoid doing anything he didn't want to. A kid like that in a family of street brawlers? He must be driving them crazy.

"Humm. No ice cream? I suppose you don't like cake or pie, either?"

"Sure I do. And brownies with walnuts are the best."

"That sounds reasonable enough. Why don't you hang around and watch some classes to get a feel for what we offer? Our hard-core martial arts might not be your thing, but you might like Tai Chi."

"Would I have to hit anybody?"

"Not in Tai Chi."

"Okay, I'll watch one of those classes."

A little later, Kieran found me in the hallway. "Grandpa would say Tai Chi is for sissies, but I like it."

"Tai Chi is a lot of things, but sissy isn't one of them. I'll talk to your grandfather. Why don't you wait in my office? If he gives the okay, we'll get you signed up."

Kieran filled out the registration form and went to get his grandfather. I looked over the form and did a double-take. The kid's name was Kieran O'Rourke. That's your maiden name, right? The grandfather signed the permission form as Kevin O'Rourke. Isn't that your father's name, Maureen?

Rico paused. I was paralyzed, barely able to breathe.

Yes, Kevin O'Rourke was my father. And, my brother, Colin, planned to name his second son Kieran. He was the nephew I'd never met, the cousin Kalayla didn't know existed. My brain struggled to absorb Rico's words. My father and my nephew had been at Matty's Way. What if Kalayla were there, too?

Rico waited for me to answer, but all I could do was nod.

I thought so. The coincidence was so bizarre that it reminded me of Casablanca when Lauren Bacall comes into Rick's and Humphrey Bogart says, "Out of all the gin joints in the world, she walks into mine." Out of all the gyms in the world, Kevin O'Rourke walked into mine with his grandson. Unbelievable!

Anyway, I told him advanced Tai Chi students can learn to use the moves for self-defense. He probably imagines Kieran will turn into the Karate Kid by next week. That's, well, that's the whole story.

I forced air in and out of my lungs, struggled to absorb the shock and anticipate the consequences. "Do you think he might run into Kalayla? If she finds out who he is, she could do something absolutely horrible!"

"Whoa, Maureen. Let's not jump to the worst-case scenario. It's very unlikely they'll meet. We don't have Tai Chi competitions he could watch the way we do for Karate, and your dad wasn't interested in observing a class. It sounded like getting Kieran enrolled and arranging transportation would be the extent of his involvement."

I hoped what Rico said was true, but how could I not worry? Bad things happened, and they happened to me. Losing my family, then Jamal, and now this made me feel like I had a target on my back.

A FRIEND

The last few school days were a waste with field trips and classroom parties. When I mentioned that to the Old Lady, she said, "Good. The world needs more ignorant, unemployable people. You can live with your Mama, take care of her in her old age, and me when I get old."

Cow turds! If Lena had her way, I'd be stuck taking care of Lotta, too! Anyway, I might stay in school. I heard about a girl who competed in gymnastics in the Olympics, had a tutor, and didn't have to go to school. Step-dancing wasn't in the Olympics now, but it might be by the time I got good enough to try out.

I needed a bike to get places faster, so I asked Lotta if I could add hours. She was a wicked witch boss most of the time, so it flipped me out when she gave me one the next day.

"Don't fall all over yourself thanking me," she said. "It needs greasing and new bearings. A bike shop near here will show you how to do a tune-up and lend you the tools."

The bike had fat tires, no gears, and scratched blue fenders, but it was awesome. I was good at fixing things, and the guy at the bike shop gave me a special rate on parts. If Eddie let me put it in the back of the Eatery, I wouldn't have to lug it up and down.

I had to cut out supervising at Clean Duds 'cause I spent time at Matty's Way, Animal Friends, and the dance studio. I kind of missed hanging out with the Old Lady.

Everybody but me forgot about Clarence. I wasn't home much, so I told Mama to tell me when he was coming 'cause I didn't want to miss seeing my favorite uncle. I never would have fooled Lena with that lie, but Mama smiled and said, "That's so sweet, Kalayla. I didn't realize how much you like him."

Yeah, right! The one good thing about Rico coming around was that Clarence wouldn't be stupid enough to mess with him.

Working at the gym was a blast, especially after Rico said, "Let me know if you hear any complaints."

Being an undercover snoop was cool. All you had to do was slouch against a wall and pretend you were a piece of furniture. I'd hang around the locker room while some hot babe revealed every detail of her sex life. I might do that for the police or become a private detective.

I'd watch classes when I had time to kill between jobs. A funny-looking red-headed kid who looked like a nerd did the same thing, and we started saying, "Hey." One day, he said, "What classes are you taking?"

"I take step-dancing and work here to pay for my lessons."

"That's cool. My grandfather wants me to learn to fight, so he's paying for my lessons."

"I want to learn how to beat the crap out of buttholes. Could you teach me?"

The kid laughed like I told a funny joke. He was as skinny as a green bean, shorter than me, with a freckle-covered face and hair sticking out in five directions. He could impersonate a scarecrow easier than a fighter. I was pretty sure I could deck him with my little finger. The idea of him teaching me to fight was funny, and I laughed, too.

We were gasping for breath when he puffed out his chest like a weight-lifter with more brains than muscles and said, "Beware of Monster Man II in disguise!"

That set us off again.

After we calmed down, I said, "Let's team up. I'll kick the buttholes in the balls, and you break their bones."

He gave me a thumbs-up. "Everything they teach here is vicious except Tai Chi. But I told my grandpa there were a lot of great classes. He patted me on the head and said, 'Good boy.' Adults are so dense."

I knew right then I liked this kid. I bet he could get away with any-thing 'cause he looked innocent and harmless. Maybe he could show me how to fake out the old lady.

His name was Kieran, and we started hanging out and called ourselves the Two K's.

After I watched one of the Tai Chi classes, I said, "The moves are like a dance routine. I didn't get how you could beat up anybody with them."

"Me either, but Rico told my grandpa you could use it for self-defense."

I told Kieran if he rode his bike to the gym, we could ride to Animal Friends, but he said, "That'd be neat, but my bike got trashed."

"Did you crash it?"

"Nope. My brother Col did."

"Is he getting you another one?"

Kieran laughed, "He said he would if I beat him in a fight."

"Could you?"

"Nah, he'd kill me, but he's not so bad. He just acts tough when he's with his friends."

"It's probably too complicated to ride here from Brighton anyway."

"No, it's not. I pay attention when people drive me here and home. I know how to go."

"Yeah?"

"Sure. It's a game."

"That's a weird game."

"Not for me. Once, Col's friends thought it would be a joke to drop me off in Newton. They said they'd give me twenty-five bucks if I could get home without calling anybody."

"Did you?"

"Sure. I asked directions from people a few times, but the jerks never paid me."

"Why didn't you just call somebody?"

"They'd have called me a sissy. Anyway, I can take care of myself."

Watching students spar in karate classes was fun. Kieran spotted the kids who looked like losers but weren't, and I spotted the flashy show-offs who'd lose.

If Rico was teaching the class, sometimes he put his hand on a kid without saying anything.

"What do you think he's doing?" Kieran said.

"Don't know. Maybe those kids are nerve cases, and he's giving them a blast of The Force."

When I asked Kieran why his Grandpa was so hot to have him fight, he said, "Grandpa thinks I'm weak. He wants me to be like Col."

"No offense, but your grandpa sounds like a jerk. At least you know him. I never met mine."

"Why not?"

"My Mama said he was dead 'cause she didn't wanna tell me what a butthole he is."

"What'd you mean?"

"They kicked my mama out of the family when she married my dad."

***

When I told the old lady I was hanging out with a kid at the gym, she said, "Is this a living, breathing kid, or somebody you made up?"

That old lady was a real pisser!

"I didn't make him up! Rico knows him. His name is Kieran. When he gets a bike, I'll bring him here, and he can meet Mama, too. Make sure you cough up one of Lotta's desserts for us."

Lena got a funny look on her face, but that was nothing new.

WHEN WILL OLD AGE GET BORING?

Kalayla never said a good thing about another kid, and when she finally did, he was the cousin she didn't know existed! When Maureen told me her father showed up at Matty's Way with his grandson, I felt trouble coming. I sure do wish that feeling had been wrong.

It felt like an invisible force relocated my apartment to an earthquake zone without me knowing it, and someone was getting a laugh from trying to dump an old woman on her butt.

Not only that, Napoleon and Petunia took over like they owned me and the apartment, sprawling out on a bed I used to call my own. They snuggled into my life, and I admit I liked their furry bodies stretched out next to me, purring.

Compared to my four boys, the cats weren't a worry even though the litter box was a permanent fixture and diapers were not. I worried about the boys at school and on the streets. I worried because the twins were together so much, and Mark was alone so much. I worried JJ admired his dad so much. And I worried about what Joey was teaching them.

That said, the cats' distinctive personalities could be annoying. When I asked Lotta why they constantly meowed, she laughed. "What did you think two Siamese would do, Lena? Talking is a characteristic of the breed. At least now you have somebody to talk to besides Kalayla."

Lotta was digging for information about Mattwo and me, but she wouldn't ask directly. I finally told her he hadn't called.

"Well then, you should call him," Lotta said. "You turned my brother down; he is not the mind-reading type. You'll both be dead before he figures out you gave up wearing black because you're hot to trot with him."

"That's not why I—."

"Pooh-bah! Your motives are perfectly transparent to anyone who knows you as well as I do."

Humph. Lotta was right about one thing. Life for women in 2000 was different from what it was in the 1950s. I suppose I could ask Mattwo to meet me for coffee. Kalayla will never believe I might be turning into a modern woman at age seventy-two!

TRYING TO STAY CALM

Kalayla charged out of her bedroom, poured half a cup of coffee, and added half a cup of milk, her version of a Café au Lait.

"Layla, honey, slow down."

"Can't. Places to go, things to do." She smeared chunky peanut butter and strawberry jam on toast. "Gym, Shelter, class. Later," she called, a whirlwind going out the door.

With dancing, two jobs, and biking to all of them, Kalayla needed more than one sandwich with globs of peanut butter and jelly running out the sides. I'd make another batch of her favorite snack later.

I saw her dart across the street and run down the alley beside Eddie's. I had no idea how far a star was from Earth, but Kalayla had traveled that distance since winter, morphing from a sassy-mouthed girl to a dependable employee and an enthusiastic dance student. And she was being civil to Rico!

Kalayla kept asking if I'd heard from Clarence. She was rude and unpleasant to him when she saw him. Why would she suddenly call him her favorite uncle and wonder when he was coming?

Despite that, it might be better if Kalayla were here when Clarence came, given what happened last week. Rico and I had planned a walk, so he met me at Eddie's. I noticed Clarence's car parked in front of the apartment building, and we crossed the street as he was leaving.

"So this is what you've been up to, Maureen," he said rudely as if I were doing something sleazy.

Clarence's sneer didn't faze Rico. He extended his hand and said, "You're Jamal's brother, Clarence, right? I'm Rico Eccli, a friend of Maureen's."

Clarence did the only thing he could to avoid looking like a jerk. He shook Rico's hand, gave me a nasty look, and said, "I'll stop by when you're not so busy, Maureen."

"That went well, don't you think?" Rico laughed after Clarence drove away.

Rico could joke about it, but I couldn't. I hoped Clarence wouldn't make up something about Rico and me and tell Lucinda. Rico didn't ask about Clarence, but he must have wondered why Clarence acted like he had a claim on me.

Instead of drinking coffee and dwelling on grim thoughts, I had to get busy. I washed my coffee cup, cleaned the apartment, and made a batch of raisins, peanuts, and granola for Kalayla. The phone rang, and when Rico said we needed to discuss something that had happened at the gym, my heart sank!

It was a gorgeous afternoon with a warm breeze, and Rico said he'd come over, and we could walk to the Common. He seemed relaxed, so I thought it wasn't too bad, but I found out it was.

RICO

Don't look so worried, Maureen. I've been impressed with how respectful and helpful Kalayla has been. You can be proud of her. She keeps an hour-by-hour log of what she does and told me her goal is to go to the dance camp for two weeks in August.

That was all good. If what happened was the worst of the worst, Rico would tell me that first, wouldn't he?

"That's good," I said. "But?"

Rico hesitated and then told me the rest.

I need to explain how it went to give you the whole picture. I was on the way to my office when I got a text from Jen at the front desk: COME NOW! I jogged past the classrooms, rounded the corner, and knew why Jen called me. I asked her to alert me if Kieran's grandfather stopped by when Kalayla and Kieran were in the building because they liked to hang out together.

Your dad was leaning on the front counter chatting with Jen. I had seen Kalayla and Kieran laughing in the back hallway, and I figured, with luck, I could snag Kieran and steer him and his grandpa out of the building.

"Hey, Kevin. How's it going?" I said.

He glanced past me like he was expecting to see Kieran behind me.

"Better for me than for you if you have to jog instead of walk. I gave that up when I retired."

"My dad says the same thing. If you hang out here a minute, I'll find Kieran, and you two can take off."

Instead of saying okay, Kevin moved closer and lowered his voice. "So, how's my grandson doing?"

I knew I had to be careful about the way I answered. "I've watched Kieran in class, and he's remarkably agile and intuitively understands how Tai Chi movements flow and connect."

Maureen, the thing is, Kevin wanted to know if Kieran was developing a fighter's instinct. He hasn't shown any sign of that, but somebody could hit Kieran's trigger point, and we'd see it flare up suddenly.

Kevin seemed to accept what I said, and I was halfway down the hall when I saw Kieran and Kalayla approaching me.

"Kieran, your ride's here. Kalayla, why don't we go over your hours," I said.

Kieran looked at Kalayla, "That's my grandpa. You want to meet him?"

"Yeah! Can we do the hours after, Rico?" The two of them zipped past me before I could veto that idea.

The kids stopped near your dad, and Kieran launched into a demonstration of would-be fighting moves.

"Better watch out, Grandpa! I might knock you over!" Both kids giggled, and Kalayla mimicked Kieran, exaggerating the moves.

The old man shifted his attention to Kalayla, and his expression changed from curious to puzzled. He squinted and put a hand over his eyes like you do when you try to block sunlight.

"You look familiar," he said, "but I can't place——."

Kieran said proudly, "This is Kalayla, Grandpa. She's my friend."

You might not believe this given how your parents treated you, Maureen, but watching the old guy was heart-wrenching.

Kevin looked uncertain and confused, the way a person with memory loss might if he was walking on the street where he lived but couldn't find his house. I was afraid Kevin might have a stroke or a heart attack.

Free-floating crap was bound to hit the fan somewhere, and it landed in the gym. All I could do was meet the situation head-on.

I plunged in, "Kalayla's last name is LeeRoyce. She's Maureen's daughter. Kieran's grandpa is Kevin O'Rourke, Kalayla. He's your mom's father."

The old man turned white, staggered, and used the counter to steady himself. He stared at Kalayla. She looked at me and then at Kevin.

Kieran cleared his throat and, going step by step, worked out what that meant. "So, if my grandpa is Kalayla's mom's dad, and he's my dad's dad, then my dad and her mom are brother and sister. And my grandpa is Kalayla's grandpa, I think. If I'm right, you and I are cousins, Kalayla!"

I was watching Kalayla. Her silence was a crash of thunder compared to Kieran's soft voice. Her green eyes were dark and wide, glued to Kevin, and her body was stone still.

She backed away from your dad and spoke so softly, I could barely hear her, "That means my grandpa is the same butthole as your grandpa, Kieran."

I was prepared to stop Kalayla from charging into the old guy, but she stayed where she was, hands clenched into fists and body trembling. The thing is, Maureen, tears were streaming down her face. I put my arm around her shoulder and pulled her close. That's all I could think of doing.

Kieran watched his grandpa and Kalayla. Then, he straightened up, pulled his shoulders back, and grew two inches. His voice was quiet and composed. "Are you going to do the same thing to me you did to Kalayla's mom, Grandpa? Are you going to kick me out of the family if I don't fight back when kids tease me or because Kalayla's my friend?"

The old man's face crumbled. He would have fallen over if he hadn't been holding on to the counter. "You don't understand, boy. You can't understand what it was like for your grandma. Grandma couldn't—she couldn't—."

Kevin didn't find the words. He turned and shuffled toward the door, bent over and broken. There were no tears on his face, Maureen, but I was sure your dad was crying inside.

When he reached the door, he stopped and turned to Kieran. "You coming with me now, boy, or do you want me to send somebody?"

Kieran looked at Kalayla, gave her a little wave, and said, "See you tomorrow, K."

He took his grandfather's hand and led him through the door like you'd lead somebody you knew couldn't make it alone.

Seeing the three of them was enough to break your heart.

I took Kalayla into my office, and we sat quietly until she looked at the clock and said, "I have to work at the shelter, Mr. Rico. Thanks for, well, thanks."

I'm not making excuses for your dad or trying to defend him, Maureen. But for whatever reason, he was forced to choose between you and your mom.

He had to decide who held his life together. He had to decide which of you was his load-bearing wall and he decided it was your mom.

Kieran wasn't willing to make that choice. He was keeping his grandfather, and he was keeping his friend. That was good for Kalayla to see, and frankly, it was damn inspiring.

SOMETHING ELSE?

Kalayla scared me half to death, pounding on my door so hard I thought she'd knock it off the hinges. I could see the only way to keep her from disturbing the cats' peace and giving me a heart attack would be to give her a key.

She strolled past me like she owned the place, chanting at the top of her lungs. "Piss, dung. Piss, dung. Dungy, pissy, dung, dung."

The idea of giving her a key vanished. I put my hands on my hips and gave her a look that would have stopped the monsters in any horror film. "Why are you shouting garbage like you crawled out of a cesspool? Stop that this minute!"

I pointed to the kitchen. Kalayla stomped in, sat down at the table, and mumbled, "Old crab ought to be in jail for the way she tortures poor, harmless kids," which I chose to ignore.

I got out the peanut butter cookies and milk and said, "Did you get bitten by a nine-headed serpent and come here so I could suck out the poison?"

Her face fell to her feet. I'd never seen her so dejected or heard her voice so sad. "Only one head, one crappy old head."

I made hazelnut coffee while she worked herself up to tell me who the crappy old head was and what they did.

Petunia sauntered in and brushed against Kalayla's leg. "Why'd you pick such an ugly cat? Old people have crappy eyesight." She picked up the ugly cat, who circled then nestled against Kalayla's stomach and cranked her purr volume to high. She was sweet-tempered enough to put up with that girl's nonsense.

"It's not fair," Kalayla said. "It's wicked, not fair."

"That probably would cover more than eighty-five percent of what happens worldwide. Are you referring to one particular unfair thing?"

"It's not fair if you hate somebody for being a jerk, and when you meet him, you find out he's a pathetic old man."

"So, who might this pathetic old man be?"

"Kieran's grandpa."

If I'd been keeping score on my prediction success, I'd be batting zero. I knew I might be wrong when I tried reassuring Maureen they'd likely never meet. And I never would have predicted that when they did meet, the old man wouldn't come across as the vicious person Kalayla imagined.

"So," I said, "Just so we're clear here, that would also be your grandpa, correct? And he isn't what you thought he'd be. It sounds like you feel sorry for him."

"Don't know. Shouldn't. Maybe. Not feeling anything."

It didn't seem likely Kalayla would go from full-tilt hating to feeling nothing. Even in her sad times, I sensed the feistiness below the surface. Now, it was buried so deep that I didn't see any sign of it.

Kalayla had more thrown at her these last few months than some folks have in a lifetime. She needed time to regain her balance, and I could give her that.

I looked out the window—nearly seven-thirty and not dark, a gift of summer that'd disappear soon enough.

"I suppose you told your mama you were coming here for dinner. Will a turkey melt suit you?"

"Haven't been home. Turkey's okay."

"All right. Put that cat down, and tell your mama you're eating here."

BEING NUMB

The second I opened the door, Mama said, "Are you okay? It must have been such a shock. I mean, seeing my father."

What a pisser! Couldn't she say hi like a normal person?

"Eating at Lena's. Back later," I said and closed the door.

At least sometimes Lena left me alone. When I went back, she was at the stove, flipping turkey melts. "Get a plate, the pickles, and the chips."

When I felt like talking, I'd ask her when she planned to promote me. I was sick of being a private.

"How come only one plate?" I said.

"My old stomach can't wait to eat until the middle of the night. I might munch on a few chips."

Middle of the night? Her kitchen clock said eight-thirty, which was normal dinner time for Mama. As soon as we sat down, Petunia jumped onto the Old Lady's lap. The ugly brown cat sat next to my chair.

I was starting my second sandwich when Lena said, "You're eating so fast, I'm getting indigestion."

"I'm keeping that vulture cat from jumping up and stealing my turkey!"

"Oh, for goodness sake! Napoleon is keeping you company. Now, Napoleon, if you're a good boy, I'll give you a treat."

It'd be a pisser if the cat answered, "Okay, I'll take the minnows."

I finished eating, but my brain was as empty as Lena's walls, and I could barely move my body. I decided to go home and sleep for the rest of my life.

Lena said, "Do you want a few cookies for the road?"

"Nah," I said and dragged myself home. The second Mama saw me, she talked non-stop, but I walked into my room, flopped on the bed, and slept.

Mama shook me before she went to work at eight the following morning. "My goodness, Kalayla, won't you be late?"

"Lemme sleep."

"Should I call Rico or Lotta and tell them you overslept?"

"Lemme sleep." I buried my head under my pillow.

I was sleeping when she barged in again.

"Kalayla, honey, you slept all day. You must be coming down with something. Oh, dear, your forehead is warm. I better get Lena."

"No! Leave me alone. Lemme sleep!" I buried my head under the pillow again.

The next time Mama woke me, the clock said seven-fifty a.m.

"Kalayla, honey, you've slept more than thirty-six hours. Lena said to let you sleep, but maybe I should call the doctor."

"Mama! I'm not sick! I'm tired!"

She kept sputtering, so I turned my back, and she left.

The next thing I knew, the old lady was shaking my shoulder.

"What?" I said. The clock by my bed said eleven-thirty a.m.

"I brought lunch," she said, all cheery like that was a big thrill.

Cow turds! Did they think sleeping was against the law? At least Lena stopped bugging me when I ignored her.

Sometime later, I heard the phone ring. Lena came in, pulled the covers off me, and said, "Get your butt up, now! Lotta needs to speak to you."

Lotta never called me, so it must be something important. I dragged myself to the living room phone. "Yeah?"

Lotta said, "Well, if it isn't sleeping beauty! Do you remember the dog with two broken legs that you insisted I take to the vet? She's back at the shelter with her hind legs in casts. Should I drop her at the intersection where we found her? Or, could you take time from your sleep schedule to help me with her?"

How could I forget that funny-looking, reddish-brown dog with floppy ears and sad eyes? I didn't think Lotta would leave her on the side of the road, but I wasn't taking any chances!

"I'm coming! Don't you let anybody mess with her! She knows me, and she'll want to see me."

"Of course, Your Majesty. Whatever you say, Your Majesty."

The old bag hung up on me. I ran to my room, splashed water on my face, and pulled on clean clothes.

When I went to the living room, Lena said, "I called a taxi. This bag has two peanut butter and jelly sandwiches, two chicken salad sandwiches, chips, cookies, and root beer. Call me when you're ready to come home."

***

I almost cried when the dog put her head in my lap like she'd been waiting for me. If I ever found out who abandoned her, I'd break their legs and see how they liked it when I left them on the side of the road.

Lotta explained everything we'd need to do, including how to put a diaper on her without hurting her.

"I can stop by three times a day and sleep here 'cause she might need something at night," I said.

"You are not sleeping here! The dog will be fine. I'll check on her." Lotta stood with her hands on her hips, daring me to say no. I nodded and muttered, "Thanks."

The next day, I told Lotta we had to name the dog. She said animals already had names, and I had to figure out what this dog's was. When I asked how I was supposed to do that, she said, "Ask her and see what she says."

Lotta was a pain in the butt, but I knew for sure she wasn't whacko. I opened the dog's cage door and reached in to pet her. I tried a bunch of different names, like Lassie, Tammy, Winnie, and Cookie. The dog looked like she wished I'd hurry up and find the right name.

Then I looked at her leg casts and said, "Hi, Hopalong."

I couldn't believe it! She thumped her tail and curled her lips like she was smiling!

***

When I told Rico I'd make up the missed time, he said he'd count it as vacation days. I was getting to like him better. He posted the class schedule near the front desk, so I knew when the back hallway was empty. When I took a break, I'd go there to practice the steps.

The first time I saw Kieran after the thing with his grandpa, he seemed shy when he said, "Would you like a drummer?"

"Sure. Why wouldn't I?"

"Well, you know, I went home with Grandpa instead of telling him he was a butthole."

161

"The old lady would probably give you a gold star for admirable behavior."

Kieran smiled and said, "How come I haven't seen you the last few days?"

"I was on vacation."

"I thought maybe you didn't want to hang out with me anymore."

I grinned at him. "Hanging out with you is better than eating worms cooked in hot sauce."

We laughed.

"I've been at the shelter with a dog. Her name is Hopalong, and her back legs are broken. She's kind of funny-looking. When the vet says she's ready for adoption, I'll see if Mama will let me keep her."

"Hopalong? I never heard of a dog named Hopalong."

"So? You never heard my name until you met me. Anyway, she likes that name. You can come to the shelter and meet her if you want."

"Do you think you'll be able to keep her?"

"Don't know. Mama might say okay 'cause she's trying to make up for being a liar. And Lena used to be a crab about pets, but she's gone whacko since she got the two cats. You can help me convince her when you get a bike."

He raised both arms and yelled, "The two K's strike again!"

We laughed, and Kieran slid down on the floor, and we slapped out a dance rhythm. I'd go loud when he went soft, and then we'd play loud and soft together. Kieran was a weird kid, but I liked him.

* * *

On Sunday, two weeks later, Mama didn't want me to go to the shelter until we had one of our Sunday morning talks.

"Say what you want quick 'cause I have to go!" I said.

Naturally, Mama sighed as she put down her coffee cup. "It's not what I want to say. It's what I think we need to discuss."

"Okay. So discuss."

"You haven't told me anything about the day you met my father. Please tell me about it."

Why'd she always have to make me feel like a jerk?

"Okay, so when I found out he was your father, I wanted to punch him in the face and tell him he was a butthole. But I didn't, and I don't know why. Are we done now?"

If she sighed one more time, I was leaving.

"How did he look? Did he seem okay?"

"Mama! He looked like an old man. He was upset. I thought he might fall and Rico would have to call 911. But he didn't."

Mama hesitated. "But, did he ask about me? Did he ask how we were doing?"

If Mama thought he'd suddenly care about his daughter or granddaughter, she was just plain dumb.

"No, Mama. He didn't ask about you. He didn't ask about us. Kieran took his hand and led him out the door when he acted like he might fall over. Can I go now, please?"

Mama said, "Okay," even though I knew she didn't want to.

I was glad she didn't see what a pathetic old man he was. He needed more help than we did, and I didn't know what Mama would've done if she saw that.

TIME ON MY HANDS

Cambridge was deserted during the summer. Business at Eddie's was slow and tedious without the hustle and bustle of customers.

I could amuse myself by planning Kalayla's birthday party, but March was months away. She never wanted a party, but she might say yes if I suggested an Ides of March celebration. She could take that as permission to assassinate anyone she wished, Julius Caesar style, with me at the top of her list.

After work, I cut a hunk of zucchini bread and went to Lena's. She laughed when I told her I could hardly wait for Eddie's to be busy again.

"What about your art? Doesn't that keep you busy?"

"Yes, it always did."

"Then why aren't you doing it?"

"When Jamal was alive, we lived in a much larger apartment. The only way I'd have a space now would be if Kalayla and I shared a bedroom. That would be a total disaster. So, I keep my art supplies in a storage unit."

"Let me talk with Dom. He might be able to find space somewhere in the building."

"Oh, Lena, that would be wonderful!"

"Hold on. I'm not promising, but I will explore the idea."

I decided to call Rico and tell him the news. I loved discussing things with him. He had a different perspective, such as when he suggested the reason my father sided with my mother was that she was his load-bearing wall. That's what Jamal was to me, and I fell apart when he died. Maybe my father was afraid that would happen to him.

The phone interrupted my thoughts. When I said hello, nobody answered. I was going to hang up, but then a man's voice said, "Maureen, it's your dad."

I almost dropped the phone.

"Maureen? Are you there?"

Was I there? I wasn't sure where there was. I took a deep breath and heard Jamal say, "Steady now, sweet babe." I had hoped to hear my father's voice for so long. Maybe I was imagining it the way I did Jamal's.

The man's voice went on. "I called to ask if it would be okay for me to take your daughter for ice cream. With her friend Kieran. With Colin's son Kieran."

My father called to ask if he could take Kalayla for ice cream with no idle chit-chat, straight to the point. That was like my father, a man of few words who didn't add dressing to his salad, sauce, or gravy to anything he ate. He called to ask if he could take Kalayla for ice cream.

How could I say no?

My throat was tight, and my voice sounded strange when I said. "Yes, that would be okay with me."

"All right then. I'll, ah, I'll ask your daughter if she'd like to go. Thanks."

My father hung up.

I stood holding the phone, the magic wand that conjured up my heart's desire. For the first time since Jamal died, I cried with joy. My father was taking our daughter for ice cream.

FINALLY DOING SOMETHING

Well, it was about time I could do something specific to help Maureen.

When Dom and I met for our weekly check-in at my office in Home Base, I had a space for Maureen on the agenda.

Dom cocked his head and gave me a knowing look. "I might be able to find one. How much are you willing to invest in this, Lena?"

"Dom! I own the building! Don't make it sound like I'm asking for new construction! I'm asking for space in the building where I live!"

"I understood what you asked for. Did you think I could pull an extra room out of my hat along with a magic bunny? So, I ask again, what are you willing to invest?"

"I swear, Dom, sometimes you are such a pill! What do you mean?"

"Three weeks ago, I found old man Spencer wandering near Margeson's flower shop. He didn't know where he was. I walked him home and called his daughter. He's moving in with her."

"Ah! I didn't know it was that bad. I could have—."

"You couldn't have done a damn thing, Lena! His family is taking care of him as they should. His apartment will be vacant at the end of the month. You can pay the rent since you treat Maureen like your newly-acquired daughter. I've got a bottom line to think about."

Dom and his bottom line! It was just like him to act as if the rent on one bed-sitting room apartment would make or break Manzetti Properties!

"Well, damn it all, Dom! Don't I at least get a family discount?"

He actually smiled. "I'll think about it. I suppose you'd want it painted?"

"Maureen will paint it and pay for the paint herself! Now, I have two other things."

His smile faded. "By god, Lena, you never stop, do you? When are you going to retire?"

"Don't you dare lecture me about retirement! You're two years older than I am! Why are you training Marita and Marco to fill your gigantic shoes if they're going to be ready to retire before you step down?"

"Oh, bug off. What are the two other things?"

"It's time we looked around for an internet package deal and picked up service for all the buildings instead of having tenants do it."

Dom screwed up his face like the Grinch he wasn't.

"Don't get apoplectic! We can raise the rent to cover it. It will enhance our public image if we do it before everybody else does, and it will cost the tenants less. We got through Y2K without the great computer in the sky crashing. Have a little faith."

"Okay, okay. I'll do the figures."

I almost laughed at how quickly he caved in.

When Dom noticed my frown, he said, "All right. I'll have Marco do it! What else?"

I raised my eyebrows.

"Damn it, Lena! I do not favor the boys! I'll have Marita do it just to keep you quiet."

I smiled sweetly. Dom knew Marita was better than her twin brother at business projections. She considered unintended consequences and suggested creative solutions for stumbling blocks in addition to calculating long-term/short-term costs and benefits.

"Lastly, I've been considering getting stackable washer and dryer units for the apartments. If they pass muster with Maureen and me, we'll put them in all the units in my building and go from there. We can include that in the rent, too."

"Okay," he said, "I'll have a proposal ready for our next board meeting. Please tell me that's all."

I smiled sweetly, "It is a pleasure doing business with you, as usual."

"Yeah, right." Despite the grumpy tone, he hugged me on his way out.

***

Maureen was gleeful when I told her about the new space that evening. Then she gulped and said, "But Lena, I can't afford rent on another apartment."

"Don't worry. I've got it covered. We'll work out a barter system like Rico has with Kalayla. You can help out with this and that. First, you'll need to buy the paint and paint the studio yourself. How's that?"

"Oh, that's wonderful! Your apartment makes me feel peaceful, and I might paint the studio white. The funny thing is that Kalayla mentioned she might want her bedroom white. I could do that, too."

My, oh my, white walls were taking over the world! Maybe I wasn't the only one changing.

Maureen babbled about needing to move her stuff out of storage. To aggravate Dom, I assured her he'd arrange that, which should remind him not to push me too far!

Then, I thought of another way to aggravate him. We had two other small apartments on the first floor that we could advertise as artists' studios. The ceilings were six inches higher than the other apartments, and the lighting was excellent. The idea of turning the entire building into an experimental nightmare for Dom gave me a good chuckle.

I thought about Dom's comment that I was treating Maureen like a daughter. Maybe I was. When she told me that her dad asked to take Kalayla for ice cream, I could have kissed that old man!

I mistakenly thought I could shape my kids like clay pieces, as did Maureen's mother. When she found out she couldn't, she turned away. It made me wonder if I'd done something similar by focusing on what I didn't like and ignoring everything else.

I decided JJ worshipped Joey because he was blind to Joey's vicious side, but maybe Joey was different around him. Maybe Joey's construction crews also saw a side of him that I didn't.

One night, when I picked Joey up at work, the foreman said, "Come for the Boss, Mrs. Barzetti? You know, the guys like working for Joey. He's a fair boss, and the pay is good, with bonuses when the job is harder. That's why there's low turnover."

That was a couple of days after Joey taught me a lesson, and I dismissed the foreman's words as those of a suck-up and a liar.

I assumed Joey was teaching the boys to be callous and think only of themselves. Did I let my tunnel vision overshadow the thoughtful things they did?

I thought about JJ's gentleness when he sewed on Cody's ear. I remembered the first time Jimmy raced his bike and fell. Mark led him into the bathroom, cleaned up his bleeding arm, and said, "Come on. I'll show you the trick to turning when you're going fast." And, I recall a night when Mark dressed up for a date. His face lit up when Mikie punched him in the arm and said, "Looking sharp, Bro."

And Mark, no word from him for fifteen years. Why did I wait for him to contact me instead of reaching out to him?

I thought about my granddaughters, JJ's two girls. I barely knew them. I'd missed their sports, drama, and music recitals because I was obsessed with solidifying my place in the business.

Sadness came at me from every direction, and then I thought about Kieran's grandfather. After all these years, he called Maureen and asked to see his granddaughter.

That was an act of bravery.

If that old man could be brave, maybe this old woman could, too. I could contact my granddaughters, and Mattwo would help me find Mark. He knew how to search dark alleys and avoid trouble spots.

I suddenly felt nervous. What if Mark didn't want to see me? What if the girls didn't want to see me? But what if they did? I guess it was time I found out, and late was better than never.

ICE CREAM

Mama didn't freak out when I mentioned getting a dog, maybe 'cause I told her I'd pay for food and the vet. The old lady said, "I suppose I'll be stuck walking Hopalong when you're busy."

When Lotta told me Hopalong was one hundred percent mutt, I said, "That's awesome! She's like me!"

Lotta looked startled, which was kind of funny. Maybe she thought I was a purebred something or other? Then she said, "I imagine she's more mixed than you are. From her sweet disposition, I'd say she got the best of whatever she is."

I decided I'd ask Mama where I got my sweet disposition.

Adopting a dog was a big responsibility, and I had a list of stuff to do, like have a chip in Hopalong so if she got lost, whoever found her could call us and buy a collar and a tag with her name and our phone number.

One of the techs at Animal Friends rigged up a cart with wheels so Hopalong could rest her back legs on a bed and move the cart with her front legs. It looked weird and it took her a while to get used to it, but she wasn't stuck in the crate. The vet said her casts would come off in three or four weeks.

I could hardly wait to walk her down Mass. Ave. I decided that if we saw Ray Ray and Thor, we'd go in the opposite direction. Thor must weigh a hundred and twenty pounds, and Hopalong weighed thirty-five.

Hopalong didn't respond when I called her Hoppy for short. Lotta said, "What'd I tell you about naming a dog?"

Fine! So, I had to ask Hopalong. I got a piece of paper and crossed off names she didn't like: Pal, Longie, Alo, and Hopa. When I said Opa, she rubbed her head against my hand and slapped her tail on the floor!

When I told Lena, she said she'd seen a movie called *Zorba the Greek* where they shouted "Opa!" while dancing. I bet anything Opa liked dancing as much as I did.

I planned to attend the dance camp for a week in August, but that was seven hours a day. Now that Opa was my responsibility, I also had to think about her. She'd be home by then, and I didn't want to leave her alone while she was adjusting to the apartment and Mama was adjusting to her.

When school started again, I decided to throw a fit in the front office and tell the principal I needed my service dog to prevent my attacks.

* * *

Rico volunteered to drive me and Kieran to Animal Friends so they could meet Opa. I took Rico and Kieran to the back of the shelter. When Opa saw me, she slapped her tail and barked twice.

"That's how she says hello to me," I said, opening Opa's cage door.

Kieran got on the floor to pet her like I always did.

"You could bring her to my house, but she might get scared with so many kids around," Kieran said.

"Yeah," I said. "And some are jerks."

Rico said, "Opa could stay at my house during the day while you're at dance camp. She'd have the backyard to herself, with shade and sun when she wanted it."

"That'd be awesome, but I might not go."

Rico sat with his back against the wall. "Whoa, Kalayla. You've been working and saving money to go to that camp."

"I know, but I'm responsible for Opa, so I have to be around to take care of her."

"Sometimes, we have to choose between two important things, but this isn't one of those times. Dancing is important to you, and Lena, Lotta, and I can make sure Opa has everything she needs while you're at camp."

I would've kissed him, but I don't go around kissing people. I held my hand to shake, which made Kieran and him laugh. Rico tried to hug me, but I twisted away, and he fell over. We were on the floor rolling around, laughing, when Lotta came in.

"Oh my God! Three beasts that nobody checked in. I'm not sure I have a crate big enough for that one!" she said, pointing at Rico. "I'm positive I don't have a big enough muzzle! I'll have to quarantine him!"

171

It was pretty funny.

I decided to thank them by making Halloween cookies. Mama could cut out Casper, the friendly ghost, cats, and pumpkins, and I could prepare the batter and bake them.

***

About a week later, I was working at the gym when Kieran came down the hall with his grandpa. My stomach turned yucky, and I thought I might puke.

Kieran waved, and even though I didn't wave back, his grandpa said, "Hi, Kalayla. Kieran and I are going for ice cream. How about coming with us? Your mom said it was okay."

Cow turds! What made him think he could come here and ask me to go for ice cream like it was an ordinary thing instead of a reason for me to drop dead from shock? He had a nerve talking to me and standing next to me.

But I kind of wanted to go.

Lena told me that flipping a coin was an excellent way to figure it out when I didn't know if I should do something. If I didn't like how the coin landed, I'd know I should do the opposite of what it said.

I didn't have a coin, and my stomach felt weird, but it didn't feel like I'd puke.

Kieran smiled and said, "Come on, K. We go to a place where you can get mix-ins like M&M's, nuts, and chocolate bits. You'll like it."

I kind of wanted to go 'cause it wasn't like I got a free ice cream every day. But, no way was I calling him Grandpa.

I said, "So say I do go with you. What am I supposed to call you?"

Kieran's grandpa frowned as if I were speaking a foreign language. Well, tough turds to him if he couldn't understand.

"A lot of kids call me Mr. O. I guess you could, too."

Calling him Mr. O. made him sound like someone I barely knew. I could do that.

"Why's Kieran going? He doesn't like ice cream."

I looked at Kieran. "Is he making you go?"

"Nah! It's a cool place. I usually get the mix-ins without ice cream."

Kieran was weird, but I liked him and knew he was telling me the truth. So, I said, "That sounds okay."

"All right, then. Come on." Mr. O. turned and walked down the hall. Kieran put his hand up for a high five, and we slapped hands.

Mr. O. was parked out front like he was planning a quick getaway. He said, "You kids can get in the back. Seat belts on."

His car was twice as big as ours, and a lot of kids could've piled in back with us. Kieran read my mind and said, "How many kids do you think we could fit in here? I say five."

"We could get more if we only took kids that didn't have big butts, and some sat on the floor. I say nine."

Mr. O. said, "Nah. You two are underestimating. You've got to think of layers. You put four little ones on the floor. You put three hulks on the seats. Then, a layer of four medium-sized kids sit on the laps of the hulks, and you squeeze as many little kids as you can on top. I say fifteen, and that's not counting how many you could put in the front seat."

"Fifteen!" Kieran and I said together. And Kieran added, "You're smoking something, Grandpa!"

"What would you know about smoking, young man?"

"Nothing, but you do. Daddy told me he started smoking at my age, and you quit to be a good example."

"That's your Uncle Colin, Kalayla. Everybody knows he lies all the time!"

"Grandpa! He does not!" Kieran said.

"Sometimes, he does," Mr. O. said.

We laughed, and it was kind of fun.

We parked a block from the ice cream place. Mr. O. stood in line while Kieran and I went to the counter to check out the flavors and mix-in ingredients. When our turn came, I decided I'd do what Kieran did. I got gummy bears, heath bar bits, and almonds in a medium cup.

Mr. O. shook his head. "Kids nowadays! I can't believe neither of you got ice cream! Next, you'll tell me you don't like chocolate cake!"

Kieran looked at me; I looked at him. We giggled and said together, "We don't like chocolate cake."

I added, "But we're kidding!"

Mr. O asked if I wanted him to drop me off at home, but I had to get my bike from the gym and see Opa.

As I was getting out of the car, I said, "How'd you know it was okay for me to go for an ice cream?"

"I called and asked your mama."

"You called my mama?"

"Yeah. I called her."

"It's about time," I said.

He nodded, and Kieran waved as they drove away.

I biked to the shelter, strapped Opa onto her cart, and took her to sniff around in the grass area. She was sniffing, and I was thinking. When Mama asked how I liked going with Mr. O. and Kieran, I'd tell her the truth. I had fun.

COMING UP TULIPS?

The bed-sitting apartment was perfect for my studio. The large room was my workspace; a couple of chairs and a coffee table from the Salvation Army formed a sitting area, and the compact kitchen and bathroom were just the right size.

Lena said Dom scrounged a refrigerator, but the Sears sticker was still on it. When I told her it was brand new, she pursed her lips and said, "Humm, my brother assured me it was a discard."

When I told Dominic I was glad I wouldn't be paying storage for my art supplies, he grunted and said, "You're thrifty. My sister is a spender!"

Layla and I discussed every shade of white with the clerk in the Sears paint section. I chose white with a tinge of orange to remind me of the sunrise, and Layla decided on the same color for her bedroom. She moved everything into the center of the floor and cleared her walls. When she saw it painted, the smile on her face lit up my world, and she hugged me!

Lena gave me a clock with gigantic numbers as a studio warming present. "Keep track of the time!" she scolded me. "Don't forget about eating with Kalayla." I put the clock where I could see it and promised Lena I'd pay attention.

***

A few days later, Kalayla came home and said, "Mr. O took me and Kieran for ice cream."

Mr. O. took her and Kieran for ice cream. All the neighborhood kids called my father Mr. O.

I took a deep breath. I thought my father might change his mind, but he didn't. I said, "How did it go?"

"We went to this ice cream place where you can add mix-ins. Kieran doesn't like ice cream, so he just gets mix-ins. I did that, too. Mr. O. asked if I wanted to go again, and I said sure."

My father asked Kalayla if she wanted to go again, and she said sure.

My father called me the next week and the week after to ask if he could invite Kalayla for ice cream. The third time, I told him Kalayla decided things like that herself and he didn't need to ask my permission.

My father was a stick-to-the-rules type of guy and said, "I'll call anyway, so everything's on the up and up." We didn't say more than a few words to each other, but I was so happy to hear his voice.

Then, last week, he said, "You and the kid doing all right? Do you need anything?"

Did we need anything? I couldn't believe he asked that now.

"No," I said. "We're all set. Thanks."

I stewed over his question for two days. Tuesday was my day off, and as soon as Kalayla left, I took a coffee cake to Lena's, hoping she wouldn't mind having company at seven-thirty in the morning.

Lena opened the door wearing a blue blouse and a black skirt with silver jewelry. Her hair bun was as neat as usual. "Well now," she said, "is the Welcome Wagon paying early morning visits to longtime residents? Did they send you around to make sure I didn't croak?"

Despite my glum mood, I smiled. "I need your advice."

"Well, you lucked out. Advice is my specialty."

Lena brewed Hazelnut coffee, and we sat at the kitchen table. I breathed a sigh of relief.

"It's about my father," I said. I'd built up so much steam over the last two days I couldn't hold it back. "On the phone a few days ago, he asked if Kalayla and I needed anything! Why didn't he ask that when I married Jamal? Why didn't he ask that when Jamal died? That's when I needed him. Why would I want his help now?"

I was so agitated if I kept talking, I'd repeat the same thing, so I stopped.

Lena sipped her coffee and took a small bite of coffee cake. "Being a parent is the hardest job anybody could ever have."

"I know that, Lena. I'm awful at it, and you've helped me so much—."

"Oh pooh-bah, Maureen!" Lena interrupted. "If I tried walking on water the way you think I can, I'd sink to the bottom of the ocean with a thousand-pound weight of mistakes to hold me down. Your father called you, which shows he has more courage than I ever did. Don't look so shocked. Let me say my piece.

"I do not know where you got the idea I was an ideal mother. I wasn't. For one thing, I made a terrible mistake with my boy Mark. If I find out where he is, I hope he'll listen when I apologize. Your father knows what he did was wrong, and he's trying to fix that as best he can. I admire that.

"I hope you give him some leeway. When he asked what you need, he meant what you need now. He knows he can't give you what you needed five or ten years ago. You won't have a relationship if you're determined to punish him. I'll tell you what I told Kalayla. Don't cut off your nose to spite your face."

My feelings were chaotic. One minute, I wanted to throw my arms around my father and tell him how glad I was that he called and wanted to spend time with Kalayla. The next minute, I wanted to scream at him and tell him how much I hated him because he'd let me down and hurt me.

I didn't know if I could let my father be my daddy again, but I was positive I wanted Kalayla to meet her O'Rourke family.

I looked at my watch and saw that it was nine-thirty. "I have to get the studio set up, Lena. Thank you for helping me think it through."

* * *

I loved that the studio was on the first floor, close to the front door. The building had two entrance doors. The first one wasn't locked. The next, a security door, was up four stairs on a landing and always locked. A panel on the wall beside it had an intercom/buzzer system with a list of apartment numbers and occupants' names.

I emptied boxes, set up my easel, and was carrying a garbage bag out of the apartment when I heard a knock on the security door. I turned and saw Clarence standing at the door. He'd appeared out of nowhere like a menacing cloud on a sunny day. Keeping him behind a locked door wouldn't make him go away, so I opened the door and said, "Hi. This is an odd time for a visit."

"Eddie said it was your day off. I came to find out if you're coming for the Labor Day cookout." He pointed at the trash bag. "Are you cleaning apartments?"

"Oh, no, I'm getting my studio set up. Let me go dump this." I walked to the end of the hall and put the bag down the garbage chute.

177

"What's the deal? Did you move to a different apartment?"

"No, a friend is letting me use this one as a studio."

"A friend? You mean the guy I saw you with? That's a friendly gesture. I bet I know how you're repaying him."

"Rico had nothing to do with it! The friend is Lena. She owns the apartment building."

"Yeah, sure, that old lady owns the building and loves it so much she lives on the fourth floor for fun. Tell me another story, Maureen!"

Clarence moved closer to me. Jamal said I shouldn't take Clarence seriously, but my back was against the wall, and Clarence didn't sound like he was joking.

I heard the landing door open and saw Mrs. Meade come in with a bag of groceries.

"Oh, Mrs. Meade," I called. "How nice to see you! Let me carry your groceries."

"Maureen, dear, you're so kind. Is this your uncle? Lena says he checks on you."

Lena must have told everyone in the building about Clarence. "He's not my uncle, Mrs. Meade. He's Kalayla's uncle."

"Oh, of course, the girl's uncle. I remember now. Hurry up, dear. I have ice cream in the bag."

Clarence scowled, and no doubt wished Mrs. Meade would fall down the garbage chute.

"I'll tell Kalayla you stopped by, Clarence. We'll see you at the cookout." I followed Mrs. Meade up the stairs.

"You can bet on that," Clarence said as he left.

Oh dear!

LABOR DAY PARTY 2000

Mama was nervous about going to Grandma and Grandpa's, but I didn't know why. Grandma said Opa would have to stay in the backyard, but I didn't care. Grandpa grilled there, and I could sneak a hot dog for Opa.

Mama brought her four-bean salad, and I had Opa's tennis ball and plenty of treats. Grandma and Grandpa invited a ton of people, so I kept Opa on a leash so nobody would bother her.

We parked half a block from their house, and walking there, I told Opa who she'd meet and what we'd be doing. The first person we saw in the backyard was Clarence. What a pisser! He strolled over like a big shot, ignored me, and said, "You are something, Maureen. First a studio, and now a dog. You're settling into some kind of life."

I pushed ahead of Mama and said, "The dog's mine. If you bug me or Mama, I'll tell her to bite you." Nobody who saw Opa's friendly face and wagging tail would believe that, but I didn't care.

"Well, aren't you the grumpy one! Did your mama's new boyfriend get the dog for you?"

Mama got flustered and said, "Rico's not my boyfriend. And the dog was a stray Kalayla adopted from a shelter."

Mama got me so pissed. She acted like she had to explain everything to Clarence, but she didn't tell me anything! Maybe she was scared of him, but I wasn't!

"I got the dog myself, and Rico is a good friend. He's a karate expert, so watch how you act with Mama."

"Layla!" Mama said, "Don't be rude. Clarence didn't mean anything by that."

Yeah, he did, but Mama was too dense to know that!

"Chill out, Kalayla. I was joking," Clarence said.

Cow turds! Clarence never joked when it came to Mama. I tugged on her arm, "Let's find Grandma and introduce her and Grandpa to Opa."

We walked toward the grill, and everybody wanted to pet Opa. When Grandma saw Opa, she said, "She is a sweet-looking thing, isn't she? And she seems to be walking fine now. Get her a bowl of water, Kalayla." Grandma rubbed Opa's head, and Opa licked her hand.

"A dog can't just exist on water, Lucinda," Grandpa said. "She'd like a hot dog, wouldn't she, Kalayla?"

I knew Grandpa would like Opa. The yard was too crowded to throw the tennis ball, so I gave it to Opa to chew on. Shanese came over and said she'd beat my ass at ping pong. I could wipe her out, but I was busy with Opa.

I filled my plate, and Opa and I ate on the front steps. When we went to the backyard, Mama was by the fence talking to Clarence. Mama should've pulled away when he took her arm, but she never wanted to make a scene.

I got there fast and said, "Mama! Opa threw up, so we better go home before she does it again. Watch out, Uncle Clarence, she might mess up your shiny shoes." Under my breath, I added, "I hope." I didn't care if he heard me.

When we were driving home, I asked Mama why Clarence grabbed her arm. She shrugged and didn't answer, which aggravated me. School started in two days, plus I was working and dancing, and I might not be home when that jerk came.

What a pisser! I'd tell Lena to be sure Mama wasn't alone if Clarence was there.

THE PERFECT STORM

When Kalayla was at a dance camp in August, Lotta and I divided the Opa-sitting time. We each went to Rico's for a couple of hours every day, and I have to say, playing with that dog added a spark to my life.

Kalayla came dragging in from dance camp around five-thirty. The first day, she said, "They're trying to kill us! All we do is stretch, strengthen, and go over the same steps a million times."

"Too bad it's such a waste of money," I said. "Will the camp give you a refund?"

"I never said it was a waste of money! Didn't you tell me working hard never hurt anybody? Anyway, everybody sits around and talks during lunch."

"Huh!" I said. "Are you inviting any of them to meet Opa?"

"Nah, they don't like dogs."

That girl came up with the worst excuses for vetoing something that might be good for her! She wasn't much different from me, which got me thinking about what-ifs, like whether I should suggest coffee, lunch, or dinner to Mattwo.

Which was a waste of time because when I called him, he said, "How about lunch the day after tomorrow at Dimitri's, the Greek place down the street from you?"

Then I had to gnash over what to wear and whether to get my hair cut like Lotta nagged me. I'd worn my hair in a bun so long it was a permanent fixture, but I was in a mood for change. I felt like a new woman when I walked to Dimitri's.

I was nearly at the restaurant when I saw Mattwo park across the street. I got goosebumps of excitement and felt like I was seventeen again. How ridiculous can an old woman get?

Dimitri's was long and narrow, with tables for two or four on either side of a center aisle. It wouldn't get a high score on intimacy, but was a good spot for getting reacquainted.

After we ordered, Mattwo said, "I don't know what you did to your hair, Lena, but I like it! Tell me, to what do I owe the pleasure of your company?"

That was Mattwo, right to the point! The flush of heat on my face told me that the seventeen-year-old was blushing, but she wasn't the one about to make a fool of herself. Before I walked into the restaurant, I told myself, "Lena, you might die tomorrow. You better say what you want to Mattwo while you can."

So, I said, "I want you to know I've been thinking about you for a long time."

The smile on Mattwo's face was so open and warm it would have convinced the Grinch not to steal Christmas! And it convinced me to keep talking. "I wanted to call you, but I felt like a dunce. So, I didn't, except when I needed help with Kalayla. I need help again, but I want you to know I would have called anyway. What do you think of that?"

Mattwo reached over, took my hand, and said, "My Lady, I am at your service! What is it you need?"

"I need to find Mark, and I don't know how. The last I heard, he was in Chicago, but that was fifteen years ago. I thought you might know how to find him."

Mattwo nodded. "I can give it a try. Does JJ know anything?"

"JJ told me I probably wouldn't hear from Mark, so he knows something."

"Let me think about it. Now, on another subject, seeing that you've been wanting to see me, how about a movie on Saturday? We can sit in the back row and hold hands."

I blushed and laughed at the same time. That sounded fine to me.

A week later, Opa and I went to do errands. It was Maureen's day off, and I told her I'd keep Opa while she was in the studio. When we got back, I knocked on the studio door. No answer.

When Opa and I reached the third-floor landing, Mrs. Meade opened her door. She must have been looking out the window for me because she said, "Thank goodness you're home! I didn't know if I should call the police."

"What's wrong?"

"Maybe nothing, but I'm not sure. I heard noise from upstairs. You know, from that young woman's apartment. The girl went to school, so I think her mother is alone. I saw that uncle parked across the street, and a little while later, I heard loud arguing."

"When was that?"

"Just before you got home. Do you think I should have called the police?"

"No, you did the right thing telling me. I'll take care of it. You go enjoy a nice cup of tea."

Mrs. Meade smiled and closed her door. I got up the last flight of stairs faster than I had in twenty years. I listened at Maureen's door, but I didn't hear anything. I unlocked my door, put down my packages, unleashed Opa, and told her to stay put. I didn't know what I might have to do, but having her underfoot wasn't part of it.

I remembered what Joey told me and the boys when the twins asked if they could bring friends to see the guns. "Guns aren't for show and tell! You use them to get food, compete, or defend yourself. If you need to defend yourself, shoot to kill!"

I didn't know what was happening in Maureen's apartment, but I wasn't going there unless I could defend her and me. I went into my bedroom closet, unlocked the steel box, loaded my pistol, got my master keys, and went to Maureen's door.

I opened and closed the door as quietly as I could. I heard Maureen's angry, frantic voice say, "Stop it, Clarence. Leave me alone!"

Clarence said, "Come on, Maureen. I know you want it. I got more than that jerk-off you've been seeing!"

I marched into the bedroom. Maureen was on the bed, struggling with Clarence. He held her arms and was trying to get on top of her.

Memories flashed through my mind of Joey on top of me, holding me down, taunting me. I'd never let that happen again.

I felt the weight of the pistol in my hand, walked to the bed, and said, "Get off, or I will put a bullet in your brain."

Startled by my voice, Clarence turned toward me, let go of Maureen, and said, "What the f–k?"

"Lena—thank God," Maureen said as she rolled away from Clarence and pushed herself off the bed.

The puzzlement on Clarence's face turned to terror when I pressed the pistol against his cheek and said, "You are wrong if you think I won't pull this trigger."

And then, the world tilted.

What happened to Clarence was so shocking I froze as I watched a slow-motion transformation.

His expression was dazed and confused as if he didn't understand what was happening. He groaned, and then, slowly, gracefully, like a building imploding, one floor after another, he curled into a ball, rocking back and forth, moaning and calling out so faintly I wasn't sure what he was saying.

Then I realized Clarence was calling for his mother.

I lowered the pistol. The man who had intended to rape turned into a terrified child calling for his mother.

Maureen grabbed my arm. Her voice shifted my attention away from Clarence.

"Oh my God," she said. "This is what happened that day at Fresh Pond. Jamal told me, but I never imagined how traumatic and terrifying it was for Clarence. I couldn't imagine how helpless Jamal felt watching those boys torment him."

I had no idea what Maureen was talking about.

"I have to call Lucinda," Maureen said. "They have to come."

Maureen, the panicky, uncertain woman, told me what needed to be done. She picked the phone up on her nightstand, dialed, and waited. "Lucinda. It's Maureen. You need to come. It's Clarence. You need to come right now."

I swear, talk about scaring a mother to death! "Give me that phone!" I said.

"Mrs. LeeRoyce. This is Lena Barzetti. I live across the hall from Maureen. Clarence is here in Maureen's apartment. He's had some kind of breakdown. He's curled up in a ball and crying for you. You'll need help getting him home."

"Oh no," Lucinda said. "What happened?"

"He tried to rape Maureen. I stuck a gun in his face and told him to stop."

"Oh, my poor boy. My poor, sweet boy." I heard her call her husband. "We're coming," she said. "Tell my boy we're coming."

I hung up the phone and realized that I was still holding the pistol. I put it down on the nightstand. Maureen and I looked at each other while Clarence rocked back and forth, crying for his mama.

She called him her poor boy, her poor, sweet boy. I looked at the figure on the bed. I saw a little boy curled into a ball, calling for his mama like any of my boys. Much as I might despise the man, the little boy needed help.

I did what any mother would have done. I sat down beside him, gently rubbed his back, and whispered, "She's coming, Clarence, don't you worry. Your mama is on her way. Shhhhhh, now. You'll be okay. Your mama and daddy are coming." I said over and over and over.

I had no idea where Maureen was until she came into the room with Clarence's parents and a neighbor friend of theirs.

I got up, and Lucinda took my place on the bed with her boy. She put her arms around him and pulled him close, crooning, "I'm here now, Clarence. Daddy's here now. We'll take care of you."

Tears ran down my face as I cried for her and with her. No matter what he had done, if he were my child, I'd be holding him like Lucinda was.

When Clarence stopped crying, Lucinda said, "Now, Clarence, honey, we're going home. Daddy and Raymond will help you get to the car, and we'll go home. Everything's all right now."

Mr. LeeRoyce and Raymond helped Clarence to his feet. "Put your arms around us, boy," Mr. LeeRoyce said. "We're taking you home."

Clarence put an arm around each of them, and they helped him, one shuffling step at a time.

Lucinda linked her arm to mine and said, "Thank you. My boy had a bad time when he was little, and we lost him back then."

She turned to Maureen. "Thank you for calling. I'm sorry for what Clarence tried to do."

For the second time that day, Maureen surprised me. She wrapped her arms around her mother-in-law. "I know, and I'm so sorry, too. I misunderstood when Jamal died. I thought you wanted to take Kalayla away from me. But you didn't. You wanted me to take care of her."

"When Jamal married you, you became part of our family. His dying didn't change that. Nothing will," Lucinda said.

The two stayed wrapped together, and finally, I said, "They probably have Clarence in the car by now."

Lucinda and Maureen walked out of the apartment arm in arm. I followed them down the stairs and waited on the landing. Lucinda got into the back seat with Clarence. Maureen stayed at the curb until they pulled away. Then she turned, came back inside, into my arms, and said, "I'm so glad Kalayla wasn't here, and I'm so grateful that you were."

We went up the stairs to her apartment. I retrieved my pistol, went home, and put it away.

Opa greeted me at the door, along with Petunia and Napoleon, as if they knew what I had witnessed and understood that love was the only remedy for pain.

Afterward, Maureen told me the story of Jamal and Clarence, two little boys exploring on their bikes on a summer day, caught in the wrong place at the wrong time and treated viciously. One boy was more resilient. The other was forever changed, a shattered child living inside a man's body.

If only Clarence and his brother had stayed at home that day or ridden their bikes someplace else, if only the young men in that car had driven by or gone to see a movie instead of choosing to terrorize, if only we could turn back time and rewrite the story, Clarence would be a different man.

But we couldn't. It was enough to break any mother's heart.

FALL 2000

THE RED SOX

Mama said Clarence was sick and wouldn't be around for a while. She must've cared 'cause she talked to Grandma way more than usual, but I didn't have time to worry about that jerk showing up. I was taking two weekly dance classes, working at Matty's Way on Saturday and at the shelter on Sunday.

Plus, Mr. O. was so jacked up about the Red Sox, he was giving Kieran and me a back-to-school present and taking us to a Red Sox home game on September twenty-third. Kieran said Mr. O. loved the Red Sox no matter how bad they were. They might be doing great in July, but be in the toilet by September. They were second or third now, which was okay unless you were panting for them to be in the World Series like Kieran's grandpa. Anyway, Rico said I could have the day off.

Kieran rolled his eyes when I told him my daddy loved every sport except baseball. He said it was boring, and the players stood around more than they played.

"Do not say that to Grandpa!" Kieran said. "He'll give us a two-hour lecture on why baseball is the most challenging and interesting game ever invented."

I met Kieran downstairs the day of the game, and it turned out his brother, Colin, and their father, Colin, were going with us. When Mr. O introduced me to Colin, the kid, I said, "Do you both answer when somebody says Colin?"

The kid said, "I'm Col. My dad's Colin."

I looked at Kieran's Grandpa, pointed at Colin, and said, "What am I supposed to call him?"

Mr. O said, "You could call him Uncle Colin, or you could call him Mr. C. Is that okay with you, son?"

Mr. C. nodded.

Kieran sat between Col and me in the back seat on the way to Fenway Park. I figured this was an excellent time to help Kieran out, so I said, "So, when are you getting Kieran a new bike, Col?"

"I never said I'd do that!" Col said. "Did you tell her I said that, Kieran?"

I didn't give Kieran a chance to answer. "Kieran's says you're a great brother. So, I thought since you wrecked his bike, you'd get him a new one."

Kieran gave me an elbow. What he really said was, "Col will say anything to get out of trouble. He's a bigger liar than his dad."

Mr. C. turned toward the back seat and said, "Col, you told me Kieran wrecked his bike."

"Yeah, well—," Col said.

Mr. C. frowned. "Kieran! Who wrecked your bike?"

"I didn't," Kieran said.

"Col!" Mr. C said.

"Maybe I did wreck it, but it's not like I did it on purpose. I was planning to get it fixed when I got the money."

"I have a simple solution," Mr. C. said. "I'll pay to get the bike fixed, and you will pay me back. Seems fair to me. Seem fair to you, Col?"

Col gave me a dirty look. "Yeah, I guess."

Awesome! There was no point stopping when I was scoring so many points! "That's cool," I said. "Then Kieran can ride over to my house and meet my mom, right?"

Mr. O. started laughing. "I told you, Colin. She's Maureen's daughter, all right."

"I can see," Mr. C. said. "Did your mom tell you the nickname we gave her, Kalayla?"

"Nah, she said you were dead."

"Jesus, Mary, and Joseph! Dead! Only Maureen would come up with something like that! That's why we called her Miss Sharp Tooth."

Sharp Tooth? Maureen, as in my Mama, Maureen? He must've got his sisters mixed up. If I had given Mama a nickname, which I wouldn't have, it would've been Miss Toothless. "That's funny 'cause Mama calls me Miss Smart Mouth."

Col muttered, "Because that's what you are and a few other things, too!"

Everybody laughed like it was a jolly family joke. Kieran gave me a double-quick elbow and a big-eyed look, so I knew he wasn't mad.

Kieran and I looked out the windows while the three of them discussed baseball. They said the Orioles could beat the Sox 'cause even though Hector wasn't great, he was better than Kohlmeier.

Col asked me if I knew "Sweet Caroline." They booed when I said I didn't. They said I couldn't get into Fenway if I didn't 'cause there was a dumb tradition that everybody in the crowd sang "Sweet Caroline" at the eighth-inning stretch. They taught me the words, and we spent the rest of the ride yelling whenever we got to, "So good, so good, so good."

It was funny.

They could hardly wait for me to see the Green Monster. I figured that'd be something scary, but it was a wall. Yeah, it was like thirty-seven feet high, but showing me a dumb green wall gave them a big thrill? I could see why Mama was whacko, coming from a family that thought it was the coolest thing they'd ever seen.

We ate Fenway Franks and sang "Sweet Caroline" in the eighth inning stretch. The game went into overtime, and the Sox won in the tenth, 8-7, so everybody was jacked up on the drive home.

Mr. O. dropped Mr. C., Col, and Kieran off and then took me home. He usually dropped me off, but today, he said, "Would you mind if I came up and said hello to your mom?"

"Opa likes meeting new people, but I don't know how Mama will feel."

"No time like the present to find out," Mr. O. said. As we went by, I knocked on the studio door, but Mama must've been upstairs.

Opa jumped all over me, but I made her sit and shake hands with Mr. O. so he'd see how well-trained she was. I didn't see Mama, so I called, "Mama, we've got company."

Mama came into the living room saying, "Is Lena—." She stopped mid-step. Her eyes were wide, and she put her hand over her open mouth.

"Mr. O. wanted to see you, so I invited him for one of Lotta's desserts. I'll see what Lena's got. He can stay here and tell you about the game. The Sox won, and Kieran, Col, and their dad went with us. Stay, Opa. You're on guard duty."

Mama stood like a statue. As I beat it out the door, I heard Mr. O. say, "I wanted to see for myself that you're all right. You've made a beautiful home here, Maureen."

I banged on Lena's door, and when she came, I said, "Get some desserts and bring them over quick! I left Mama alone with Mr. O. and Opa."

"Get in here and help me carry the food," Lena said, getting lemon squares and five kinds of cookies.

"That's enough, Lena! We have to get back!"

I guess I didn't need to worry. Mama was where she'd been when I left, and Mr. O. was looking around. Opa was watching Mr. O. She didn't understand that her job was to keep Mama from turning into her whacko self and not protect her from Mr. O.

Anyway, Lena took charge. "Well, hello, Mr. O'Rourke. I heard you know the best place for ice cream mix-ins. How did Hector do today? Any strikeouts?"

Cow turds! Lena knew less about baseball than I did, which was zero until today. How did she know who was pitching?

Mama stared at Mr. O. like she was scared he might disappear in a puff of smoke if she blinked or turned away.

As soon as we sat, I got busy scarfing down lemon squares.

Mr. O. turned to Mama and said, "You used to keep track of the stats for us, Maureen. You still doing that?"

Up until then, Mama hadn't said a single word. She blinked several times and said, "Counting today, they're 81-74 and ranked third. Carrasco has zero starts, 18 finishes, including today."

"See, what'd I tell you?" Mr. O. said.

I stared at Mama.

Lena said, "Don't look so surprised, Kalayla. Your mama and I talk baseball all the time."

Cow turds! Liar, liar, pants on fire!

"Oh, yeah," I said. "I must've forgot!"

Lena smirked. I ground my teeth. Opa wagged her tail. Mr. O. and Mama talked about stats.

DADDY

When my father said he had to shove off, Lena jumped up from the table. "I forgot I have to feed the cats. Come with me, Kalayla. You need to learn something useful."

Kalayla looked at Lena like she had three heads, but she followed her to the door. "Come on, Opa," she said. "You better learn, too. See you, Mr. O. Thanks for an awesome day."

I couldn't stop staring at my father. He looked older and tired, like he needed sleep. His belt was under his belly now instead of around it. He was prying open a closed door by taking his granddaughter for ice cream, inviting my brother to a baseball game with them, and taking the chance I wouldn't slam the door in his face when he came to visit.

After Kalayla closed the door, he said, "I'm glad to see you, Maureen. Your daughter is just like you. And I'm grateful you were willing—."

"She's like me and Jamal," I interrupted. "She got his good traits and some of my bad ones, but she's her own person."

He laughed. "Colin thought she was a lot like you."

Colin. What made him go to the game? He must have known our father was taking Kalayla. He and I used to fight constantly, but once, he punched Jimmy McDonald for saying I was a know-it-all. That was funny because Colin said that's exactly what I was.

My family hadn't seen the vulnerable and frightened side of me. Kalayla had. She said I was nervous and jumpy, a scaredy-cat. My father would have been shocked by that. He would have said, "Since when is Maureen afraid of anything?"

"Does my mother know that you've been seeing Kalayla?"

"She does. She disapproves but doesn't have the energy to fight me."

My mother, always the fighter, no longer had the energy to fight. How was that possible? She wasn't the person I depended on or whose opinion I valued now, but the thought that she didn't have the strength to fight for what she believed wrenched my heart.

When my parents kicked me out and I married Jamal, I realized how intolerant and narrow-minded people could be, and that frightened me. My white skin was a protective covering when I was alone. Jamal never had that, and when we were together, I was vulnerable, too.

Lena hurried home to give my father and me time alone. She said what my father did now counted for a lot, no matter what he'd done in the past. She said people could change if we let them. I'd changed, and my father had, too.

"I'm glad you're seeing Kalayla," I said.

"There's no point making excuses or giving reasons. What we did when you married Jamal was wrong," my father said slowly. "The fact is the fact."

"Would you feel that way if he was still alive?" I said. "Would you have come here if Jamal lived here, too?"

My father sighed. "I'm not good with what if this happened or that happened. I hope I would."

My father. Always honest, like Jamal. I think they would have liked each other.

"I can live with that," I said.

He smiled. "Would you be willing to let a foolish old man give you a hug?"

"Yes, Daddy. I would."

LENA
LATE FALL SURPRISES

When I told Lotta I was planning Maureen's thirty-first birthday party, she said, "I suppose you'll want to borrow my china and linens, seeing that you gave yours away when you joined the nunnery."

"Lotta, you know that no respectable nunnery would take me!"

"Well, they sure wouldn't now. No matter what you say, there's nothing platonic about your relationship with my brother."

I scowled. "I was thinking of a yummy buffet. What would you like to make? I thought I'd do the three-cheese lasagna with hamburger. You could do fried chicken."

"There you go, changing the subject, which is an obvious sign of guilt, probably leftover from your Catholic girlhood training! And suggesting fried chicken proves you have no imagination, Lena!"

I told Maureen it would be a small celebration and asked if she wanted me to invite Rico, which she naturally did. Little did she know this would be a chance for her in-laws to check out Rico.

Just to irritate Lotta, well, maybe not just to irritate her, I invited Mattwo. She insisted on spiffing up my apartment by contributing accent pillows in orange, brown, yellow, and gold, along with gorgeous flowers from her garden. She volunteered to send invitations, but I vetoed that idea.

It came together seamlessly. I was in the kitchen chatting with Lucinda while Harmon, Lotta, Mattwo, and Rico watched Kalayla show Opa's proficiency at sit, down, shake, and stay.

When the buzzer rang, I pressed the lock release and said, "Maureen, will you get the door?"

When Maureen opened the door, she pressed her hands to her cheeks like she was holding her face together. Luckily, she didn't faint from shock. Her father came in carrying a cake box, followed by a lovely young woman and a handsome man. Both resembled Maureen.

"Look what the cat dragged in," her father said.

Some cat in the O'Rourke family must have been a hunter because all of them, Maureen included, burst out laughing.

The young man said, "Remember when our cat, Oscar, caught a rat and put it in Maureen's bed? Maureen put it in my bed. I put it in Kate's, and Kate put it in Leah's. And Leah was so mad she put it in the refrigerator, and Mummie freaked out."

Maureen recovered enough to say, "And we told Mummie Leah was the one who did it."

"Then Mummie told Daddy, and he said I had to make a casket for the rat. We each picked a bouquet from Mummie's garden and buried the rat in the backyard."

By that time, everyone was laughing. It was a perfect start to the party!

Maureen's father had put the box on the coffee table and said, "This is for you, Maureen, a little late but freshly baked."

Maureen opened the box, sucked in her breath, and said, "An orange crunch cake!" The writing on the cake said, "For all the missed birthdays."

"Katie's home with your mother," her father said. "The two of them made it this morning. It was as much as she could do, Maureen."

Maureen's tears had to be a mixture of sadness and joy. Her mother reached out as best she could and let Maureen know she wasn't as unforgiving as she once had been.

Love and redemption overflowed, and it was hours before anybody went home.

***

Mattwo and I made a date for Tuesday dinner. To my surprise, I didn't hear from him until that afternoon when he called to say he had news about Mark.

After we'd eaten, Mattwo sat on the sofa, and I took the overstuffed armchair facing him to use his expression as a gauge for what he was thinking. The cats sensed my nervousness and snuggled on either side of me like bookends.

"Mark is in Denver," Mattwo said.

"Denver, that's a surprise."

"He's been there for fourteen years. He and his partner started an industrial cleaning business, which has expanded and is well respected. He settled, Lena."

My Mark, alive, settled, a businessman. "That's wonderful news! Is he married? Does he have kids? JJ must not know."

"He knows Lena."

"JJ knows how much I've wanted to hear about Mark. Why didn't he tell me?"

"You'll have to ask him. Mark called him after he got to Denver, and JJ advised him to stay there away from the family."

"That can't be right. You know what our families are like, Mattwo. When you're in, you're in. Six feet under is the only way out. Mark must have misunderstood."

"No, he didn't, Lena. I went to Denver to check it out. I flew out Sunday morning after I left here and took the red-eye back this morning."

"But I don't understand why JJ would tell Mark to stay away?"

"I think JJ didn't know what to do. He wanted to keep Mark safe, and he knew that Mark was, well, he knew that Mark was gay."

My brain went on strike. Mattwo said Mark was gay, but that couldn't be true. Mark was the brawler who fought to be the alpha no matter what. He never let anything go, and he got even for any supposed wrong.

Mattwo took my hand.

"Lena, sweetheart, Mark is happy. He has a partner, a guy named Frankie Gonzales. Mark met him when he first moved to Denver, and they've been together ever since."

Mark had a partner. Joey would have called him a queer. Joey would have said we didn't allow queers in the family, and other relatives felt the same. Joey would have killed Mark if he came out as gay.

Joey couldn't have known, even if JJ did. How was that possible? Nothing got by Joey. Somebody had been on Mark's side, protecting him from Joey and the family.

It had to be JJ. Was that why he was so hard on Mark and tried to toughen him up? Did he tell Mark to move to Boston, to get out of Joey's sight? Boston was too close, so Mark went to New York and Chicago. Farther and farther away from Manzetti Properties. Farther and farther away from Joey's orbit.

And yet, JJ and Mark were as different as summer and winter. JJ's first-grade friends still came to his Thanksgiving open house. With him, it was once a friend, always a friend. Mark went from one new friend to another as if they were tea-light candles that flared, burned out, and were discarded. He never had a steady girl like the other boys. Joey once bragged that Mark had a different girl for every night of the week.

I assumed that was a phase and thought Mark would meet the right woman and raise a family. That's what the Manero men did. That's what the Barzetti men did. But it wasn't what Mark did. He didn't meet the right woman. He met the right man.

I finally understood that Mark was trying to prove his toughness to himself and everyone else. He never cared if he got hurt, how many he took on in a fight, or how big they were. He was trying to be the type of man the family would accept.

I remember when JJ carried Mark home after he'd been beaten so severely he could barely walk. JJ was bruised and bloody, too, and when I asked him why he'd gotten into the fight, he shrugged it off, "I couldn't let them kill him, Ma."

JJ knew the family would look weak if it ignored Mark's sexual preferences. In our business, weak meant vulnerable, and vulnerable meant easy prey. The family wouldn't allow that.

I worried about JJ's attachment to Joey and prayed that JJ's marriage to Amelia wasn't a carbon copy of mine. I promised myself I'd help Amelia get free if she ever came to me. I assumed JJ was a clone of Joey, but I was wrong. He was my boy, my boy, and Joey's.

* * *

I took some time to think, and a few days later, I asked Mattwo if he wanted to take a trip.

"Sure," he said. "I have the plane schedules and found a good B&B near Mark's house. Depending on the weather, we can do some sightseeing, maybe drive into the mountains. How long do you want to stay?"

I smiled. Mattwo knew I'd have to see my son.

The drive to the airport and four and a half hours in the air were a blur. As we were landing, I vaguely recall Mattwo pointing to the mountains, the airport shaped like a string of desert tents, the wide-open space between the airport and the outskirts of Denver.

Random thoughts went through my mind during the shuttle ride to the rental car agency and the drive into Denver. When Mattwo told

198

me we were almost at Marks's, I noticed on street signs: Washington, Grant, Lincoln, no women, unless Logan or Corona were women I'd never heard of.

Mattwo said our B&B, Molly's Nest, was named for a woman, Molly Brown, whose face was on the barroom floor in Central City, which was close enough to Denver that we might go and see it. Mattwo, the tour guide, said we could also walk from the B&B to the gold-domed capitol near downtown Denver. He knew I was half-listening. He knew I was anxious to see my son.

"I let Mark know our arrival time so they expect us. Their house is a couple of blocks from here, an easy walk," Mattwo said. "I can drop off our bags, or we can freshen up before we walk there."

I cocked my head but didn't answer. Mattwo nodded, pulled our suitcases from the back seat, and said, "I'll be right back."

The day was cool and dry. I pulled on my sweater and wondered if this was typical early November weather in Denver. During the drive from the airport, all I saw was the sky. Now, the neighborhood density made it seem less expansive.

Mark's house was a dignified two-story brick with a wrought iron fence around a well-maintained yard. Succulents and rocks of various shapes and sizes covered the area between the street and sidewalk. The succulents inside the fence were more prominent, and the stones were boulder-sized. I would never have imagined Mark living in such a quiet, orderly neighborhood.

Mattwo took my arm as we walked up the stairs onto the concrete porch, a functional space with a wooden swing with floral cushions, garden tools in a large woven basket, and a pair of rubber boots beside the front door. I rang the bell and waited.

The Mark who opened the door was older but still had an athlete's body. His brown eyes looked into mine. "Ma," he said, reaching for my hand.

"Let me look at you," I said, holding off his hug.

I could see so many differences. Mark, the boy, was in perpetual motion, ready to slip away instantly. Mark, the man, was rock solid and comfortable in one place. The boy's eyes constantly roamed, and I could hear myself repeating, "Mark, I'm talking to you. Look at me!" The man looked at me with clear, unwavering eyes. My son had found peace.

I let him pull me close. I had my boy back.

Frankie steered Mattwo past us into the living room. I heard Mattwo asking about their yard and Frankie explaining that Mark was the head of the Neighborhood Conservation Association, which was currently fighting an uphill battle on issues like water use.

I kept my arm in Mark's when we joined them.

"This is Frankie," he said. Frankie was shorter than Mark, darker-skinned with penetrating black eyes, wavy black hair, wiry, narrow-shouldered, and slim. His demeanor was dependable and mature. He was likely close to Mark's age. He put out his hand, and I took it.

"Welcome to our home," Frankie said.

The next day, we walked downtown Denver as far as Larimer Square. "They took down most of the old buildings," Frankie said. "When I was a kid, I looked in Gano Downs and Neusteder's windows. We couldn't afford to shop there. Woolworth's was our haunt." We had dinner at the historic Brown Palace Hotel and drove into the mountains the next day.

"Please stay with us the next time you come," Mark said. "I'd come there, but—."

I shook my head. "JJ tracks the undercurrents. He'll tell you when to come."

On the return drive to Denver International Airport, we passed a gigantic sculpture of a blue Mustang with fierce red eyes, his front legs rearing toward the sky, challenging anyone driving by, "I'm proud of what I am. Are you?"

I imagined Mark standing beside the Mustang. At long last, he was living openly and without apology.

If Mark could do it, maybe this old woman could, too.

The day after we returned, I saw JJ at Home Base. "Hi," I said.

JJ looked up from his papers. "Ma, what brings you here on Sunday?"

"Mattwo and I went to see Mark."

"I thought you would. I knew Mattwo would find Mark if you asked him to. How is he?"

"He's better than he's ever been. But I guess you know that."

JJ nodded.

"I didn't realize you kept in touch with him. Thank you."

JJ nodded again. "No need for thanks. He's my brother."

We stared into each other's eyes, and for the first time since he was a boy, I saw into his heart.

"So," I said after a bit, "I've been thinking about your two girls, about spending time with them and getting to know them. I thought I might take them to Denver to meet Mark."

JJ said, "That's a surprise. It's fine with me, but it's up to them. Taking them to see Mark is fine, too. The world is different now, and I doubt finding out their uncle is gay will be a big deal. But you won't get off cheap with Juliana. She'll go if you fly first class. She's a sophomore, but she's already got her eye out for a guy who'll make her more of a princess than she already is—if that's possible."

I laughed. No wonder JJ didn't bring them to my place for dinner. She probably equated my apartment with the baggage section.

"What about Ronnie?"

"She's looking at colleges now; whatever she does, you can bet it will be on her terms. I was going to talk to you about her. Would you be willing to take her on as your apprentice? The kid has ideas. One day, out of the blue, she said, 'You should be building parking garages, Dad. Design them to fit in with the surrounding area and make them beautiful instead of functional and ugly.'"

That took my breath away! "I'd be happy to. Why don't the three of us meet and talk it over?"

***

On Friday night, Mattwo came with a shopping bag and a massive bouquet of white and yellow roses. "Special order from Magneson's," he said with a kiss. "Let's talk."

Well now! Did that man have proposing on his mind? If he did, there was no doubt how I'd answer him!

"About what?" I said.

"How about taking a trip by ourselves? You can make goo-goo eyes at me, and I can pinch your butt, and nobody will care."

It wasn't a proposal but a step in the right direction.

"Yes," I said hesitantly, not sure how to tell Mattwo what I knew I had to.

Suddenly wary, Mattwo said, "There's a 'but' coming, isn't there, Lena?"

"It's not about being with you, Mattwo. I'd love for us to spend time together away from here. And I like the goo-goo eyes and butt-pinching agenda."

Mattwo's sigh of relief made me smile. "Okay, so, what's the problem?"

"I was waiting for the right time to tell you, and if we're going globe-trotting, I better tell you now."

He frowned, waiting for me to go on.

"It's about the night that Joey died."

"Damn, Lena, that's ancient history, the same as your life with Joey is."

I took a deep breath. "It's ancient history that I lied about to everyone, Mattwo. If you and I are going to be together, I don't want a secret along as baggage."

"OK," he said. "So, tell me."

I took a minute to focus on that night in June 1969. I kept the secret for so many years, but it came out quickly, like a story with a beginning and middle, but I didn't know what the ending would be.

THE NIGHT JOEY DIED

Part of it happened the way I said then. Joey always waited until the twins were gone to start drinking, but that was the weekend after their high school graduation. Jimmy and Mikie had steady girlfriends, so Joey didn't expect them to come home.

He and I were in the kitchen, and booze always put him in a mood for sex. I told him we should wait because I had a special outfit to model before we went to bed. I knew Joey would get whatever he wanted when he went to UG's and would pass out when he came home.

Instead of going there right away, he grabbed me, twisted my arm around my back, and pressed me against the counter. The pain was excruciating.

The twins came home to pick up Miss Clementine, and when they came in through the kitchen door, they saw me crying. I never told the boys what Joey did to me. It was my problem, not theirs.

It was obvious that Joey was hurting me. Maybe the twins knew he had a vicious side, but they'd never seen him turn it on me. They were outraged.

Mikie glared at Joey, "What the fuck are you doing, Dad?"

When Joey turned to face them, I slid to the kitchen floor. The tiles felt cold and smooth against my skin, but I was sweating. I had no idea what Joey would do. He was the ruler in the house, and the twins had crossed his Maginot Line.

Joey screamed, "What do you mean, what the fuck am I doing? I'm teaching this bitch a lesson!" He kicked me in the side.

The twins looked at each other in the private way they had, silently sorting their options, deciding what to do. They were eighteen and strong as bison. Not even Joey stood a chance against them. They lunged at him, and each grabbed one of his arms. They slammed him against the counter and pinned him there.

"You're a fucking coward," Jimmy said so quietly it terrified me.

"You ever touch Ma again, and it'll be the last thing you do. We will kill you!" Mikie said just as quietly.

They let Joey go, and he stumbled out the kitchen door. I heard the tires screech as he pulled out of the driveway.

After the twins helped me up, I assured them I was okay and shooed them off to see their girls. What I said was true. I was better than I'd been after many of Joey's lessons.

I was afraid to go to bed. If I fell asleep and Joey found me, I'd be helpless no matter how drunk he was. I stayed in the den watching videos. I was halfway through Butch Cassidy and The Sundance Kid when I heard him slam the front door.

He screamed, "Lena, you bitch. Get out here!"

I knew that he was going to kill me. His sons had shamed him, and he'd make me pay. I ran to the kitchen, thinking I could get out the back door before he caught me.

Drunk as he was, Joey was fast, ever the athlete. He lunged for me and grabbed my blouse. When I twisted away, the blouse ripped and threw him off balance. He spun around and tried to steady himself but slipped; one hundred and ninety pounds went into free fall. Joey cracked his head on the counter and landed with a thud on the ceramic tile. He lay there, not moving.

A blood puddle pooled next to his head. My first thought was, what if he's dead? My next was, please, let him be dead because if he weren't, I would be.

What I did then still haunts me.

I ran to the den, grabbed a throw pillow from the sofa, and returned to the kitchen. I put the pillow over Joey's face and held it down with both hands. He wasn't moving, but I knew Joey. He could be faking, waiting for a chance to grab me.

I pressed as hard as I could. The kitchen clock said two forty-five a.m. I kept the pillow on his face for twenty minutes. Not even Joey could hold his breath that long. He had to be dead.

The pool of blood had expanded, but I didn't see any on the pillow. I left everything as it was: lights on, the half-empty bottle of Glenfiddich 18, and his glass on the counter.

I returned to the den, turned off the video player, and arranged the pillows so the one I used was underneath the others. I turned off the lights, went upstairs, took a shower, and two Advil to stave off the pain. Then I went to bed.

JJ came at seven-thirty the following morning to pick Joey up for work. He found his father's body, rushed upstairs, and woke me up from a dead sleep. When I saw Joey's body, I became hysterical. JJ took charge and called the police.

Mattwo slowly shook his head. "I remember. The police report said he'd been drinking and had fallen and hit his head."

"Yes," I said, "and there was no reason to doubt that. The twins said he was drunk when they came to get Miss Clementine, and he got angry because they told him to sleep it off. They would never have said Joey was abusing me. That was a family matter.

I didn't tell the twins what happened after they left that day, and I don't know if I ever would have. Joey had been dead for thirty years, and what happened that night was as murky now as it was then. I still didn't know if I had killed him.

"JJ took Joey's death harder than the other boys. Mark was living in New York but came home to help him through it. Then the twins died, and you know the direction I went until Dom, Lotta and my mother helped me pull myself together."

"You kept that buried for a long time," Mattwo said.

"That I did. And I've never stopped wondering if Joey was already dead or if I killed him."

"There's no point digging up a murky past," he said. "It's time to let it go, Lena. You've done your best to lead a decent life. That's enough for me."

"Are you sure you want to travel with a woman who could be a murderer? That was my intention, even if I didn't kill him."

Mattwo reached over and gently ran his fingers over my face, and said:

"I'm planning to travel with the woman I've loved all my life, and I say let's get on with that."

LATE FALL 2000

LEAVING THE PAST BEHIND

When Mattwo and I started spending time together, I was getting a second chance to do what I didn't have enough sense or guts to do in high school. Back then, I did what the family told me to do.

I wasn't silly enough to think I could erase fifty years, but I was smart enough to know I'd be dead and buried if I waited much longer.

A blanket of November clouds parked itself over Massachusetts, and seeing Mattwo was the best way to clear out the gloominess. I invited him for a romantic dinner with candles and soft music.

I soaked in a hot bath of lavender bubbles and pampered my skin with an almond oil rub. I picked out a soft-pink silk blouse, a navy skirt, heart-shaped silver earrings, and a matching necklace; no need to over-advertise my seductive intentions.

I'd covered the beef chunks with Lotta's special marinade of Worcestershire sauce, olive oil, garlic, mustard, and spices and was about to make a salad. Mattwo was bringing red wine, and I had a cheese tray and mixed nuts ready on the coffee table.

I buzzed Mattwo in, hustled to the refrigerator, and concentrated on the salad fixings. A hand circled my left arm, and a shockwave shot through me. How could I have been so mindless and let down my guard? Joey was an expert at sneaking up behind me when I switched laundry from the washer to the dryer, dead-headed marigolds, or focused on food in the refrigerator.

My mother said my fear was a narcotic that fueled Joey's power, and I had to learn to hide it. I heard a voice in the background, but it couldn't be Joey. Silence was his most cunning weapon.

"Lena!" the voice said louder and more insistent. "Lena, sweetheart, are you okay?"

I looked around the kitchen. There were no broken dishes strewn on the floor. Joey wasn't here.

I realized the voice was Mattwo's. The hand on my arm wasn't Joey's. I slumped against the refrigerator, felt cold air on my cheek, and heard the soft dinging, warning the refrigerator doors had been open too long. My heart was racing.

Mattwo took my arm, guided me to a chair, and sat beside me, "When I came into the kitchen and touched your arm, you froze." Mattwo rubbed my arm, "You're looking better now. Your face is back to normal instead of stark white."

I couldn't explain what I didn't understand. "I don't know what happened to me, Mattwo. When Joey was alive, he'd sneak up behind me, and I never knew how he'd hurt me. When I felt your hand, I thought you were Joey, but that doesn't make sense."

Mattwo shook his head. "It does, Lena. I know guys who had flashbacks about their experiences in Vietnam after they came home. And a gym member told me her car was rear-ended when she was driving to the grocery store. Months later, she'd flinch if she heard the screech of brakes or a car got too close to her. Flashbacks are awful. Living through it once is bad enough."

Mattwo's voice was soft and calming, and what he said made sense. I'd lived alone for years. Joey was the only man I'd known until I welcomed Mattwo into my life. His unexpected touch triggered the fear I lived with when Joey was alive.

Mattwo gently caressed my cheek.

"I'm not Joey, Lena. I'll do my best not to startle you, but we'll deal with it together if this happens again."

I felt the gentleness of Mattwo's hand and saw the love in his eyes.

"I've been thinking we should go someplace without cats, family, or friends and see how we do on our own," Mattwo said. "Are you wild enough to let a sexy guy like me have his way with you?"

I laughed, and I nodded. I was likely the only person in the world who would consider Mattwo sexy, and on a scale of wildness, I'd be ranked even with a toenail. We were meant to be together, and I wasn't about to pass up this chance.

"Okay then," Mattwo said and gave me a very sexy kiss.

We didn't waste time hemming and hawing. Rome, Florence, and Assisi were logical places for old Italians in love to spend time together. We planned to leave soon because I wanted to be home for Christmas.

CAT SITTING INSTRUCTIONS

After the old lady and the old guy decided to sneak off to Italy, she gave me a list of stuff I was supposed to do:

Feed the cats twice a day.
Clean the litter twice a day.
Change their water once a day.
Clean up fur balls they throw up.
Check on Mrs. Meade every day.
If any tenant has a problem, call Dominic.

That old lady acted like I didn't have a brain. Mr. Rossi was the building superintendent, and if anybody needed anything, I'd tell him, not her brother!

Naturally, Lena left copies of the list with Mama and Lotta so they could bug me every five minutes. I'm surprised she didn't tell me to wash dishes for all the tenants. She must've forgot.

Lena stacked thirty cans of cat food, a fifteen-pound bag of dry food, a cat brush, and ten treat bags on her kitchen counter. Two fourteen-pound bags of litter were beside the litter boxes. Unless that old lady was never coming home, the only thing I'd run out of was my good humor.

The old lady said they'd be home for Christmas, so I told Mama she better quit hanging around with Rico and finish Lena's painting.

When I told Mama I wanted to knit the old guy a scarf for Christmas, she said, "Why would I waste time teaching you to knit? You said the only thing knitting needles were good for was to stick up the butt of kids you hate."

No wonder Mama's brother and sisters said she was a pain. She was lucky I was too mature to stick out my tongue at her.

"I'm asking Rico to help me make a coffin for Clarence to encourage him to croak. Rico probably knows how to knit and would be nice enough to help me."

"Layla! Don't you dare ask Rico to help you make a coffin! Clarence is sick, but he is not going to die!"

Blah, blah, blah!

I was going to make a hundred for Grandma and Grandpa, the old lady and her old guy, a bunch for Lotta and her staff, the staff at Eddie's, a few for Kieran, Dominic, Rico, and Mrs. Meade, one for Clarence and Mr. O.

Lotta gave me a recipe for dog biscuits, and I already made a double batch for Opa. If she had a recipe for cat treats with arsenic, I wouldn't have to take care of the cats. But Lena would have a stroke, and the old guy would have a heart attack, and I'd be stuck taking care of them.

Maybe Opa and I could visit New Zealand or the North Pole so I won't be available for cat duty. What if Opa didn't like flying and threw up on the airplane? Cow turds!

If we stay home, I can make up a bunch of lies about how beautiful, sweet-tempered, and quiet the cats are and advertise for a sucker who wants to rent two Siamese for three weeks.

DECEMBER 2000

ITALY

Lotta might tout the luxury of flying business class, but my old bones could tell a makeshift bed from a real one. The bathrooms were the size of a phone booth, and the flight from Logan to Leonardo da Vinci was eight hours long, no matter where you sat.

When we got off the plane, Mattwo commented, "That was a heck of a pricy way to get a hot towel at the end of a meal."

When we found our driver at the airport, he smiled and said, "Two beautiful Italians! I take you to see the wedding cake. Your hotel is close by."

Mattwo's square face, olive skin, bushy eyebrows, and dark brown eyes would fit in a mafia movie, but I didn't resemble Sophia Loren or Gina Lollobrigida when I was young, and I sure didn't now. Our driver needed glasses, and I hoped he didn't prove it in Rome's traffic.

Rome natives nicknamed the gigantic monument in honor of Victor Emmanuel II "the typewriter" or "the wedding cake," decorated by someone who added flourishes to use excess frosting.

Our boutique hotel was small, with an ivy-covered front and an enclosed courtyard that would be a glory of flowers in spring. The elevator was big enough for two humans and two medium suitcases, and our room was old-fashioned cozy. The concierge assured us the owner planned to update soon.

After resting, we walked to the enormous Christmas tree in front of the monument and explored the streets surrounding our hotel. Gigantic trellises were draped from one side of the road to the other at street-light height and covered with colored lights in the shape of angels, stars, and animals. We got sore necks from looking up.

I was entranced with everything I saw!

"Lena," Mattwo said, "if you keep poking me, I'll end up black and blue before we find our way back to the hotel."

Finding our way around became our standing joke. The concierge gave us maps and directions, but we'd veer off to explore side-street windows of handcrafted gifts and ornaments with holiday lights.

We layered up, walked everywhere, and stopped frequently. We ate a big breakfast at the hotel before setting out, but bakeries duplicating the smell of Lotta's kitchen forced us to sample sfogliatella and cannolo. We burned our fingers on roasted chestnuts from street vendors and sipped cappuccinos in small cafes.

In Assisi, we found a wooden statue of young St. Francis with a dog curled up at his feet for Kalayla and a green leash decorated with red and white candy canes for Opa. We found a fall-colored silk shawl highlighting Maureen's hair and skin tone.

When we visited the St. Francis Cathedral, Mattwo said, "Wouldn't you know my sister was right? This is my kind of church."

Frescos covered the walls in earth tones of tangerine, mellow orange, sand, rust brown, lemon, mustard, and celestial blue. Even a non-church-goer like me could appreciate the quiet beauty.

The day we arrived in Florence, Mattwo said, "You know, it'd be fun to rent a couple of motorscooters and explore the hillside towns."

"Did you have that in mind for today?" I said, wondering if the enthusiasm of our lovemaking clouded his good sense.

He laughed, "Twenty or thirty years ago, I would, but today, I've got snoozing on my mind."

We laughed that the beds were too soft, rigid, or narrow, but my body went on strike when I woke up with every muscle aching.

We planned to search for examples of Michelangelo's work, but I looked at Mattwo standing at the bathroom door brushing his teeth and said, "How about going home and sitting for a couple of weeks?"

He fist-pumped. "My feet say yes to that! I'll change our flights. How soon can you be ready?"

I was halfway out of bed, stuffing my feet into my slippers. "Now!" I said.

* * *

Lotta picked us up at the airport, saw our contented faces, and said, "Well, thank God! If tortoises took as long to get together as you two,

216

they'd have been extinct years ago! Tell me everything you saw and did, but leave out the nighttime romps."

Kalayla was sitting on the front steps when we drove up. Never mind that it was thirty-three degrees and threatening snow. Before she grabbed my suitcase and charged up the stairs, she actually let me hug her!

CAT SITTING DUTY

Napoleon and Petunia lived in a feline palace with scratch pads in every room, two litter boxes, and a three-tiered climbing post with a top platform big enough for both. They could curl up on Lena's precious white sofa or chairs if they got bored.

The first morning, the cats circled my legs, walked in front of me, and meowed nonstop to let the world know how neglected they were. Napoleon's fire alarm yowl almost broke my eardrums and made Opa whine.

I wasn't running a five-star restaurant and decided I could forget about the canned food. I loaded two bowls of dry food and put them on the floor.

Napoleon took one sniff, jumped on top of a case of canned food, and screamed like I was torturing him. I wasn't wasting my time in a stand-off with a stubborn cat. If I didn't give in, he'd pee or poop on Lena's white furniture to get even. And how would I explain that?

Opa did her best to help by nuzzling the cats, but Napoleon hissed at her, and Petunia walked away. I felt guilty about leaving after feeding them, so I sat on the sofa. The cats jumped up, snuggled, and shared my lap while Opa used my feet as a backrest. I felt like the prize exhibit in their human zoo.

I thought it'd be fun to pig out on the stash of cookies Lena left for me, but sitting alone at her kitchen table was weird. I could eat cookies alone at home. I'd been in Lena's apartment when she wasn't home, but I knew she'd be back soon, and the cats did, too. They'd be asleep on her bed and wouldn't bother to yawn if I went in to say hello.

This was different. The apartment was empty and lonely without that crabby old lady. It was as if the lights were turned off, and I didn't know how to turn them on. I kept telling myself she'd be coming home, but what if she didn't? I woke up at night thinking about that.

When she came home, Lena promised to take me and Kieran to Bartley's Burgers. She thought I'd look forward to that, but she was wrong. The night my daddy and Clarence went drag racing, Daddy promised we'd make blueberry pancakes for breakfast and then go biking around Fresh Pond, but we didn't.

Lena thought she was coming home, but that didn't mean she would. What would the cats do if she croaked? What would I do?

***

Fifteen days after Lena and Mattwo left for Italy, the phone rang.

"Yeah," I said, expecting it was Lotta checking on me for the ninetieth time.

"It's me, Lena. Are you home?"

"How'd I be answering the phone if I wasn't at home? Did you call to say you're tired of hanging around with that old guy?"

"Of course not! Mattwo and I are at Logan Airport. Lotta is picking us up, and we should be home in about an hour."

I hung up the phone, hugged Opa, and shouted, "Yes!"

I zipped to Lena's to tell the cats and filled a plate of Lotta's cookies for the old guy. I bet he missed those more than he missed the cats. Then I ran to Eddie's to tell Mama.

I put a folding chair in the No Parking Zone in front of the building and sat down. I didn't like freezing my butt, but I didn't plan on carrying suitcases two blocks. When Lotta pulled in front of me, my teeth were chattering.

Mattwo groaned and helped Lena out of the car. "I can't believe so many muscles can ache all at once," he said.

Lena grunted and said, "Get over here and hug me, Kalayla!"

So I did.

"I can't park here, Kalayla. Get their suitcases out of the trunk," Lotta, the boss, said.

So, I was stuck carrying their junk. Lena and Mattwo huffed and puffed so hard I thought I'd be stuck carrying them, too.

They were resting on the third-floor landing when I said, "How'd you get so out of shape, Lena? Were you guys too lazy to use the stairs in Italy?"

Instead of snapping at me 'cause I asked a rude question, Lena smiled! I wouldn't've believed it, except I was looking right at her!

"No, we weren't, Kalayla," she said. "The plane ride was long, and there's a six-hour time difference, so it feels like we've been awake for days. We'll go up and down these stairs just fine when we're over the jetlag."

And then, she smiled again!

I was sure she'd take a fit when I said, "The cats didn't notice you were gone."

"I knew you'd take good care of them," Lena smiled.

The Lena who left here would've told me she didn't come home to listen to my smart mouth. The Lena who came home was Ms Smiley Face!

That's when I knew something was wrong, but I wasn't sure what it was.

WINTER 2000/2001

GETTING ANSWERS FROM LENA

The old lady was nothing like her old self. Two days ago, she was standing on the third-floor landing when I came home from dance class late. Before she went to Italy, she would've asked if I had to stay 'cause I told the teacher her class sucked.

Instead, she said, "Do you think Opa would like a biscuit?"

Lena wasn't only acting weird. She looked different. She was bright and shiny like somebody dumped silver polish on her and rubbed it until the tarnish disappeared.

Plus, the old guy practically lived at Lena's. He had the nerve to tell me I could come over anytime. What'd he think I usually did? I would've told him to bug off, but he played with Opa and gave her treats.

Lena was alone when Opa and I stopped there after school yesterday. I ate two peanut butter cookies. She didn't say anything when I wrapped two in a napkin and stuck them in my pocket with an extra biscuit for Opa.

Two weeks ago, a wooden rocker showed up next to one of the white-cushioned chairs, and I said, "Where'd you get such an ugly old rocker? I won't charge you much to paint it white."

"You will do no such thing! That is an antique oak Lincoln Rocker, the oldest thing in this apartment. The caning on the back and the seat gave out years ago, and I finally got it re-caned."

If the chair was older than she was, it could fall apart any minute, with or without new caning. Nothing was different in the kitchen, living room, or bathroom. The old guy probably stuck his junk in the spare room where I used to stay.

I ate another cookie to work up the nerve to say, "Something happened in Italy, right? Like, you got a disease or cracked your head?"

"Kalayla!" Lena said, staring at me. "Why would you say anything so ridiculous?"

I almost cheered. The crabby old lady voice and I-will-turn-you-into-a-centipede look were back!

"You're different, and I thought that might be why." That wasn't true. I also thought an alien might have taken over her body, but saying that would've pissed her off.

Lena frowned, then pointed at her face. "Look at this face, Kalayla. Does it look different to you?"

I gave her a long look. "Your wrinkles are still there, and you're frowning, so you look like your crabby old self. But you've been smiling so much I thought you were auditioning for a job as Santa's jolly wife."

"Kalayla," she said, "do you honestly think I'm smiling because I have a disease or because I fell on my head?"

When she put it that way, it did sound kind of dumb. "Well, not a life-threatening disease, but an Italian mosquito bit you, or you tripped on a curb and hit your head."

Lena laughed and came and sat in the chair next to Opa and me.

"The reason I'm smiling is that I'm happy."

Any dumb turd could see she was happy. I wanted to know what that meant.

"Okay," I said. "If going on a trip made you happy, when will I be stuck with the cats again?"

"Ah," Lena said, nodding. "Being away wasn't what made me happy, Kalayla."

She reached over and took my hand. I felt like pulling away and going home, but I didn't.

"Didn't I send you postcards so you'd know where we were and what we were doing?"

"Yeah, but what good are postcards? What if you woke up one morning and felt like taking another trip? How will I explain that to the cats?"

Lena glanced at Petunia nestled on my lap.

"Kalayla, I missed you and the cats, and I don't want to go on another trip. The flight was too long, the beds were uncomfortable, and my feet got sore from walking. One of the reasons I'm smiling so much is that Mattwo is in my life."

"So if he wants to go someplace, you're going, too?"

Lena laughed. "The only place Mattwo wants to go is up four flights of stairs. I'm glad to be home, and so is he. Kalayla, I am happy because of Mattwo, and I'm also happy because you, your mama, and the cats are in my life. I am very grateful for that."

I wish the old lady hadn't said that. I remember when my daddy told me how happy he was 'cause he had Mama and me. I knew how that worked out.

I gave Petunia a few pats and said, "I better take Opa for a walk before she poops on the floor. Tell the old guy I left a cookie for him."

Lena looked like she had more to say, but I was done talking.

Opa sniffed while I thought about what I didn't tell Lena. She better not count on staying happy. Mattwo could die, and her life could collapse the way Mama's did. I hoped it wouldn't, but what if it did?

WHO TELLS KALAYLA?

I watched Kalayla and Opa bounce down the stairs, ready to take on the world, and I couldn't help smiling again.

Kalayla was like a finicky water faucet that drove a person crazy. When you wanted her to be quiet, she kept talking, and she clammed up when you wanted her to speak. Something about our conversation bugged that girl, but she wasn't ready to tell me what it was.

Kalayla seemed to relax when she saw Mattwo and me in a comfortable, home-bound routine. After her dance class, she stopped by on Saturday morning and said, "I'm on my way to work and can't stay. I just came to find out what you think."

If anybody but Kalayla had said what she had just done, I wouldn't have given it a second thought. But she didn't look or sound like the girl who roamed Cambridge streets almost two years ago. Somewhere along the way, she had grown up.

When I met Kalayla, she was wearing what appeared to be her whole wardrobe in multiple layers of clashing colors and patterns. Today, she wore a dark blue sweater and jeans that were no more than one or two sizes too big, and nothing sarcastic or Lena-baiting came out of her mouth.

My twins never did outgrow their smart-mouthed attitudes, but it seemed Kalayla could control hers when and if she chose to. Maybe teenage girls were more skilled at subtle changes you might miss without paying close attention. I never raised any, so how would I know? My boys were as transparent as cellophane. They liked sports, cars, girls, competing with friends and each other, and pleasing their father. If something was happening below the surface, it stayed there.

"Lena? Did you hear me?" Kalayla had been waiting while I'd been lollygagging about the past.

"Of course I did. You want to know what I think about something."

"Not something. Someone. Clarence," she said.

Ugh! I knew, sooner or later, Kalayla would notice her uncle's absence. She might not like Clarence, but he was her daddy's only sibling, and he'd been halfway consistent in his drive-by visits. She'd want to know why he dropped out of sight.

I was sure about one thing. I wasn't the one who ought to tell Kalayla what happened to him.

"Why are you asking about Clarence?" I said.

"I made a special Christmas cookie for him with mayonnaise, garlic powder, hot pepper sauce, and lemon flavoring. I wanted to see his face when he took a bite, but he didn't come to Grandma's for Christmas and hadn't seen us in a long time. I don't care, but it seems weird."

I didn't think it was weird because I knew why Clarence was in the no-show category. I said, "Did your Grandma say why he wasn't there?"

"I didn't ask her."

For the second time in five minutes, Kalayla caught me by surprise. She never shied away from asking anybody anything.

"Why not?" I said.

Kalayla sighed. "When Grandma has something to say, she says it if you like it or not—just like you and Lotta."

"Maybe you should ask your Mama."

Kalayla frowned. "I'd have a better chance of getting an answer from Opa. Mama never tells me anything unless she has to."

"Did it occur to you that your mama might be trying to protect you?"

"Why would she need to protect me from knowing where Clarence is? If I ask her about him, she'll probably say he won the lottery and is cruising the world."

I didn't know what Maureen might tell Kalayla, but I suspected Lucinda would tell her granddaughter the truth. If life threw crap at you, you had to deal with it.

"Maybe you should ask your grandma when nobody is around. If she wanted to say anything about Clarence, I doubt she'd have done it at a Christmas party."

Kalayla said, "I can understand that, but she hasn't said anything since then. I have to go now. See you later, Lena."

Kalayla left, and I sat at the kitchen table thinking, "Here we go again."

I didn't understand why Maureen hadn't told Kalayla about her maternal grandparents, but I could see why neither Lucinda nor Maureen told Kalayla about Clarence. I doubt there was a good way of telling her.

Maybe the best thing would be to say it right out: "Clarence tried to rape your Mama. Lena stuck a gun in his face to stop him, and he regressed to his childhood when something terrible happened to him."

Or maybe not.

A NEW PLACE TO LIVE?

I heard a knock and knew it was Mattwo. Why that man didn't use the key I gave him was beyond me, but I shooed Napoleon off my lap and went to the door.

Mattwo had a big smile and a small box. "Sweets for my sweetheart," he said, handing me a box of chocolate-covered caramels before kissing me.

I laughed as I took the candy, "If you keep this up, I'll be your pudgy sweetheart."

"You want to know what I was doing while walking up the stairs?"

"You mean besides hoping you'd make it to the top?"

"I was counting steps."

"And why would you be doing that?"

"To get facts. I was calculating how many stairs I climbed in the last few weeks. But I decided that was a dumb approach," Mattwo said.

"Dumb approach to what?"

Mattwo got up from the sofa, used the arm of my rocker to get down on one knee, took my hand, and said, "The only way I'll get you out of this apartment and onto the ground floor is if we get married. So, how about it?"

I laughed. I imagined Mattwo proposing during a romantic candle-light dinner in Italy, but I wasn't turning my nose up at a cloudy, late afternoon in Cambridge!

I kissed him and said, "What took you so long?"

He snorted, "I've been figuring the odds on whether I could get up once I got down on one knee." He pushed himself up. "I guess they were pretty good. I might not have bothered getting up if you turned me down."

I snuggled next to him on the sofa. "So what does getting married have to do with counting the stairs?"

"Let's face facts, Lena. I don't mean to jinx us, but we'll be in our eighties in a few years. I say we get married and get ourselves a little ground-floor house. What do you think about that?"

What Mattwo said was true. When I moved here over thirty years ago, I ran up and down the stairs, but now my muscles and joints rebelled if I went up more than once a day. Living on the ground floor sounded fine.

Kalayla was as smart as I gave her credit for being. She knew things would change if Mattwo and I got together, and she wanted to know what we were doing before we did it, not after. Our trip to Italy was the spur of the moment, and it surprised her. She didn't want that to happen again.

"I am definitely in, Mattwo, but," I hesitated.

"I'm not surprised you want to think about it. Moving would be a giant step."

"I'd love to move in with you, Mattwo. I'm thinking about Kalayla. I don't want her to feel like I'm abandoning her. Maureen does her best, but Kalayla relies on me. Who will she turn to if I'm not across the hall? Her grandmother has her hands full with Clarence right now."

Mattwo nodded. "So, we'll find a place near here, and Kalayla can come over whenever she wants. How does that sound?"

That sounded better than good. Finding a house and moving would take time and planning, but getting married would be simple. I was too old for falderal and fussing.

The next day, I called Dom to see if he'd heard any scuttlebutt about houses going on the market within about eight blocks of me.

"Why would you be asking that, Lena? Did you or Mattwo develop a sudden allergy to stairs, or are you inquiring for somebody else?"

"I'm inquiring for me and Mattwo. Please don't give me a hard time!"

"My dear sister, I would not dream of doing such a thing! There is a potential tear-down about six blocks from you. It is a small white Cape Cod with enough land that somebody can bulldoze and put up a house that fits the neighborhood."

"Do you think I'd build a Victorian monster that Dracula would love? I might like something from the Frank Lloyd Wright school."

"Not going to happen, Lena. You know how things work in Cambridge. The neighbors would hate that as much as they do the Cape. The new house can be ultra-modern inside but must be a Victorian. The neighbors are planning a block party to celebrate when the current owner moves. They're sure the new owner will tear it down and increase their property values."

"Well, I'm glad you have time to keep up with the local gossip. Mattwo and I will walk by and see what we think."

I put together a respectable engagement dinner with candlelight, chicken cacciatore, roasted potatoes, salad, and chocolate-covered caramels for dessert that night.

The following morning, Mattwo and I went to see the house. I'd appraised thousands of homes, apartment buildings, and business sites, from potential tear-downs to rehabs, and I knew better than to sign on to a deal before considering all aspects.

Cape Cods come in many forms, but this particular one was the original design: a long rectangle facing the street, two stories with a slanted roof in front and back, no front-facing windows on the second floor, but good-sized ones at either end of the house.

The lot was between Massachusetts Avenue and Oxford Street, sandwiched between Victorians. The one-car garage looked adequate for Mattwo's monster car, and the fenced backyard was decent-sized.

"Let's cross and look from the other side of the street," I said. I wanted to gauge the distance from the other houses. "We'd get light despite the houses on either side, and it doesn't look like we'd have to take down trees. The outside seems to be in good repair. Do you think it's worth checking out the inside?"

Mattwo nodded, and I could tell he liked it. "It's nothing like the grandeur of your Brattle Street house or JJ's Weston house, Lena."

I laughed. "Mattwo, the apartment is nothing like the Brattle Street house, but I didn't have a reason to move until now. This little house looks homey and welcoming. I'll make the arrangements for us to get a full tour."

WHAT'S OVER AND WHAT'S NEXT

Riding to Matty's Way or the shelter was faster than walking, and so far, this winter wasn't a pisser of snow and ice like last year. I told Mama I wore a helmet and rode on the sidewalk so she wouldn't get all jacked up. Sometimes, I did ride on the sidewalk, but I waited until after I got through Harvard Square 'cause students and tourists hogged the sidewalk. I could zip around cars stuck in traffic or stalled at red lights. Today, I got to Matty's Way in less than twenty minutes.

I whizzed by the desk with a half-wave and angled to the back hall where Kieran would be waiting for the Tai Chi class. He was sitting against the wall, and when I saw him, I burst out laughing, fist-pumped, and said, "It's Michael Jordan!"

Kieran looked startled, but then he laughed, too. Michael Jordan was six and a half feet of solid muscle and black. Kieran was five feet five, skinny as a telephone pole and white.

But they both had shaved heads.

Kieran's used to be bright red and stuck out in every direction.

"Did you have to shave your head 'cause one of your cowlicks caught fire?"

"Ha, real funny," Kieran said.

"You ruined your chance of getting a job as a scarecrow. Do you polish your head to make it shiny?"

"Keep it up, Kalayla, and I'm going to smash your nose."

No matter how much I teased him, Kieran wouldn't do that, but I said, "Stay cool. So, why'd you do it?"

"I'm sick of kids laughing at my hair."

"I get that. Never give the buttholes a reason to zero in on you. But why'd you do it in February? What if you get frostbite on your head?"

"I always wear a hat. Col told me I better not embarrass him and his friends by looking like a wimpy nerd. He said this was an improvement."

"Col? You mean your brother Col, who wrecked your bike and wouldn't pay for it until your dad forced him to, and whose friends dropped you off, so you had to walk home about ten miles, right?"

"You don't get it, Kalayla. He won't bug me so much if I do some of the things he wants. He said I had to go out for a sport. I'll try out for cross country in the fall and track in the spring. Give a little; get a little is what I'm doing."

"Maybe I'll shave my head, too. We could go on stage as the Bald K Cousins. I'd dance and tell jokes; you could be the straight guy. I could start a lunch table for skinheads at school."

Kieran laughed, "You could get a t-shirt printed with Boys Prefer Bald Girls. Your mom could do the artwork, and you could sell them as a fundraiser for Animal Friends. Do you think anybody would sit at a table for skinheads?"

"Maybe. At my school, the black kids sit together, and the white kids sit together."

"They do?"

"Kieran, are there any black kids at your school or kids who look like me?"

He frowned. "No, but there might be at high school because it's bigger."

"So, I'm the only mixed-race kid you ever met, and you've never met any black kids, right?"

"So?" Kieran said, rubbing his bald head.

It wasn't Kieran's fault he didn't know anything. He was a white kid in a white school, and I bet there wouldn't be any black kids at his high school—no wonder he didn't have a clue.

"You get I'm a mix of black and white, right?"

"Yeah, so why don't you sit with the black kids one day and the white kids the next day?"

"If I sat with the white kids, the black kids would say I was passing for white. If I sat with the black kids, the white kids would say I was black. My daddy said I got the best from him and my mama. Why would I choose one over the other? I'm proud I'm both."

Kieran made a ghoulish face, laughed, and said, "You could sit with me if you went to my school."

I laughed. "Yeah, and if Col's friends gave him a hard time, he'd beat the crap out of you."

Kieran looked down and made another face. "He might. Doesn't thinking about this stuff make your brain ache?"

"Nah, I'm used to it. Anyway, I wanted to tell you I won't be coming to Matty's Way as often."

Kieran frowned.

"Rico didn't fire me," I said. "I've been working here to barter for my step dance lessons, but I'm not dancing anymore. I'm telling Rico today I won't need to work here."

"I thought you loved to dance."

"I did. I mean, I still do, but the teacher wants everybody in the recitals, and there's one coming up in June."

"So?" he said.

"You have to buy costumes, and they cost seventy-five bucks each. Last year, I didn't have to be in the recital 'cause I just started, but the teacher expects me in this one."

"Maybe the teacher will give you a break on the price for the costumes."

"I'm not getting on a needy kid list. I'm not telling my mama. She doesn't have extra money. I could ask Lena, my grandma, or maybe even Rico or Lotta, but I won't."

Kieran thought that over and said, "My grandpa pays for my Tai Chi lessons. He's your grandpa, too, so maybe he'd pay for your costumes."

"He didn't offer to help me and Mama after my daddy died. I'd never ask him. Besides, there's free stuff I can do. This kid, Shanese, stays at my grandma's sometimes. She goes to the high school, and she'll help me even though she gets pissed when I beat her at ping pong."

"I get beat at games, and I don't get pissed."

"Kieran, you are not a normal kid, and I'm not either. You should keep shaving your head 'cause it looks cool. I only laughed 'cause it was a surprise."

Kieran blushed, but what I said was true. He didn't look nearly as weird as he used to.

TIME WITH KALAYLA

This morning at Eddie's, another waitress said, "You're in a fine mood, Maureen. Did you get a good night's sleep?"

I'd gone to the studio around ten-thirty and worked until two a.m. I'd gotten less sleep than usual, but Nellie was right. I felt great, and I didn't remember dreaming.

That gave me an idea. If I went to the studio after dinner instead of before, Kalayla and I could eat together. I didn't cook when Jamal was alive because he enjoyed that and taught Kalayla to cook, too. Now, she bought what she needed at Mickey's and ate whatever and whenever she wanted. Cooking dinner could be an excellent way for us to spend time together.

***

During our Sunday morning talk, I said, "Why don't you and I cook dinner and eat before I go to the studio?"

Kalayla frowned. "You mean tonight?"

"We could do that every night if we wanted to."

Kalayla looked at me like I had two heads. "Why would you want to? You hate to cook."

My lack of enthusiasm had nothing to do with my lack of skill. My mother insisted I learn to cook and show off my skills by making a special dish whenever we had guests. I was like a prize racehorse being groomed for sale, and my reaction was to avoid the kitchen whenever possible.

Finally, I said, "No, I don't. It would be fun."

Kalayla's green eyes flashed. "Yeah, fun like when we make Christmas cookies? I prepare and bake them, and you mess with the decorations. So your idea is I cook dinner, and you create an artistic masterpiece on the plate?"

"No," I said, hoping I didn't sound as defensive as I felt. "We can plan the menus, shop together, and decide who cooks what."

"Fine. My menu is sweet potatoes and mac and cheese. What's yours?"

"Kalayla, that can't be all you eat."

"It isn't. Lena invites me, and she makes great mashed potatoes, gravy, and chicken."

Oh, dear! Kalayla had turned this into a separate but equal use of the kitchen space. But I wasn't giving up. "Mickey's isn't open on Sunday night," I said. "Let's make a shopping list and go tomorrow night."

"I can't, 'cause that's my last—ah, how about Tuesday?"

On Monday, Kalayla moaned that she had too much homework. On Tuesday, she remembered she needed to study for a test she had on Wednesday.

I was afraid she'd make up endless excuses. So, before she went to school on Thursday, I said, "Why don't we invite Rico for dinner tomorrow night? We can shop tonight. Or we can decide on a menu, and I can shop."

To my surprise, she said, "That might not be so bad. Rico probably doesn't have anything else to do. Anyway, I've got some coupons."

"Coupons for what?" I said.

"Mama," Kalayla said, "You shop at Mickey's. They don't have sales. I go to Star Market. They have sales and specials."

"Kalayla, you told me you only eat sweet potatoes and mac and cheese."

"That's when there's nothing good for sale. The special this week is chicken wings. We'll need a ton of them 'cause they don't have much meat."

On the way to Star Market, I told Kalayla I'd been thinking about lasagna with chicken sausage and mild cheddar cheese rather than chicken wings.

She looked surprised and said, "We can stuff Rico with pasta and throw in a little sausage. That'll be cheaper than chicken wings. Sherbert is on sale, and I can get cookies from Lena. We should invite her sometime if we don't poison Rico."

When we got to the check-out counter, Kalayla smiled at the cashier and said, "Hey, Connie. This is my mama."

"Working two jobs is tough," Connie said. "We all help Kalayla find bargains."

As we loaded the groceries, I said, "Kalayla, Why didn't you tell Connie I stopped working two jobs?"

Kalayla shrugged. "Why would I bother? You still didn't go shopping with me."

****

Opa greeted Rico when Kalayla opened the door, and I could tell from the combination of noisy humans and growling canine that they were playing tug of war with one of Opa's toys. I turned off the oven so the lasagna could rest and joined them in the living room.

Kalayla and Rico were on their hands and knees, and Opa was trying to wrestle a football-sized stuffed turtle from under Rico's armpit.

"Foul on the human for using his right hand," Kalayla, the referee, said. "Ball turnover and five-point penalty. The next penalty means no hand use for the human!"

"I object! Referee bias!" Rico shouted.

"You can't object before it happens. You used both hands to grab the ball. The rule is you can only use your left hand. You saw him, Mama."

Unconcerned by the controversy, Opa picked up the turtle and retired to the corner.

Rico said, "How am I supposed to get the turtle if my hands are behind my back?"

"Use your mouth, same as Opa. Right, Mama?"

I laughed. "As a neutral observer, I can't comment, but Opa seems satisfied with the ref's decision. If the human wishes to contest it, he can request an investigation."

Rico scowled and shook his head. "Yeah, and who'd investigate? I'm asking Lotta or Mattwo for our next match. Either of them will be a more impartial referee and neutral observer." He made a face at me.

I decided the best approach was a change of subject. "Will you open the wine, Rico?"

Kalayla gave me a thumbs up when Rico ate two helpings of the lasagna and salad, raved about the lemon sherbet, and ate three of Lotta's cranberry and macadamia nut cookies.

Everything was perfect until Kalayla went to her room, and Rico and I went into the living room to enjoy Irish Crème coffee.

237

"Kalayla seems good," Rico said. "I wondered how she'd do without step dancing."

"I don't understand what you mean."

Rico saw my shocked expression and said, "Uh oh, I think I just waded into a mud hole and got stuck. A couple of weeks ago, Kalayla told me she planned to quit dance. I said I'd pay her if she wanted to keep working, but she hasn't taken me up on the offer."

Why would Kalayla give up dancing when she loved it so much? I wish she'd asked me for advice before doing something so drastic. I would've asked my mother for advice.

That thought stopped me cold.

I stopped confiding in my mother or asking her for advice long before I met Jamal.

"Things have been peaceful lately, and I assumed everything was fine," I said.

"Maybe it is fine. You should ask Kalayla."

"I'm going to. I hope she doesn't explode."

Rico squeezed my hand. "If you don't mind, I'll hang around and see how it goes."

When I told Kalayla I needed to talk with her, she returned to the living room, sat in the armchair, looked at me, and said, "Rico told you, didn't he? I was going to, but I was afraid you'd think it was your fault and get depressed."

I was stunned. I closed my eyes and took a deep breath. "Were you going to tell me?"

"Sure, after I decided what I was doing instead. Don't worry, Mama, I won't turn into a couch potato no matter what Lena says."

"But you loved step-dancing."

"Yeah, but I got tired of the sore muscles and blisters."

Kalayla busied herself, patting Opa, and avoided looking at me, a sure sign that there was more to it than that.

"Really?" I said.

Kalayla looked up, "No, not really. I quit 'cause I don't have the money for costumes. I'm not asking you or anybody else to pay for something I'll wear once. I'm not dancing anymore, no matter what anybody says. Please don't make a big deal of it, Mama."

Kalayla's eyes pleaded with me to understand I didn't need to fix anything.

She was asking me to show I respected and believed in her decisions. "I can do that, Kalayla."

Two big tears ran down her face.

I wrapped my arms around her. Rico whopped and said, "Okay, Opa, we can relax! Guard duty takes a lot of energy. I need a cookie, and you deserve a biscuit."

Rico rubbed Opa's ears. She followed him into the kitchen, and I hugged my daughter.

SPRING 2001

LENA'S NEW LIFE

Ray Ray and his monster dog, Thor, owned the sidewalk on Mass. Ave., so I walked the long way to the old lady's new house. If Ray Ray gave me a hard time, I could kick him in the balls and tear ass out of there. But Opa couldn't outrun that drooling bull mastiff.

About a month ago, when Opa and I went for a snack, Lena said, "Don't get comfortable. We're going for a walk."

I knew something was going on 'cause Lena never went for a walk without a reason, like going to Mickey's or Eddie's. So I said, "The wind is cold. You might want to stay inside for the next couple of months."

"If you're afraid of a little wind, the world is in worse shape than I thought. That poor dog needs sun and exercise. Don't turn her into a couch potato because you want company on the sofa."

"This way," Lena said. We crossed the street and walked down Mass. Ave. toward Arlington. "Where are we going?" I said, keeping a sharp eye out for Ray Ray.

"You'll see," Lena said. "At least you're turning into a decent cook. Your mama must be a good teacher."

"Yeah," I said. "I didn't know she could cook. She kept it a secret, so Daddy got stuck cooking while she worked on her art."

"That could pay off. Your mama's artwork is intriguing."

"Does that mean you like it?"

"It means I think she should show it. We turn right here. See that little house across the street? What do you think?"

I liked it 'cause it looked like Grandma's house. "Somebody should write a children's book about the little house surrounded by monsters and fighting to save itself."

Lena laughed. "Mattwo and I are the ones fighting the monsters. We bought the house, and you and Opa can come over whenever you want."

A bowling ball slammed into my stomach. The old lady was moving. She wouldn't live across the hall anymore. I thought she and the old guy might take trips, but I never thought she'd take off for good. And here she was, smiling like Santa Claus gave her the world's best present.

What was I supposed to say?

When Lena told me I should be nicer to my mama, she said, "When it comes to people you love, Kalayla, you can't only think of yourself. You have to think about them, too."

I wanted to take Opa, run home, lock the door to my room, and never come out again. But if I did, Lena would be standing here alone, and she wouldn't be smiling.

I thought about when Lena invited me to supper, how she let me sleep with Cody, listened to me, and gave me lectures so I'd be a better person.

How could I tell her I hated the house and didn't want her to move?

I swallowed and said, "You better stock up on a lot of good stuff in case Opa, and I come and stay a week or two."

Lena laughed. "I hope you do."

I didn't say anything the whole way home, and Lena didn't either. Mama would have asked me if something was wrong, but Lena didn't, and I was glad.

After I got Lena up the stairs, I went home, curled up on my bed with Opa, and thought about the worst things that ever happened to me.

Mama lying about her family was one, but it wasn't the worst.

Kids at school acted like I was different, but it wasn't the worst.

I didn't want Lena to move, but it wouldn't be the worst if she did.

The worst thing was that Daddy died. He couldn't take me for ice cream, tell me dumb jokes, or hug me. Having Lena move was way better than Daddy being dead.

***

I saw a dark-haired girl with wraparound sunglasses pushed on top of her head standing in front of Lena's house, laughing. At first, I thought she was on a cell phone, but when I got closer, I could see she wasn't.

The girl laughed again, so I said, "What's so funny?"

She turned and saw Opa sitting awkwardly on her left hip, with one ear up and the other down, showing off her scruffy, light-brown coat and trim thirty pounds. She said, "What a sweet little dog!"

"What's so funny?" I repeated.

"You'd have to know my grandmother to understand. She lives in this house."

I'd never seen Lena's grandkids. When I asked her if she had any family, she said, "Of course I do. Just because you haven't seen them doesn't mean they don't exist. My son used to bring his two daughters here every Halloween. I'd load them up with candy."

This girl must be one of the kids who came for the candy haul.

"That's kind of hard to believe," I said.

The girl laughed. "Why is it hard to believe my grandmother lives here?"

"You don't look like her. You're tall, and she's my size. Maybe you'll look more like her after you get wrinkles and white hair."

The girl laughed. "What's your dog's name?"

"Opa," I said, stroking Opa's head. "I got her at the animal shelter where I work. Her back legs were broken, and I adopted her after she got better."

"That's why she sits funny. I'm president of the Animal Rights Club at my high school. I'm trying to talk my dad into donating to People for the Ethical Treatment of Animals. He won't because he blamed them for throwing blood on some lady's fur coat."

"He can give money to Animal Friends instead. We don't throw blood on anybody. Lena's best friend, Lotta, owns the shelter. Do you know her?"

"I don't know my grandmother's friends. I barely know her."

I said, "When I first met Lena, I thought she was too crabby to have friends, but I was wrong."

I looked the girl over again. If her dad could donate money to animal organizations, he must be rich, but she didn't advertise it like some kids at school did. Her gold hoop earrings had the initial "R" in the middle and might be one-of-a-kind, but her blue jeans were old and faded, and her light-blue t-shirt, denim jacket, and blue flip-flops were stuff I'd wear.

"Lena used to live across the hall from me and my mama."

"You live on the fourth floor? That's awesome," the girl said. "When my Dad took my sister and me to Grandma's, I wanted to hang out the window and yell stuff, but my dad would have grounded me forever. Did you ever do that?"

If I had, Mama would have freaked out.

"Nah," I said, and then I heard Lena's voice.

VISITORS

"Hey, you two! I don't allow loitering in front of my house. Kalayla, get in here and stop depriving that poor mutt of her treats. And you, Ronnie, are you waiting for the wicked witch to invite you into her lair?"

The girls looked at each other, laughed, and strolled up the brick walk. I held the screen door open and gave Opa a treat.

"Hey, Lena," Kalayla said. "Anybody croak in the old folks' home last night?"

I smacked her arm. "You better mind your mouth if you want to stuff it with Lotta's cookies."

"Are you going to starve me for telling the truth? You guys are old, and this is your home, right?"

I couldn't very well argue about that. "Since when do you two know each other?"

Kalayla said, "We don't. She says she's your granddaughter."

"She says she used to live across the hall from you," Ronnie said.

"Kalayla LeeRoyce, meet Ronnie Barzetti. Ronnie is my son JJ's youngest daughter. When I wore black, she thought I was a witch."

Ronnie laughed, "That was because Dad brought us to visit on Halloween. Remember when I asked you where you kept your broomstick?"

"How would I forget such a question?" I said.

Kalayla smiled. "I bet you told her it was where it was supposed to be. In the broom closet."

"How did you know?" Ronnie said.

"That's where I found it," Kalayla giggled.

"Maybe I should have invited Opa in and left you two on the sidewalk. Let's sit on the patio and give Opa sniffing time."

I put my stern face on, hoping it would cover how unsettled I felt. Both girls were strong-willed teenagers who knew how to work around adult roadblocks. Ronnie's parents spoiled her, and she out-maneuvered them. When Kalayla decided she wanted something, she could bull-dose or out-smart anything in her way. Having them here together was enough to give anyone a case of jittery nerves.

I walked toward the kitchen, past the pile of boxes on the living room floor, clear evidence that the predictability of my old life was gone.

Boxes with sticky notes indicated contents circled the living room like a protective wall. Mattwo built floor-to-ceiling cherry bookcases along one living room wall, and everything in the boxes would find a home on the shelves.

Mattwo also built a cherry entertainment center for our new thirty-two-inch TV, VCR, and CD player. Rico was coming to set up the electronics so he and his dad could watch the NBA playoffs tomorrow afternoon.

We had enough in place to show we were here for the long haul with Mattwo's deep-orange recliner and my Lincoln Rocker side-by-side near the cinnamon-colored sofa and matching armchair. Mattwo's woodworking magazines cluttered the cherry coffee table.

Ronnie went to the kitchen door sliders and saw Opa giving herself a back rub in the grass.

"I guess Dad won't come here to play on your tennis court, Grandma," she said.

"Ronnie, you do realize that most people don't have private tennis courts, don't you?"

"Sure, but I bet Dad told you to buy this house and the one next to it, remodel the Victorian, and put in a tennis court on this lot, right?"

Kalayla opened the slider for Opa and said, "Opa loves to chase tennis balls if you've got any extra. If you and your dad want to play tennis, the courts aren't too far away."

Ronnie wrinkled her nose. "We have a court at our house, so Dad plays whenever he wants. He's a fanatic about staying in shape."

Kalayla tilted her head to look squarely into Ronnie's face, "Do you think Lena should tear this place down?"

Ronnie said, "Most of the time, I don't do what my dad says, so why should my grandma? Dad and I get along okay when I keep my mouth shut. We agree that my sister Juliana's goal is to find a rich husband.

She's brainless."

I wondered if Ronnie knew her father described her as a charging bull because she was so direct. He nicknamed her sister Juliana of the Veils because she was skilled at hiding her motives while manipulating you.

Kalayla carried the plate of lemon squares to the patio and said, "I'd rather sit on Lena's patio than on a tennis court."

I asked Lotta for advice about patio furniture, and she suggested Olefin fabric, which was easy to clean, durable, and sun-resistant. Four chairs, a chaise lounge with blue-red cushions, and a round table left space for the gas grille, side table, and additional seating.

Kalayla and Opa liked sharing the chaise lounge. Ronnie and I took chairs. The temperature was slightly over sixty degrees, a blessing in April.

We no sooner sat down than Ronnie said, "My dad told me to come over here so you could plan my life. Am I the next one in line for CEO of Manzetti Properties?"

That explained her impromptu visit. Talk about the charging bull. "You'll have to apply to the Board. Your lack of education and experience won't impress them much. They might offer you a job pushing papers for a few years and see how you do."

"Too bad for Dad and his great ambitions for me. Working at Manzetti Properties is about minus twenty on my choices. He's hoping if I hang around with you, you'll talk me out of standing on street corners carrying placards about social issues. Dad's in la la land. Really, he actually thought he could convince you and Mattwo to move to Weston."

I stifled a laugh.

Ronnie said, "I'm joining AmeriCorps no matter what Mom and Dad say. I only applied to colleges so they'd stop nagging me. After AmeriCorps, I'll attend college and become a civil rights lawyer."

When Ronnie told her father she was going to law school, JJ would assume she'd become a lawyer for Manzetti Properties. My eldest son had more than a few shocks coming his way!

"Cool," Kalayla said. "I was thinking about working at an animal shelter, but Lotta is afraid I'll go after people who abuse animals with a baseball bat. She says if I become a vet, I'll be less likely to wind up in jail."

"I can see her point," Ronnie said. "You can't help animals if you're in jail. You just gave me an idea, Kalayla. I'm sure the Animal Rights Club members would like a shelter tour. Could you work that out?"

"Sure, if you tell them we need donations of blankets and carrying cases for pets or money to buy stuff like that."

Ronnie nodded.

Kalayla and Ronnie had more in common than I thought. Their interests could intersect positively, but I wasn't sure what the fallout would be for the people who loved them.

SCATTERED THOUGHTS AND WORRIES

When Kalayla came into the studio to tell me she was off to Animal Friends, she said, "Mama, I wish you'd quit staring at me. It's creepy like you're stalking me."

Since Kalayla stopped step-dancing, I had been worrying more about how she was spending her time, but I didn't realize I'd been staring at her.

"Mothers don't stalk their daughters, Kalayla."

Kalayla rolled her eyes, implying I was out of touch with reality, but I wasn't. I knew someone had been stalking Gwyneth Paltrow, but Kalayla didn't read newspapers or watch the news.

"How do you know about stalking?" I said.

"Everybody knows, Mama. This girl in my class was dating an older guy, and when she broke up with him, he stalked her 'cause he was pissed."

"Oh, my goodness! Was she a friend of yours? Did she tell her parents? Did they make him stop?"

Kalayla shrugged. "How would I know? Don't go all nutsy on me. It's just stuff I heard."

"You'd tell me if that happened to you, wouldn't you, Kalayla?"

"Maybe. Anyway, how come you're staring at me? Do you think I'm hiding some sexy tattoos?"

Sexy tattoos! I didn't want to think about how Kalayla learned about sexy tattoos. Her green eyes were twinkling, so maybe she was teasing me.

"I've been worried since you quit step-dancing. If you changed your mind, I could—."

"I'm not changing my mind, so stop staring, okay? I'll take Opa out later."

Off she went, leaving me a puddle of agitation and worry. Hearing her talk about stalking and sexy tattoos was terrifying. I had no idea how to keep her safe. I sounded like my mother, whose priority was keeping her family safe. I never intended to sound like her. I never intended to have children.

I didn't discuss that with Jamal, and when I got pregnant soon after we married, it was too late. He saw that I didn't have the single-minded stamina a mother needed. I don't know what I would have done if he hadn't been willing to share the burden of caring for Kalayla. I trusted he would keep her safe, but that was my job now, and I had no idea how.

And here I was, falling in love with Rico, which complicated everything. He liked Kalayla, but what if he wanted biological children? I couldn't agree to that. I was having trouble raising the child I had, and the idea of more children was overwhelming and depressing. And that wasn't the only complication. I had no idea how Kalayla would feel about him as a stepfather or what Lucinda and Harmon would think. I had to talk with Rico soon.

I scowled at the watercolor on my easel. My art studio was supposed to be a refuge from the outside world, but I couldn't check my brain at the door. My thoughts scattered like sand in a dust storm.

I flopped down in the armchair and looked around. Jamal's UMass college chair and an oblong crate doubled as a coffee table in a small seating area at the end of my workspace, where three windows looked onto Massachusetts Avenue. Tangerine-tinged white walls mimicked sunlight on dingy days.

Despite that, my creative juices weren't flowing, which would have pleased my mother. She was horrified that I intended to be an artist.

"Don't be ridiculous, Maureen!" she said. "Irish artists cut off their ears, commit suicide, and are sent to mental institutions. Do you want to be with inmates who roam the halls drooling, stinking of feces, and talking to people who aren't there?"

I tried to explain that Van Gogh, who cut off his ear, and Rothko, who was suicidal, weren't Irish. And they weren't women. If I'd married an Irish Catholic, my mother might have bragged that art was my hobby. But I didn't. Jamal wasn't Irish, Catholic, or white. Her fears materialized and triggered the mood changes my siblings and I dreaded.

My mother thought life was a matter of simple choices. You would be safe if you did the smart thing and lived in a community that shared your values. If you stepped outside that boundary, bad things would happen like they did to her family in Belfast.

Belfast had nothing to do with my siblings or myself. Our father owned a business, a house, and a car, and we lived in a tight-knit Catholic community. My brother and sisters did what Mother wanted by chance, not intention. I was the exception long before I met Jamal.

After I met him, I learned what it was like to be afraid for someone you love. Even simple pleasures could go sideways like the night we went to see *Men in Black*. We were standing in line to get tickets when one of the men in front of us said, "You think they oughta let niggers in this theatre?"

Jamal tensed, and I was horrified. I glanced around and saw white faces. I was terrified Jamal would confront the guy, terrified that people would gang up on him.

"The line's too long," I said, pulling on Jamal's arm. "Let's go someplace else."

I could see Jamal breathing slowly, deciding what to do. When he said, "You're right," I was so relieved I could have cried.

Afterward, Jamal said, "The guy was showing off to his friend. He'd have done more than taunt me if he wanted to push it."

I understood life differently after I fell in love with Jamal. I understood my mother's fear for her family. I did my best to protect Kalayla, but I couldn't control her decisions any better than my mother could control mine.

Memories of my mother's love and rejection intermingled like a pretzel twisting in on itself. Mother kissed away my tears after I fell and gashed my knee, baked my favorite key lime pie for a summer BBQ, and kept my report cards in a three-ring binder to show to friends. And she turned her back on me.

I threw my watercolor brush on the workbench, spraying an arc of yellow across the wooden surface. I stared at the canvas on the easel and suddenly understood what I saw. Maybe this wasn't a botched landscape. Was it a new direction for my art?

I'd painted a tree dressed for different seasons. Some branches were bare winter skeletons, others covered with changing fall leaves, fresh spring greenery, or summer's deeper green. The branches were connected to the trunk as if to suggest that the potential for the past, present, and future simultaneously existed under its bark. The tree's essence lived below the surface: what is, what was, and what would be were waiting for the proper season.

I jumped up, rejuvenated and inspired. Get busy, I told myself! You have work to do!

MY FATHER

When that girl, Ronnie, told me about her big-bucks dad, I could have said my father was good at sports and won tons of trophies. But I didn't talk about him 'cause it reminded me how much I missed him. He was my best friend.

Ronnie and her dad didn't agree on nearly anything, but Daddy and I agreed on almost everything. We did fun things when Mama was busy, like going for banana splits 'cause Daddy said I needed fattening up.

For my fifth birthday, Mama made Daddy an octopus costume with eight extra-long arms, and he couldn't figure out how to hug me with more than two arms, no matter how hard he tried. Mama kept laughing and making suggestions to help, but suddenly, she said, "Oh, this gives me the best idea. I need to make a few notes." She rushed to her studio and forgot to come back. We were used to that.

The night before I started kindergarten, Mama went through my closet and picked out a yellow dress with bows across the front that I hated. "You must look your best to make a good first impression."

"But I want to play on the jungle gym."

"Oh, Kalayla, honey, you'll forget about the jungle gym when you see how much fun it is to meet your teachers and make new friends."

The next morning, I put on the dark blue romper and tights I wore when Daddy took me to the playground. Mama was working on a clay sculpture when we went to say goodbye. She glanced up and said, "Have a wonderful day. My hands are covered, so I can't hug you." She blew me a kiss but didn't notice I wasn't wearing the yellow dress.

Daddy always paid attention to what I was doing. That's how I learned to cook. When Mama was in her studio, she didn't think about dinner, so we'd eat at eight or nine o'clock. Neither of them cared, but my stomach did.

I decided if Mama could make a grilled cheese sandwich, so could I. All she did was melt butter, stick cheese between two slices of bread, and fry it. I put half a stick of butter in the pan and waited for it to melt when Daddy came home and called, "Hey, Skinny Girl! Where are you?"

"In the kitchen making dinner."

When Daddy saw me standing on a stool at the stove, he said, "What are you making?"

"Grilled cheese."

He looked at the stove. "I see you figured out just about everything. Let me show you a few tricks. See that red burner in the back? That's the one you turned on."

The pan with the butter was on the front burner.

"Oh," I said.

Daddy pointed to the front section of the stovetop. "See how those half circles are in the same position as the burners, each with an on/off dot? That's how you know which burner to turn on. Use the plus and minus to turn the burner up or down."

The next day, Daddy gave me *My First Cookbook,* and I learned to cook stuffed baked potatoes and teddy bear pancakes.

I wish I knew what Daddy was like at my age. I wonder how he learned to cook. I might ask Grandpa about him when we go to their house Friday night.

***

I dropped Opa off with Grandpa and went down to play ping pong. After I won a few games, I loaded up with chips and root beer and went to Grandpa's den.

Mama carved a Snoopy with the words "Harmon's Dog House" for the sign on his door. Grandpa loved dogs, but when I asked him why he didn't have one, he said, "If I adopted dogs the way your Grandma adopts kids, there wouldn't be any room for her and me!"

Grandpa was sitting on the floor next to Opa.

"Hey," I said.

"Hey, yourself. Watch this," he said.

Grandpa tucked his legs and arms into a ball, grunted, and rolled over. Then he said, "Roll over, Opa!"

Opa cocked her head, barked once, and held up her paw.

I giggled.

Grandpa shook his head. "I ask you, granddaughter, did I tell this dog to shake hands?"

Opa waited patiently with her paw up until Grandpa rewarded her with a biscuit.

"Grandpa! You shouldn't give her a biscuit for doing the wrong trick! Let me try!"

I got on the floor, rolled over, and said, "Roll over, Opa!"

Opa barked once and held up her paw.

"See that," Grandpa said. "You don't know any more about dog training than I do. I'm not sure that dog will ever be ready for the big show."

"What big show?"

"The one we're having in the backyard as soon as Opa figures out the difference between shake and rollover."

I crawled to Grandpa and hugged him. "I'm sorry she's not cooperating."

"Don't you worry. We're just getting started! I've got faith and fortitude, don't I, girl?" He ruffed Opa's head.

"Can I ask you a question, Grandpa?"

"Well, now, that depends on how personal it is. Some things are on my do-not-disclose list."

"Don't worry. I won't ask what size belt you wore five years ago and what size you wear now."

Grandpa laughed. "Good, because that's on my list. What would you like to know?"

"I want to know what my father was like when he was my age."

Grandpa rubbed his fingers over his lips like he was deciding which words he was willing to let out. "Your daddy was a fine man."

"I know. I want to know what kind of kid he was."

Grandpa nodded. "Your dad was a natural runner. He loved both cross country and track, which is unusual. Sometimes, I wondered if he was running away from or toward something. And Jamal was good in academic classes. Your grandmother saw to that."

"I know he was good at that stuff. What kind of kid was he?"

"Not your typical one. Most kids don't do a lot of planning, but your daddy was always thinking ahead. And he was an organizer. He'd get kids together for pick-up football, baseball games, or volleyball. No matter how many kids showed up, that boy figured out how to make it work and always included everybody.

"Jamal didn't enjoy church any more than you do, but he helped us start a program with older boys reading to younger ones. He was a natural-born teacher, but he wanted to invent things to help people instead of teaching them like Grandma. That's how he ended up tinkering with medical devices."

Once Grandpa got going, he didn't stop. "Jamal and his friends acted like this city was a giant playground, but he never took Clarence with them after Fresh Pond.

"When I told him to be careful, he said, 'Dad, if I'd thought fast enough at Fresh Pond, I could have taken Clarence into Friendly's and called you. Those kids would never have seen us. I learned the hard way that I constantly have to watch for trouble. If I need to hide, run, smile, or walk away, I will. But, I will not be afraid of leaving our neighborhood.'"

"What happened at Fresh Pond?" I said.

"Damn! I just stepped in it with both feet." He stared at me like he was trying to see inside my skin. "I guess it's time you knew some things."

That pissed me off. It meant Mama wasn't the only one hiding things from me. Grandpa and Grandma were, too.

"What things?" I said.

Grandpa rubbed his chin and said, "We decided you didn't need to know until you were older, but you're old enough now.

"Clarence idolized your dad and wanted to go everywhere Jamal went. That day, he found out his older brother wasn't a superhero. They rode their bikes to Fresh Pond, and a car full of white boys tormented them. Clarence begged your daddy to protect him. But Jamal was seven, a year older than Clarence, and he couldn't do anything to help Clarence or himself. Clarence changed from a sweet-trusting boy to a fearful-angry one, and Jamal never got over feeling guilty."

"Did Clarence think it was Daddy's fault?" I said.

Grandpa shrugged. "After that, Clarence was afraid to try anything new and resented Jamal because he was always planning, setting goals, and working for what he wanted. As early as eighth grade, your father was thinking about where he'd go to college.

"The two of them were in high school when I overheard them talking.

"Clarence said, 'Stop acting like you're going to be a big man, Bro.

You'll be picking up the white man's garbage, same as me.'

"'That's not going to happen,' Jamal said."

Grandpa stopped talking, and I wondered if he'd forgotten what he was going to say. He was staring at the ceiling, looking confused. I was afraid he was stuck between the past and the present and couldn't find his way back.

"Are you okay, Grandpa?"

He looked down and squinted at me. "Talking about the past can take you to places you don't want to go." He groaned softly.

I was about to get Grandma when he said, "You know, Kalayla, the hardest thing about being old is knowing you can't change the past, no matter how much you want to. Don't pay any attention to me. I'm an old man who ought to know when to stop blabbing. Take that puppy and join the young folks. Give me a hug before you go."

I wrapped my arms around him. "Thanks for telling me." I held out my hand to give him a boost off the floor.

He pushed my hand away. "I'm not that old and frail yet. Give that stubborn puppy an extra biscuit for me."

When I went to the kitchen, Mama was chatting with Grandma and putting food away. I grabbed a peanut butter brownie and jerked my hand away so fast she couldn't smack it.

Grandma smiled. "Did talking to that old man drive you to starvation?"

"Nah," I said. "Grandpa showed me how to snitch brownies without getting smacked, and I thought I'd get some practice."

"Harmon would have been at those brownies twice as quick as you. That man loves his sweets!" Grandma laughed. "I better take one to him so he'll have the energy to get to bed."

I didn't tell Mama what Grandpa said. One day, a long time ago, I told the old lady I wished some of the butthole kids at school would drown, and she said, "Be careful what you wish for, Kalayla. You might get more than you bargained for. One of them could drag you under, and you'd drown along with them."

"No, I wouldn't," I said. "I can swim a lot better than any of those turds."

What bothered me was that the old lady was right. I asked about my daddy, but I found out about Clarence, too. After Daddy died, I told Mama I hated Clarence. "Daddy wouldn't have died if Clarence hadn't pestered him to go drag-racing."

"Oh, Kalayla, honey," Mama said, "your daddy was a grown man who made his own decisions. Clarence didn't force him."

If Clarence hadn't begged to go to Fresh Pond, he wouldn't have gotten hurt. He shouldn't blame my daddy for something that was his own fault. If I ever saw him again, I'd tell him that.

A FOUR-LEGGED ADDITION

When I lived in the apartment, I looked down at a paved street and concrete sidewalks. Sitting in front of the kitchen slider was like watching a movie of spring breaking out all over. A sparrow pair was building their nest, preparing to sit on an egg for hours, maybe days. I'd have a seriously sore butt if I tried that, but birds might have built-in butt cushions.

The tidy forsythia hedge next to the back fence mimicked the orderliness of my life before Maureen, Kalayla, Mattwo, Opa, and a new house turned routine into chaos.

The front door slammed, and Lotta called, "Where are you hiding?"

She popped into the kitchen. "I might have known you'd be sitting and staring out a window. Living with my brother has reduced you to pitiful laziness."

"It's nice to see you, too," I said. "I trust your mouth wasn't the only thing you brought."

"Humph!" Lotta said, setting two reusable grocery bags on the kitchen table. "There's only so much I'm willing to cart around for you and him. I hope I don't ruin my taste buds by drinking your fake coffee."

I smiled the version of sweet I reserved for Lotta, which was a combination of sweet and sour.

"Pistachio muffins, cranberry-nut bread, and mini-chocolate cupcakes with a skim of icing," Lotta said as she emptied the bags. "I hope Mattwo is doing more to stay in shape than romping around the bedroom with you."

She paused, "You know, Lena, dear,—."

I interrupted before she could say another word. "Don't you 'Lena, dear' me! I know your tricks, and I'm not buying whatever you're selling."

"Oh, don't be such an old fart. You moved to a questionable neighborhood, and I'm considering your safety and well-being. You need a guard dog for protection, and I have just the one for you. She's a small German Shepherd with a sweet disposition and a perfect friend for Opa."

"I moved five blocks from where I used to live, Lotta. Don't tell me I need a guard dog. You already conned me into taking two cats."

"You didn't need protection in the apartment because no self-respecting thief would climb four flights to steal anything but a Picasso, and you don't own one of those. The ground floor is easy pickings for a burglar who'll settle for a large-screen TV like the one in your living room. Take a few deep breaths, and get your cardboard coffee going while I collect Bluebell from the car."

"Bluebell! Whoever heard of a guard dog named Bluebell?"

Lotta wrinkled her nose. "I call her BB. Stop beating your gums, Lena. She's cat-friendly, dog-friendly, and kid-friendly. What more could you want?"

She sprinted to the front door before I could throw a cat toy at her. I weighed the option of escaping out the slider, but Lotta was faster than I was in more ways than one.

Lotta returned with Bluebell at her heels, and I hoped she'd overlook my wide-eyed pleasure. The dog was gorgeous.

"BB," Lotta said, "I'd like you to meet my best friend, Lena. She's old and cantankerous, but her husband compensates for her bad traits."

"That dog can't be a German Shepherd," I said. "She has blue eyes, a long-haired gray coat, and is about Opa's size."

"For your information, BB's coat is gray and sable, blue eyes are a recessive gene in German Shepherds, and she's bigger than she looks. She weighs twenty-five pounds more than Opa. Her former owners thought she'd win Best in Show at the National Dog Show. They dropped her at the shelter when they found out she needed pure-bred credentials to compete. They should have done the research before buying her, and named her Lady Jane Gray instead of Bluebell. You're lucky they were so ignorant."

Lady Jane/Bluebell sniffed my hand, nuzzled the side of my leg, and lasered me with her blue eyes.

When I opened the cupboard to get a water bowl, Lotta said, "You know I wouldn't bring an animal without all the essentials." She pulled water and food bowls, chew toys, and treats out of her second bag.

"Her food and bed are in the car. Don't give me such a pained look, Lena. You don't have to agree until my brother meets her, but I trust you recall he and Angi always had dogs. Now, tell me what's on your mind."

BB was happily gnawing on a chew toy when Napoleon strolled into the kitchen, gave her a casual look, and flopped on the floor. Petunia arrived a minute later, sniffed BB's face, licked her long coat, and got a mouthful of fur.

"So?" Lotta said after we sat at the kitchen table with coffee.

"The so is this. When I invited Mark and Frankie to visit, Mark said Frankie won't come until they see how this visit goes."

"We're on the same page. If you try to shove a gay man down anybody's throat, the chances are you'll be cleaning up vomit. Gay rights activists may be alive and well in Massachusetts, but I'm not aware of any in your family. Are you?"

"No. I don't want to create an awkward situation for Mark, but I intend to give him a small welcome-home party."

Lotta said. "We can invite Rico, Maureen, Kalayla, JJ, and his family. What about Dom and your sisters?"

I refrained from hugging Lotta because if I did, she'd tell me to stop drooling all over her. Annoying as she could be, I'd always been able to count on Lotta for help.

"Dom may be well aware that Mark is gay, but I don't know how he will react to seeing him. My sisters are dear women, but they follow church doctrine, and the Catholic Church says homosexuality is a sin. That's the end of the discussion for them. They'd beg Mark to repent, and I won't subject him to that. Also, I've been thinking about inviting Lucinda and Harmon. What do you think?"

"I think you should invite anyone you want to."

I didn't know Maureen's in-laws well, but when Clarence curled into a fetal position and called for his mother, I imagined Mikie and Jimmy in a jungle thousands of miles away calling for me.

When Lucinda and Harmon picked Clarence up, the sadness in her eyes mirrored mine. Lucinda lost one child to death and another to a mental breakdown. I'd lost the twins to death and Mark to foolish pride. Lucinda was helping Clarence recover, and I was bringing Mark home to his family. We were both doing what we thought was best.

"This is a joyful occasion, and I'd like to share it with them."

"That's a fine reason for inviting them," Lotta said.

"Oh, Lotta, did you ever imagine our lives would turn out this way?"

"I knew I'd never stay married, you'd be the CEO of Manzetti Properties, you and Mattwo would eventually get together, and I know we'll be friends until one of us is six feet under or ashes in a crematorium. That gives me a superior score for imagining how things would turn out."

Now, what could I say to that?

A FABULOUS SURPRISE

At seven a.m. on Saturday, I staggered into the kitchen to toast an English Muffin and have coffee before going to the studio. I groaned when the phone rang. After five good hours of sleep, I was anxious to work on my latest painting, but I didn't dare ignore the call. What if it were Kalayla or someone calling about her?

I answered and heard Lena's drill sergeant voice, "We're going on a field trip, Maureen. I asked Eddie for two take-out coffees and two cinnamon buns. Pick them up and meet me on the corner. I'll swing by in ten minutes."

Lena was on a mission, and it was clear I had to get on board or be left behind!

I quickly changed into an emerald-green sweater and black slacks, added green dangle earrings, and brushed my hair.

Kalayla had taped a note to the front door: "Walking then meeting Shanese." That seemed odd. Kalayla saw Shanese at Lucinda's, but I didn't know they were friends.

It never occurred to me Lena had a driver's license until she pulled Mattwo's car to the curb.

"I'd be happy to drive," I said.

"Don't look so nervous, Maureen. This isn't my first time behind a steering wheel. I'll talk Mattwo into buying a car that doesn't use a tank of gas every fifteen miles and takes up two parking spaces. Ah, nothing like the smell of fresh-baked cinnamon buns. Make sure your seatbelt is tight."

I tightened my seatbelt. "Where are we going?"

Lena glanced at me. "I'm fine, thank you, and so is Mattwo. You'll have to come and meet BB. Kalayla is nagging Mattwo to take me on a trip so she and Opa can stay at our house with BB."

I laughed. "I'm glad you and Mattwo are fine, but you didn't say where we were going or why. Surprises make me nervous."

Lena put on the turn signal and pulled away from the curb. "Don't worry. You'll like this one. We're going to Arlington."

My concern that Lena had planned an all-day outing vanished. Arlington was the abutting town, and Mass. Ave. was devoid of traffic this early Saturday morning.

Shortly after we crossed into Arlington, Lena pulled to the curb and parked in front of an apartment building. "Hand over my coffee and bun," she said. "We'll eat and then take a stroll."

"How do you like your house?" I said.

Lena smiled, "These old legs love it. The business used to keep my brain sharp. Now, a house, a man, a dog, two cats, and a field trip like this one are doing that."

I smiled. "I hope I'll be as lucky as you are."

Lena ate crumbs off her napkin, took the last swig of her coffee, and said, "We're going down the block."

She pointed at the closest apartment building. "That's one of the first Manzetti Properties I purchased, Maureen. We eventually acquired the entire block, rehabbed the apartment buildings, and built three new office buildings."

The apartment building resembled an oblong horseshoe. Each of the three sides had a private entrance but shared a central courtyard. A master gardener had selected flowers for the canopy-covered seating area, Crab apple trees for shade, and a Magnolia tree at each entrance with Azalea, Hydrangea, and Rhododendron bushes to add color.

"Lena, this is just lovely. If I lived in one of the apartments, I'd sit here with my sketch pad."

"I convinced Dom the seating would enhance the property value. He favored a large statue. When I suggested Eleanor Roosevelt, he changed his mind."

Further along Mass. Ave., we passed two identical apartment buildings and then came to a strip mall with an insurance company and real estate broker in the first two buildings.

The marquee above the third building read "Artist's Intuition." A thirty-by-forty-inch collage dominated the window. The creativity and complexity of the work mesmerized me. Eyes rendered in every color and shape, with and without piercings or make-up, were drawn in watercolor, ink, and charcoal. The discretely placed price tag read 2,550.00. Inquire within."

"Enough lollygagging, Maureen," Lena said, taking my arm. "A good friend of my daughter-in-law manages the gallery. I asked her to open early."

Lena pressed the buzzer, and a perfectly coiffed woman with dark-brown hair wearing a powder-blue tweed suit, a silk blouse, and spike heels opened the door. Everything about her screamed Neiman Marcus and Jimmy Cho while my outfit advertised TJ Maxx, Marshall's, and thrift stores.

I hadn't noticed what Lena was wearing. Now, I did. She epitomized a successful businesswoman clad in a classic silk sheath and matching coat with satin piping, two-inch black suede heels, and a gold sunburst pendant on a delicate gold chain around her neck.

"Thank you for opening early, Nicole," Lena said. "Amelia would have joined us, but she's in a tennis league on Saturday mornings. This is Maureen, the artist we discussed."

The idea that Lena and Nicole had discussed me gave me goosebumps.

"Would you like coffee or tea before we look at the gallery? I have lovely cranberry scones."

I shook my head, and Lena said, "We're on a tight schedule."

Nicole led us through an ante-room into an enormous space divided into two galleries. The left gallery was devoted to traditional family portraits and nature scenes. The right-hand gallery displayed contemporary art, and I was stunned to see the watercolor I gave Lena for Christmas showcased near the beginning of the exhibit. It was a fanciful caricature of Kalayla in a losing battle, trying on three hats to restrain her unruly curls.

Lena said, "I asked Rico to take photos of the canvasses in your studio. Nicole promotes young artists and agrees your work deserves an audience. Nicole reserved the contemporary section exclusively for your work during July. Does that seem doable, Maureen?"

An exhibit of my own! Images of my watercolors, charcoals, oils, and pen and ink drawings filtered through my mind. Which should I use? How should I group them? Should my new work be interspersed or in a section by itself?

"Maureen," Lena said as if reading my mind, "you needn't make every decision right now. Is the timeframe doable?"

"Yes, it's doable!" I said.

The rest of the time at the gallery was a blur. I was going to have a gallery show! I had imagined showing my work at a local library or having a single piece included in a more extensive exhibit, but this was overwhelming. How could I be this lucky?

When Lena guided me out of the gallery to the car, I said, "Lena, I don't have the words to thank you."

"This is an investment, Maureen. It will be good for the gallery and good for you. Lotta has done a lot for Kalayla. You can thank me by giving Lotta one of your pieces. How about that?"

I could have cried with joy. When Lena pulled into her driveway, I was too excited to do anything but dash to my studio.

"I have to get started," I called from the sidewalk. "I'll be over tomorrow morning."

Lena called after me, "Fine. Wearing this costume reminds me how glad I am to be a homebody."

I laughed and jogged all the way home!

LATE SPRING 2001

SWIMMING

Shanese said no dogs were allowed at the high school, so I dropped Opa at home and said, "Don't worry, girl, you'll see BB later."

Sometimes, Shanese crashed at Grandma's house. She was rotten at ping-pong but nice enough and sort of funny. She was over six feet tall, with shoulders broad for a football player, and her skin was two shades darker than mine. The rugby coach tried to recruit her, but Shanese said she wasn't a fan of broken bones and bruises. She sounded like Kieran.

When I asked her about free stuff at the high school, she said, "Can you swim well enough not to drown?"

"Sure," I said. "My dad took me to the YWCA for lessons. I'm pretty close to being an expert."

Shanese snickered. "I'll believe that when I see it. If you can scull, tread water, and hold your breath underwater, you might be able to get in the synchronized swim club."

"I never heard of synchronized swimming. Can't be that great."

"If you weren't Lucinda's and Harmon's granddaughter, I'd knock out a few of your teeth. It's like dancing in the swimming pool with music. The swimmers do the stunts simultaneously. It's awesome. I'm the club manager."

"How is that fun?" I said.

"It doesn't have to be fun. Being the manager of anything is a big deal. I'm putting it on my college applications."

"Do I have to buy anything?"

"You have a swimsuit?"

"I've got two of them."

"That's enough. The practice is on Saturday mornings. Meet me at the high school, and I'll show you around. If you ride your bike, lock it or lose it, and don't bring a knife."

When I laughed, Shanese said, "I'm not kidding. If you set off the metal detector, I don't know you."

Parking my bike next to the sick-looking grey stone building didn't make me feel like doing cartwheels. I felt better after seeing the massive mural of jungle animals in the entrance hall. Going through the Security Check-in was easy.

Shanese was leaning against a locker near it, and when she saw me, she said, "Come on. I can't be late."

Two boys wearing tight t-shirts and sagging jeans walked toward us, acting like they owned the hallway. When Shanese got between them and me, one of them laughed and said, "Hey, 'Nese, don't be hiding her. I love sucking caramel cream."

"Buzz off," Shanese said. They laughed as they walked away.

"Who are those guys?" I said.

"They're jerk-offs from the wrestling team. If you're stupid and let guys like that near you, you're asking for trouble."

We passed lockers and classrooms as we walked to the women's locker room, where a small area like the YWCA check-in counter had towels on locked shelves.

A few girls were stuffing their clothes into lockers, and when Shanese said, "Three minutes," they headed to the pool door.

Three girls were at the poolside doing calisthenics. Some others were swimming laps.

"They're getting the circulation going. We keep the pool temp low so that the old farts from the community won't push for more pool time," Shanese said.

The coach, who was in a sweat suit, yelled, "Huddle up!"

The practice lasted two hours. They were supposed to do everything in unison, but sticking one leg up and rotating in a circle needed more practice than the other stunts.

It didn't look harder than step-dancing, and if Shanese showed me what to do, I could practice at the Y. It was free, the team got to choose the music, and the coach didn't yell as much as Miss Megan. Maybe that was because the swimmers were underwater half the time.

✳✳✳

Sitting on the patio with Lena and watching Opa and BB chase each other was a blast. Opa'd be on BB's heels, they'd flop down to rest, one of them would stretch out her paws, stick her butt in the air, and they'd be off in the other direction.

"Don't tell Lotta how much fun those two are having," Lena said. "She'll bring two puppies the next time she comes!"

I giggled. Lotta loved to harass Lena about fulfilling her civic responsibility.

"Did you see Mattwo at the gym this morning?" Lena asked.

"Nah, I went to the high school to check out the synchronized swim club. One of the kids from Grandma's is trying to talk me into joining it."

Lena laughed like that was the funniest thing she had ever heard. "In my day," she said, "we called it water ballet. It's an Olympic sport. An actress named Esther Williams made it famous in the movies. Ask Lotta. We'd go to the drive-in movies, get popcorn, Cokes, and Milk Duds, and watch films like *Million Dollar Mermaid.*"

If synchronized swimming was a big deal when Lena was a kid, no wonder I never heard of it. I wasn't asking her about drive-in movies or Milk Duds 'cause I already knew more about the dinosaur age than I needed to.

It's too bad Lena didn't know anything useful, like how to outsmart those turd-brained wrestlers if they tried to add me to their grab-ass score. I'd ask Shanese about the best hiding places at the high school. Maybe she also knew how to get pepper spray past the Security Desk.

Ray Ray could take those wrestlers with one hand. I'd be all set if I could get him to act like my bodyguard and let me pet Thor to show how tight we were. Maybe he'd give me a friend-of-Lena discount.

I refilled the dogs' water bowl and got them a few biscuits. Then I said, "I asked Grandpa what my father was like when he was my age."

"What did he tell you?"

"He said Clarence was a jerk."

"Why would you say that when you know, I won't believe it?"

"Okay, so Grandpa said Clarence thought my father was a superhero instead of a regular kid, which shows how dumb Clarence is. Do you know where Clarence is hiding?"

"I don't think he's hiding. Why didn't you ask your grandpa?"

273

"How come I ask you a question, and instead of answering me, you ask me a question?"

Lena sighed. "As far as I know, Clarence lives in a nearby town."

Lena got a sandwich bag and put the rest of the cookies in it. "These'll keep you from starving on your way home."

The only time Lena pushed me out the door like that was when I camped in her spare room, and she got sick of Mama talking at me through the door. There was a reason she wanted me gone then, and there was one now. She knew more about Clarence than she said, but I took the cookies, leashed Opa, and walked home.

NOWHERE TO HIDE

A DAY LATER

I heard Kalayla shout, "Later, Mama."

The front door slammed before I could put down my hairbrush and stick my head out of the bathroom door to say goodbye.

Today, the note on the door said she was meeting Kieran. Yesterday, it was Shanese. I needed to ask Kalayla what was happening, but it wouldn't be this morning. I couldn't repay Lena's generosity and kindness by not showing up when I said I would!

When I opened Lena's screen door, a blur of gray fur swept past Lena, braked before crashing into my legs, and sniffed my jeans while I massaged her back. The scent of the white lilacs near her front porch drifted into the house as a lovely reminder of spring.

Lena stood in the living room wearing dark green khakis, a long-sleeve-light-pink blouse, and slippers.

"What a beauty," I said.

"That she is, and she milks that for all it's worth. BB, come," Lena said in a quiet tone that expected obedience. BB trotted ahead of us into the kitchen and lay in front of the slider.

"I'll make the coffee while you get a couple of Lotta's pistachio muffins out of the refrigerator."

It was wonderful to see how relaxed Lena was. In contrast to her stark white apartment, this house was warm and inviting with cream-colored walls, a deep-orange micro-fiber sofa, and a matching chair.

"I was in a daze when I left you yesterday, Lena. I've sorted through my work, should be able to finish two new pieces, and am thinking about how to organize the others. Kalayla told me she's helping with the party for your son, Mark. I'd love to help with decorations."

Lena laughed. "If Lotta and Kalayla were in charge, they'd rent a hall and hire a band. I intend to have a quiet gathering where Mark can see family and meet friends like you. Did I tell you Lucinda said she and Harmon are coming?"

I nodded.

Lena swirled the coffee around her cup. "Lucinda told me Clarence is living in a house in Somerville with a few roommates while he pulls himself together."

An invading army of storm clouds suddenly smothered the sunshine. Why would Lena bring up Clarence?

I must have frowned because Lena said, "I can see why you might not want to talk about him."

"I don't. I'd rather talk about the gallery show or your party. I'd rather talk about anything except Clarence."

"You can't put it off forever, Maureen. He isn't gone for good."

I wasn't trying to put off talking about Clarence. I wanted to erase him from my memory.

Lena said, "Kalayla asked me if I knew where Clarence was. You might want to bury what happened, but things like that can come out when you don't want them to."

Lena made it sound straightforward, but it wasn't. "It isn't that I wanted to bury it, Lena. Jamal put up with more from Clarence than he should have. And maybe Lucinda and Harmon didn't expect as much from Clarence as they should have. I guess I've been doing that, too."

I realized that making excuses for Clarence was ridiculous. He wasn't a little boy anymore.

My words spilled out like water breaching a dam. "When Clarence collapsed, I couldn't confront him for what he'd done. He depended on Lucinda and Harmon, and his needs overshadowed mine."

I covered my head with my arms as the memory of that day came back. When Clarence rang the buzzer, I assumed he'd stopped by to drop off something silly like the psychedelic knee socks Kalayla hated and gave to the thrift store.

Clarence wasn't a drinker, but he slurred his words that day, and his breath smelled. "Well, look at you, Maureen, going down to play the artist? Is that how you keep the neighbors from gossiping about what you and that honky do in your so-called studio?"

"Clarence," I said. "I told you—."

"Yeah, you told me. My dear brother, Jamal the Perfect, might believe everything his Snow White beauty told him, but I don't."

Clarence sniggered, locked his fingers around my arm, and pulled me into the bedroom.

The anger I'd smothered since that day broke loose in crashing waves. "I tried to get away, but he was too strong. He straddled me on the bed and rubbed himself against me. I begged him to stop, but he wouldn't, and I couldn't make him."

I pounded my hands against my thighs, remembering how helpless I'd been.

"Maureen! Stop! You're safe."

Lena's hands covered my fists, and BB pressed her fur against my leg. Exhaustion replaced anger as my breathing returned to normal.

Lena said, "What happened to you was not okay. You didn't confront Clarence then, but that doesn't mean you can't now."

"I have no idea how to do that, Lena."

"What's making it so hard?" Lena said.

"Lucinda and Harmon have been through enough. Caring for Clarence when he was a boy changed their lives. Then, after Jamal died, they took Kalayla and me in. And they've been dealing with Clarence since his breakdown."

Lena stroked BB's head and said, "That's true, but I don't see how ignoring what he did helps them, you or him."

"I should have done more to defend myself. I hate feeling like a victim."

Lena said, "I understand that. And I understand the need to fight back. Maybe part of that is telling Kalayla so she knows she may need to protect herself from situations like that."

"How can I do that?"

"Tell her the facts," Lena said. "Leave explaining why Clarence did it and why you're angry with yourself to the therapists. Kalayla is a smart girl. You don't want her or Clarence to think what he did was okay with you."

"I'm not sure how Clarence is, and I don't feel right confronting him until he's back to normal."

"Finding out where is he might be a start."

Lena was right. It was time for me to stop spinning in place.

SECRETS AS A WAY OF LIFE

BB followed me into the living room and nestled her head on her front paws beside my Lincoln Rocker. The cherry coffee table Mattwo made was home to copies of *Fine Woodworking Magazine,* and his slippers were beside his recliner. Seeing them improved my mood.

Maureen had the darndest way of keeping secrets and turning them into catastrophes. That wouldn't have happened when I was young. What went on in a marriage, child-rearing, business, or the Catholic Church was out-of-bounds and not intended for public knowledge. We kept everything except a surprise party a secret.

My generation was glued to the *Adventures of Ossie, Harriet,* and *I Love Lucy.* Husbands were wise and benevolent breadwinners who ruled the family. Even though Ralph in *The Honeymooners* was an annoying grouch, we believed he was a loving husband. If I'd gone public about how Joey treated me, people would have questioned my truthfulness or asked what I'd done to deserve it.

Maureen would have fit right in. She didn't tell Kalayla the truth about her maternal grandparents. She didn't talk about the racism she and Jamal experienced as a mixed-race couple, and until this morning, she filed the incident with Clarence in a never-happened folder.

I was the last person who ought to give Maureen advice about her situation. Keeping secrets was part of my DNA. I felt I had to tell Mattwo how Joey died, but I didn't tell him about my marriage. The man was smart enough to put two and two together himself.

Maybe any woman who lives day in and day out with the threat of abuse undergoes a personality change. When I started dating Joey, I was a naive, stupid girl chasing popularity, status from dating a football star, and the envy of other girls.

My mother tried to warn me before I married Joey. "This isn't a game you can stop playing if you feel like it," she said.

I told her I knew that, but it didn't take long to find out how ignorant I was.

Nothing in my story would help Maureen. I had no idea what she would have done if I hadn't gone into the bedroom when I did, but that didn't matter. I wasn't the victim. Maureen was, and what she decided to do was up to her.

EARLY SUMMER 2001

BEING A GIRL

On Saturday morning, Kieran and I sat on the floor outside his Tai Chi classroom with our legs stretched out. His were at least a foot longer than when we met, and he wasn't skinny like he used to be. I bet he was pumping iron to build muscles. I kind of missed hanging out with a toothpick scarecrow, but the good part was his voice had gone from a squeak to a whole note.

"Do you like synchronized swimming as much as step-dancing?" Kieran said.

"I don't know. I thought it might be easier, but I swallowed half the pool, trying to stay above water while I stuck a leg in the air. Shanese said I better not make her look bad, so I have to practice a lot before the tryouts."

Kieran laughed, but I didn't think it was funny.

"She sounds like Col," he said. "I switched from Tai Chi to Aikido, but I stink at it. In Tai Chi, everybody makes the same moves simultaneously, like a dance. In Aikido, you have a partner and switch who attacks and defends. See this bruise?"

Kieran's arm had a mega black and blue area.

"The teacher says we have to control our actions and reactions, but that's not as easy as it sounds. I was supposed to attack, but when my partner defended himself, I backed away, so he hit me."

"I thought you hated that kind of stuff," I said.

"If you do it right, you can defend yourself and won't get hurt. I have to practice a lot, too."

"Why do you need to defend yourself?"

"Col said some of the jocks haze new kids on the team. I don't mind putting up with remarks, but I don't want to be a punching bag."

"I wouldn't be on a team if I had to put up with crap like that."

Kieran shrugged. "A guy is supposed to be into sports. I've been running to build up my endurance for cross country. Col will say I'm a disgrace to the family if I come in last in every race."

"Does Mattwo teach Aikido?"

"Nah, the teacher comes in twice a week. When I told him I didn't want to hurt anybody, he asked if I'd let somebody hurt me without trying to stop him. I decided I wouldn't."

"I get wanting to defend yourself," I said. "A couple of creeps made remarks when I met Shanese at the high school, and I've been thinking about what to do if it happens again."

Kieran nodded. "You should because you look way more like a girl than you used to."

I punched him in the arm, but I knew what he meant. "Shanese told me to be careful what I wear, or I'll send the wrong message. I told her I wanted the boys to know I was hot, but she knew I was kidding."

Kieran shifted against the wall and cleared his throat. "So, were you kidding?"

"Get a grip, K. Do I look like I'm inviting some butthole to trash my body?" I stood up so he could see the oversized shorts below my knees and the loose-fitting t-shirt under my denim vest.

Kieran blushed and shook his head. "I can show you some Aikido moves, and we can practice them."

"That might give me a chance to escape."

"Explaining and practicing the moves will help me, too. I feel like I have two left feet and too few hands, and I look like a wimp when I get nervous."

"You could wear a sign that says, *Don't mess with me. I'm Irish.*"

We laughed, but it wasn't funny, and we both knew it.

Kieran said, "Remember when we said we'd beat the crap out of kids that we didn't like?"

"Yeah."

"Did you believe it?"

"About as much as I believe I could be a star on the girls' rugby team."

"I know, but saying it made me feel good."

"Those two guys I was telling you about are scary. Shanese told me to stay away from them, and she's twice my size. I wish I knew how to turn invisible."

Kieran laughed, "Me, too. We could trip them or throw something at them, and they wouldn't know who was doing it. I thought I'd be different when I got bigger, but I'm not. Even though I'm going out for track, shaving my head, and doing Aikido, I'm still me. That sucks."

"I'm glad you're you. Who else will tell me I look like a girl?"

Kieran put his finger on his cheek like he was thinking about it and said, "Your mom."

We both laughed.

"Grandpa's coming to your mom's gallery opening, and I'm coming with him."

"Mama will be happy if Mr. O. shows up."

"Are you going to call Grampa Mr. O. forever?"

"Depends on how he acts. A real dad would come. A real grandpa would come. But Mr. O. might stay home because he stubbed his toe."

"You're tough, Kalayla."

"No, I'm not. If you were a jerk to my mama or me, I wouldn't be sitting here talking with you. If he keeps showing up, I might call him Grandpa in a few years."

THE SAME DAY: THREE-THIRTY IN THE AFTERNOON

Opa greeted me with her leash in her mouth. "You are the smartest," I said, giving her head and back a good rub. Walking to Lena's gave Opa a chance to pee and sniff, and I saw the trees and shrubs change shape when the wind blew their branches and leaves.

Lena was sitting on a little bench in the flower bed near her front door.

"Hey, Lena," I said, "are you planting yourself next to the flowers? Mama can make you a plaque saying *The Old Lady and her Flowers*."

Lena grunted and said, "I'm not in the mood for smart remarks. Mattwo made this cute little bench for me, but it needs a swivel seat and a hoist to get me up. Weeding is for the young, and I expect you'll want to help me."

Cow turds! That old lady was always finding ways to put me to work. When I didn't answer, she said, "You'll have plenty of time when school is out. Weeding will keep you off the streets."

Lena used the bench arms to push herself up, straightened, and said, "All right then. Let's take those puppies for a romp in the backyard."

Lena used the handrailing as she went up the stairs to the porch, and I was glad she didn't have to go up four flights anymore.

We went into the kitchen, and I opened the kitchen slider, and the dogs charged out, growling and circling each other.

We took our usual places on the patio.

"Have you figured out how to stay above water yet?" Lena said.

"Shanese is helping me. She said it was that or let me drown, and Grandma would boot her out if she let that happen."

"Smart girl."

"If you want me to pull weeds, could we do one of those barter things like I did with Rico for dance lessons? You know that guy Ray Ray? I need to hire him. Could you give me his phone number and tell him what a great kid I am?"

Lena was watching the dogs play, but her head whipped toward me.

"Weeding seems like a high price for one phone number," she said. "Why do you want to hire Ray Ray?"

"I want him to act like he's my friend."

Lena's eyebrows went up.

"He doesn't have to be my friend. I just want him and that monster dog to act like we're best buds."

"What has brought on this sudden need for a friends-but-not-friends arrangement?"

I could have said I wanted Ray Ray to help me train Opa to be a guard dog like Thor, but Lena wouldn't have believed that.

"I need him to scare off some jerks who might give me a hard time."

"Humm," Lena said. "I take it that means you've run into jerks like that?"

I nodded. "When I met Shanese at the high school. She cooled them down and told me to stay away from them. I've been thinking about what I'd do if I met them when I was alone."

"I can see how that could be a problem, and Ray Ray might be a solution. I'll contact him, explain the situation, and discuss his price for a fake bodyguard job. In return, you will be on call to weed the front and back gardens. Agreed?"

That meant I'd be sweating buckets while the old lady used a magnifying glass to find weeds. But any plan was better than no plan, and Ray Ray might give me a cut-rate deal if Lena called him.

"Yeah," I said. "Thank you."

"I'll supply the tools, and you can use my bench if you want to."

Fat chance I'd use that old lady's bench, but I smiled sweetly like I appreciated her generous offer.

A BODYGUARD?

Lotta told me the pluses of dog ownership when she pawned BB off on us, but she forgot to mention the downsides. We could leave dry food out twenty-four-seven for the cats, but BB's stomach didn't have a fail-safe shut-off. She gobbled anything marginally edible.

Two days after BB arrived, we left a steak defrosting on the kitchen counter while we went out for an errand. The remains of the Styrofoam plate were scattered on the kitchen floor, and BB was peacefully dozing in the corner when we came home. Lotta said Mattwo, as a former dog owner, should have known dogs were scavengers.

BB announced she was hungry this morning by whining and scratching on our bedroom door.

"It's your friend Lotta's fault we have a dog," Mattwo said. "We might as well get up. How about waffles?"

"Who's cooking?" I said.

"I'll handle waffles and coffee if you handle BB. Deal?"

"Deal."

I mixed half a can of dog food with a cup of dry, changed BB's water, waited forty-five seconds while she wolfed down her food, and opened the slider to the backyard. Mattwo stirred a cup of seltzer and cinnamon into the Belgian waffle mix, cooked the waffles to the right degree of crispness, and brewed two cups of Keurig's dark blend.

I soaked my last piece of waffle in Vermont maple syrup and said, "What do you think about Kalayla asking Ray Ray for help?"

"You took Ray Ray under your wing when he was a kid, so you know him better than I do. Sometimes, a show of force is enough. I'd guess one glance from Ray Ray probably will keep those guys away from Kalayla."

I trusted Mattwo's instincts. When Lotta decided married life wasn't for her, he convinced her first and second husbands they'd be happier if they divorced Lotta and left town.

I did have a long history with Ray Ray. His mother, Cindy Bingha, worked in a local elementary school cafeteria, and they lived in North Cambridge near Rindge Avenue in the Jefferson Park Projects. Cindy was from the Dominican Republic and shorter than I am. I never met Ray Ray's father, but giant genes must lurk in that boy's DNA.

I met Ray Ray at the Cambridge Boys' Club when he was ten. The Boys' Club was a lifeline for free-floating kids, and Ray Ray was a regular there. I helped with fund-raising and occasional math tutoring. Ray Ray was a whiz with numbers and quickly mastered every shortcut or tip I showed him.

When Ray Ray was sixteen, I told him he should plan on college, but he said, "All due respect, Mrs. Barzetti, but I like the street life. I've got other plans. I'd like to discuss a business idea if that's okay."

Ray Ray knew I had financed start-ups, but he was the youngest entrepreneur to approach me with an idea. Street businesses could include the risk of jail sentences and were not investments I'd consider making. I waited for Ray Ray to explain.

"I can pick up a tattoo business in Mattapan for a steal if I pay cash, but my cash flow is short."

Running a tattoo parlor wasn't on my veto list, so I said, "I take it you're hoping to secure a loan from me."

Ray Ray nodded. "Everyone says you're the go-to person for helping folks out."

"How much are we talking about, and how long will the payback be?" I said.

"A year tops with half paid in six months. If I do it sooner, I'd like a break on the interest. I could squeak by with ten K, but fifteen would make a site upgrade possible."

Ray Ray was asking for a drop in the ocean of monetary outlay. We settled on fifteen with a handshake. The boy paid half back with interest in six months, and true to his word, he paid the remainder four months later. Then, he switched from calling me Mrs. Barzetti to Miss Lena. I never was sure what to make of that.

I met Ray Ray in front of Mickey's. His chinos and t-shirt made him look taller than six feet five and strong enough to bench press a thousand pounds. As usual, his hair was in a neat ponytail. I'd have signed him to a long-term contract as a bodyguard if I needed one.

"What do you think of my new wheels, Miss Lena? This is the latest Chevy Silverado. You ought to see what it'll tow. If you want to move a house, I'm your guy," he said as he took my arm. "I had this two-step running board installed so someone your size could get in without any trouble. I ordered a special seat for Thor, too."

I got in his shiny black truck and was greeted by Thor, sprawled across the back seat.

"We have business to do," I said.

Ray Ray looked surprised. "Okay. How about we go to Fresh Pond Reservoir and take Thor for a walk?"

As we walked around the Reservoir, Ray Ray said, "You should have called me when you moved, Miss Lena. I have a moving business and would have given you a special rate."

I laughed. "I'm beginning to think you have more business interests than I do, Ray Ray."

"Oh, not more, Miss Lena, but a greater variety. If you need anything outside real estate or construction, let me know. I either have it or can get it."

"I need something, Ray Ray, but it involves a person. Do you remember the girl who was so hot to pet Thor a couple of years ago?"

"The skinny thing with the mouth? I haven't seen her in a long time. You told her to stay away from me, right?"

"Kalayla has enough ideas of her own. She doesn't need you to give her anymore. Yes, I did tell her to stay away from you."

"Miss Lena, you know I wouldn't bother anybody important to you. Besides, I can't see why anybody would be interested in her."

"You haven't seen her lately. She's on her way to being as beautiful as her mother and wants to hire you as a bodyguard."

"Hot damn! What do you know about that? Maybe she heard how good I took care of my sisters. I walked them down the aisle when they found the right guy."

"I want to make clear that you are not to do anything that might interest the police, no matter what Kalayla says."

Ray Ray looked pained that I would raise such a point. He said, "Miss Lena, you're hurting my feelings. Live and let live is my motto. Don't you know I don't get involved with anything that draws the wrong kind of attention?"

I didn't know any such thing. I heard rumors that a young man who grabbed Ray Ray's sister Mary in the ass wound up with an arm broken in three places. I also heard Mary had stopped her brother from cutting off the young man's balls. At least Ray Ray understood the ground rules regarding Kalayla.

"Give that little thing my phone number, and I'll help her when she calls. No charge."

"You have to charge her. She won't take handouts. I want you to meet her so you understand why she needs your services. Her mother's art is featured in a gallery show, and I'd like you to come to the opening. It's formal, so you have to wear a jacket. Don't look like I just skewered you. You looked quite handsome when you walked your sisters down the aisle."

Ray Ray smiled. "Not to brag, but you heard right. I love cookies, and my ex-girlfriend gave me a recipe for Thor's favorite biscuits. I'll take that as payment."

I bet Kalayla would make biscuits for the three dogs and trick Lotta into providing cookies for Ray Ray.

"Done," I said. "You can drop me at home. Mattwo will want to see this truck, and you can show him what it can do. We have a dog now, Ray Ray, and I don't want Thor going after her, you understand?"

"Ah, Miss Lena, have a little faith. Bullmastiffs are the best; this guy can be as gentle as a lamb. Can't you, boy?" Ray Ray stroked Thor's colossal head.

SHOPPING WITH LENA

When I left Lena's yesterday, she said, "Be ready tomorrow at 3:00. We're going shopping."

I went shopping for the old lady plenty of times, but she never went with me. I decided she was coming 'cause she loved aggravating me by doing stuff like setting her clock ten minutes ahead so she could say I was late unless I was early.

"What for?" I said.

She frowned like she was deciding which lie would shut me up.

"A dress," she said. "Mattwo will drive us into Boston, and we'll have an early dinner afterward. He wants a steak."

I didn't care what Matteo ate, and Lena didn't need me to help her pick a dress. If she was going to aggravate me, I was going to aggravate her.

"Why don't you wear one of those black dresses? Are you packing on pounds now that you're not going up and down stairs?"

Lena gave me a dirty look. "The dress isn't for me." She opened her front door, obviously wanting me to disappear.

"Oh, is Mattwo wearing dresses now?"

"For goodness sake! Mattwo is driving because he's afraid I'll put a ding in his car if I drive into Boston, which I might, accidentally, of course."

"If the dress isn't for you or Mattwo, who's it for?"

"You," Lena said.

"Me? When did you ever see me wearing a dress?"

"Never, but that doesn't mean you can't. It's for the gallery opening. You will not do, say, or wear anything that might embarrass your mother. And tell her we're taking you for dinner."

Yesterday, Mama asked if I thought Lena was getting old. I said the old lady was as bossy as ever, and this proved it. I stopped at Eddie's and told Mama Lena wanted her to go shopping tomorrow, but Mama said she had to work. Cow turds!

***

The ride to Boston was wicked boring. Lena and Mattwo pointed out stuff like I was a tourist who'd never been on Storrow Drive, heard of the Coca-Cola sign that went missing, or seen the Zakim Bridge and the Big Dig.

I got sick of it and said, "I know all that. Grandpa says they'll never finish the Big Dig—just keep adding to its cost."

"Harmon is a smart man," Mattwo said. "This might be the biggest boondoggle in Boston history."

Lena interrupted. "We're going to Copley Place. I suppose you've been there, too."

"Sure," I said. "Daddy took me to the library and the church, and then we got ice cream. The day we walked the Black Heritage Trail, it was so hot he carried me most of the way. We got ice cream then, too."

"We're not doing historic sites, and nobody's carrying you anywhere. We're going to Neiman Marcus and then to the Capital Grille so Mattwo can get his steak. Does that meet with your approval?"

I didn't bother to answer. That old lady wouldn't change her mind no matter what I said.

Mattwo drove away after he dropped us at this glitzy store. The inside was enormous, with high ceilings, mirrors everywhere, and enough spotlights to light up Harvard Square. I would have tried a few perfumes and looked inside some handbags, but Lena didn't give me a chance.

A mobile of wooden birds in flight hung from the ceiling next to the escalator. We went to the second floor, where a saleswoman was waiting. "Hello, Lydia," Lena said. "This is Kalayla."

Lydia nearly fell over with smiles, "It's a pleasure to see you, Mrs. Barzetti. I took the liberty of making a few selections, and now that I see Kalayla, I may add one or two more. Come this way, please."

Lydia led us down a center aisle, past displays of leather gloves, scarves, and clothes, then steered us to a private nook with a couple of chairs, a floor-length mirror, and a changing room.

"Is this your private dressing room, Lena?" I said.

292

Lena looked daggers at me, but Lydia said, "Oh no, Kalayla. This visit is an unusual pleasure for us. Normally, I take a selection of clothes to Mrs. Barzetti's office."

Good old reliable Lydia might be a suck-up, but she hadn't been dumb enough to lug clothes up the four flights even for her favorite customer.

Instead of barfing, I flopped in a super-comfortable chair and waited while Lena went through the rack and pulled out one dress at a time.

"Come here, Kalayla," she said. She held a dress under my chin. "What do you think, Lydia? I like the simple lines, but the champagne tone doesn't quite catch the hint of orange in her hair."

Of course, Lydia said, "I see exactly what you mean, Mrs. Barzetti. I have a scarf with champagne and orange highlights that would do the trick if we draped it across the scooped neck and capped sleeves. How does that sound, Kalayla?"

"Cover me with a tent if you want. You should have seen what I wore for my mama's birthday party." I said, hoping Lena appreciated how agreeable I was.

Lena laughed. "Kalayla dressed as a black-eyed Susan for her mother's thirtieth birthday party. That's Maureen's favorite flower."

"How sweet of you," Lydia said, smiling at me.

Yuck!

Lena handed me the dress and said, "Let's try it with the scarf, Lydia."

I was used to wearing clothes that didn't rate a first look and never got a second one. This dress was different. Mirrors on every wall of the dressing room drew attention to my breasts and buff arms, and the skirt shimmered when I twirled around.

When I came out of the changing room, Lena made me turn this way and that so she could inspect. Finally, she said, "Well, you don't look like a little girl anymore. Maybe we should unearth that black-eyed Susan costume."

"Here we are," Lydia said, returning with the scarf. "Let's drape it around your shoulders and across your bustline."

Lydia played with the scarf until Lena said, "The colors are perfect, and the scarf covers, ah, the dress looks better with the scarf."

"I was thinking dyed to match ballet slippers rather than heels," Lydia said.

"Perfect," Lena said.

"You look lovely, Kalayla," Lydia said.

"Yes, she does," Lena said in a tone that implied insisting I wear a dress wasn't the grand idea she thought it would be. That'd teach her not to stick her nose in my clothes.

As we walked toward the exit, I noticed a baseball cap with a price tag of a hundred and fifty dollars. Maybe I should ask Lena if Lydia could dye it to match the dress.

SUMMER 2001

TELLING KALAYLA AND RICO

The morning sun streamed in our living room windows but did nothing to brighten a grim conversation. Kalayla had been out of school for a week, and the gallery opening was a few days away. I finally decided no amount of rehearsal would make telling Kalayla any easier, and I was right. She was angry at Clarence but even more furious at me.

She jumped up from the sofa and glared at me. "You are unbelievable! Clarence tried to rape you, and you didn't tell anybody! What is the matter with you, Mama?"

"I told you. Clarence collapsed when Lena put the gun in his face, then Lena took charge, and Lucinda and Harmon picked him up. You just can't imagine how awful it was."

Kalayla stood with her hands still on her hips. "Oh, I get that part. What pisses me off is that anybody except you would have known what Clarence had on his mind. You should have warned him, told him if he came near you, you'd stick a pencil up his nose so he wouldn't have messed with you. Daddy said you give people a second chance, but what you really do is let them crap all over you."

Kalayla grabbed a book from the coffee table and threw it on the floor, startling Opa, who backed away barking.

Kalayla winced, dropped to the floor, and said, "Ah, Opa, I didn't mean to scare you."

Opa sniffed Kalayla's outstretched hand and then licked her face.

Kalayla put her arms around Opa, shaking her head in disgust, likely at me.

"Kalayla, I can't cut people off because they don't do what I want. People can grow and change like my father did. I hope Clarence will, too."

"Yeah, sure. Were you going to wait until that happened to tell me?"

Kalayla was right. I could have, should have told her months ago. "I don't know. I'm sorry, Kalayla. I don't know what else I can say."

"You don't need to say anything. I can ask a guy I know how much he'd charge to break Clarence's legs."

"No! Didn't you hear anything I said? I realize I need to do something, but what I do is my choice, not yours."

"That's right, but all you've done so far is think about it. Try doing something instead. If it doesn't work, do something else. Look, I've got to go. I'm meeting Shanese, and then I work at the shelter."

Kalayla grabbed her backpack, rubbed Opa's head, and said, "We'll go and see BB when I get home."

Kalayla opened the door, then turned and said, "I bet you didn't tell Rico about Clarence, either. Why would you tell your boyfriend something like that, right?"

Kalayla closed the door with a bang that was midway between an exclamation mark and a swear. On a scale of one to ten, with ten being outstanding, the conversation with her deserved a five or six. Kalayla didn't stop talking to me or take her sleeping bag and Opa to camp at Lena's. And she threw the book on the floor instead of at me.

All things considered, telling Kalayla went better than I expected. I didn't feel depressed and wasn't chastising myself for being a terrible mother. After talking with Rico, I'd ask Lucinda for advice on approaching Clarence. The conversation with him was the only one that frightened me, and I didn't want to think about it now.

AFTER DINNER

Rico and I had dinner with Lena and Mattwo at Merino's, an upscale Italian restaurant near Arlington, then picked up Kalayla from pet-sitting the menagerie at Lena's house. Once home, Kalayla announced that she was not interested in watching Rico and me play kissy face. "Besides," she said, "I already heard Mama's confession."

Rico said, "Kissy face sounds good to me. You can leave Opa as canine support if you think I need it to survive the confession."

"No way. Don't call us if you need help."

We settled on the sofa, and Rico listened without reacting. When I stopped talking, he said, "Kalayla's reaction must have been interesting."

"She said I should have told him long ago that I'd shove a pencil up his nose if he tried anything."

"That sounds like her."

Rico kissed the palm of my hand. "Look, I don't know how I would have reacted if you'd told me the day it happened. The dynamic shifted so fast from him as the villain to the victim that you and everybody else were stuck in a moral dilemma. I haven't faced anything like that in real life, but one of my professors gave us role-play situations with no-win moral dilemmas in college.

"I played a dad at the beach with his daughter, a good swimmer, and his niece, a mediocre one. A storm blew in suddenly, and both girls were far from shore and struggling. I had to decide who to save and justify my decision. It was like being squeezed in a vise."

I looked into Rico's clear, dark brown eyes and knew how lucky I was to have him in my life.

He stroked my cheek and said, "You took time to think it through. Have you decided what to do?"

"Kalayla and Lena both asked me that. I'm the tortoise trailing after the hares, but I am clear on one thing. Clarence has to take responsibility for his actions and do something to make amends."

Rico kissed me on the cheek. "I'd say the tortoise just crossed the finish line. The peanut gallery would like to suggest a reward of some serious snuggling. How does that sound?"

It sounded lovely!

THE GALLERY OPENING

JULY 1, 2001

I had everything under control except the weather. Yesterday, the temperature spiked to ninety-two, and the humidity was ninety-seven. The prediction for today was almost the same. I called the heating/air-conditioning contractor to check out the system. "Not to worry," he assured me. "It purring."

Then, I thought about the caterer's refrigerated truck with food that could spoil. But Lotta said, "Trust me, Lena. These folks are pros. They don't want the cannoli or key lime cheesecakes to melt or crostini with goat cheese and fig jam to sag."

No doubt Lotta was correct, but I asked the air-conditioning contractor to be on call, which annoyed Lotta, who said, "Don't get all dolled up to entice my brother. Maureen's artwork is on show, not you!"

"For your information, I am wearing an ankle-length silk navy dress with a matching three-quarter sleeve jacket with blue embroidery trim, plus my sapphire pendant and earrings. I hope you're not wearing fire-engine red?"

That set Lotta sputtering and made me happy I'd called.

* * *

Mattwo dropped me in front of the gallery, and I hurried inside to avoid a heat stroke. The caterer set up a drinks table near the foyer door. A calligraphy sign indicated snacks were available in the rear of the gallery. Piano selections from Michael Jones provided soothing background music. Three paintings had red dots showing art enthusiasts had purchased them at yesterday's private preview.

Business associates and friends mingled with family members like Lucinda, Harmon, Dominic, and JJ's family. Ray Ray wore a sports shirt, jacket, slacks and towered above everyone.

When he saw Kalayla, he said, "Hot damn, Miss Lena, I see what you mean. It'll take serious swatting to keep the flies away from her. The stunner standing beside her must be the Mama, right? The dude with her has his work cut out, too."

"Don't worry, Ray Ray. Maureen is in good hands. Rico is Mattwo's son. So, you see Kalayla's potential for trouble."

"No way to miss it, Miss Lena. I'll mosey over and schedule a time for Thor and me to talk with her."

"I hope you didn't leave that poor dog in the truck on a day like this!"

"Ah, Miss Lena, you know that puppy is happy and cool at home."

"Good. Would you like me to reintroduce you to Kalayla?"

"I expect she'll remember my unusual size, but she might be surprised at how fine I dress up."

There was no doubt about that.

A steady flow of guests came and went, and two more red dots appeared under Maureen's paintings. It did my heart good to see Lucinda, Harmon, Mr. O., and Maureen chatting. Kalayla and Kieran had staked out the snack table. Most guests were gone by five when Lotta strolled over and said, "What do you think?"

"I don't intend to say you're the best event planner I've ever met because another compliment would make your swelled head explode."

Lotta smiled. "And I won't mention Kalayla's appearance because your blood pressure couldn't stand it. You did notice that I switched from red to burgundy to please you, didn't you?"

I scoffed. "Yes, I did notice. It was sheer luck I didn't have a stroke when I saw Kalayla in the dressing room! Ray Ray needed to see what he was up against. I hope she goes home and changes—." I gasped and stared at the door.

I wasn't outside in the heat being treated to an optical illusion, and I wasn't tipsy from the non-alcoholic punch. Clarence was standing at the door wearing an Oxford shirt with rolled sleeves, pressed jeans, and loafers. His bald head was unmistakable.

Lotta touched my arm. "Lena! What's the matter?"

"Clarence just came in carrying a bouquet!"

"What!" Lotta whipped around. "Where in hell did he come from?"

I didn't know, and I didn't care. "You warn Maureen. I'll head off Kalayla."

Kalayla seemed to be lecturing Ray Ray, whose bulk blocked her view of Clarence. I stepped between her and Ray Ray, stuck my finger in her face, and said, "I am going to say something, and you will listen. Do you understand?"

Kalayla looked stunned, but she nodded slowly.

Ray Ray's voice came from behind me. "What do you need me to do, Miss Lena?"

"A gentleman with a bouquet is by the drinks table. Find out what he wants. Be friendly, but keep him there."

Ray Ray moved away, and Kalayla's expression changed from puzzlement to fury.

Kalayla was my size, but I learned long ago that size has nothing to do with power. My voice was soft, but Kalayla knew an order when she heard it. "I will take care of this. You will not say or do anything to spoil your mother's day. Turn around, go to the food table, and stay there."

Kalayla opened her mouth but swallowed her words, turned abruptly, and stormed toward the gallery's rear.

I had no idea how Clarence would react to me, but the conversation between Ray Ray and him seemed amiable enough. When I joined them, Ray Ray said, "Clarence, have you met Mrs. Barzetti?"

Clarence squinted. "You look like the landlady, except younger and more upscale. Are you the rich sister?"

Ray Ray tightened his lips to keep from laughing.

Lucinda told Maureen Clarence hadn't fully recovered, and I'd say that was an understatement.

"I am the landlady. I don't have a sister."

"Well, now," Clarence nodded, "Just shows what money can do. You could be the model for one of those before and after ads."

Ray Ray stepped toward Clarence but stopped when I touched his arm.

Clarence said, "Jamal would've given Maureen flowers for her big event, so I brought them for him."

Ray Ray watched me closely. "Clarence was saying how much he admired my truck," he said. "I was lucky to wrangle a parking spot out front."

"Cars are my thing, well, really anything with an engine and wheels is," Clarence said. "Maureen probably told you I keep her car tuned up."

For the first time since I sat down with my mother and heard her plan for my life, I was at a loss for words.

Lucinda, Harmon, and Mattwo joined our jolly threesome, saving me from looking like a tongue-tied dunce. Mattwo put his arm around my shoulder.

Lucinda said, "Clarence, we had no idea you were coming."

"I saw the flyers on your kitchen table. I thought you'd be glad if I came to represent Jamal."

Lucinda glanced at Harmon, who said, "We were just leaving. We can give you a lift."

"Nah," Clarence said. "I've got wheels. I want to see what Maureen's been doing, give her these flowers from Jamal, and check on my sweet little niece."

Lucinda shook her head. "Too bad you missed them, Clarence. Maureen was exhausted, and they—."

Nothing but trouble would come if Clarence went to Maureen's apartment and Rico greeted him at the door. Rico was his father's son. He'd protect anyone he cared about in any way he had to. Lies can come back to haunt you, but I didn't see any other way out of this mess.

"Your mother was about to explain that Mattwo and I moved, and Maureen and Kalayla are staying with us and our guard dog."

Ray Ray's eyes twinkled as he said, "Clarence, did you ever catch sight of my dog, Thor? He could rip the throat out of any mutt, but it shames me to say he rolls over when he sees Mrs. Barzetti's dog."

"Dogs aren't my thing," Clarence said.

"Why don't I give the flowers to Maureen for you?" I said.

Clarence hesitated, then handed me the bouquet. "That'd be better than throwing them in the trash."

Clarence gave Harmon a soft punch in the arm. "I'll catch you later, Pop. I don't plan to hang around long. Looks like they're ready to close."

After Clarence left, Lucinda said, "I told Maureen and Rico to take Kalayla out the back. Kalayla started to fuss, but Lotta shut that down fast."

After Ray Ray left, Lucinda took my hand. "I am so sorry, Lena. I never imagined Clarence would come."

"Our children are past the age when we can control what they do, Lucinda. Let's talk in a day or two."

"Well," I said to Mattwo when we were alone, "when it comes to last-minute surprises, I'd prefer a broken-down air-conditioner."

Mattwo laughed, kissed me, and said, "Let's go see our vicious mutt."

THE OPENING

When I said I wouldn't leave the gallery, Lotta would've dragged me out, but Rico said, "Now, Aunt Carlotta, Kalayla is mature enough to know this is the only way to save her mother from an embarrassing situation. Right, Kalayla?"

I glared at Rico. He knew I wouldn't wreck one of the best days of Mama's life.

When I opened the door and walked out, Lotta said, "That proves you're good for something, nephew. And Kalayla, I hope all those desserts won't keep you awake tonight. I expect to see you early tomorrow morning."

The old bat probably hid a camera near the food table so she'd know how many I ate! If I stayed, I could have practiced Aikido and kicked Clarence in the balls. But I didn't want to rip this dress.

On the way home, Rico squeezed Mama's hand and said, "How are you doing, honey?"

I couldn't hear Mama's answer, so I said, "I'm not a mannequin. It's rude to ignore me."

Mama turned around and said, "I would never ignore you, Kalayla. I told Rico I was shocked Clarence didn't tell anybody he was coming."

"I would have asked Clarence what he was doing there if you'd've let me. Those flowers might have been for my birthday," I said, knowing that would get Mama flustered.

"Kalayla, honestly, Clarence knows your birthday is in March."

"Maybe he forgot like he forgot to come to Grandma and Grandpa's house for Christmas. Are you going to punch Clarence when you see him, Rico?"

Rico snorted. "When was the last time you saw me punch anybody, Kalayla?"

"You've probably done a lot of stuff I haven't seen. You wouldn't have to punch him if Mama had grabbed Lena's gun and shot him, right?"

"If your mama had done that, instead of driving you home, I'd be taking you to visit her in prison. Life is not as simple as you would like it to be, Kalayla."

Yeah, that's what they all thought. None of them understood that sometimes the simple way was best. If I asked Ray Ray to chat with Clarence, I might be at the top of his flower-giving list.

AFTER THE OPENING

Kalayla charged into her room and changed into baggy shorts and a T-shirt. Opa waited at the door. I hoped Kalayla would leave Clarence to me, but I wasn't reassured when she said, "Don't worry, Mama. I won't take Opa with me when I go after Clarence."

I collapsed on the sofa next to Rico. He entwined his fingers in mine and said, "Saved by a back door exit! I'd say that was a close escape. Are you in a state of shock?"

"I'm mostly puzzled and angry. I don't know why Clarence would appear like that unless he intended to spoil my day."

Rico caressed my arm. I knew I could count on him for a thoughtful response.

"Frankly," Rico said, "I don't think a guy shows up with flowers if he's trying to spoil the day. If he planned to apologize, the flowers might be a peace offering. But Clarence said they were from Jamal, so your guess is as good as mine."

"He might not have intended to spoil the day," I said, "but he added a sour note."

"I only met Clarence, and it was clear he was suspicious of me and protective of you. That doesn't jibe with him assaulting you or showing up today with flowers. It makes me wonder if the guy has mental problems."

"Lucinda said the doctors were trying everything they could to get Clarence out of that immobilizing depression. The meds didn't work, but the shock treatments did enough so he could live with three other guys and go back to work. Do you think I should have stayed and confronted him at the opening?"

Rico shrugged. "That's hard to say. I don't think leaving was the equivalent of running away. Clarence picked the time and place to see you, and you decided his choice wasn't right for you. Facing him will be a major deal. You need to choose when, where, and how that happens."

"I could have called the police instead of calling Lucinda and Harmon. But I was terrified of making things worse. Clarence was in a helpless state, and who knows how the police would have reacted to a black man accused of assaulting a white woman."

"You did the best you could," Rico said, "and it gave Clarence a chance at recovery he might not have gotten otherwise. Nobody knew how to handle his arrival at the gallery. We just wanted to prevent an unpleasant scene."

I nestled my head against Rico's shoulder. "Thank you for helping with Kalayla. It would have been awful if she'd flipped out."

"If Lena hadn't sent Ray Ray to head off Clarence, Kalayla might have told him to take Clarence out and bash his face in. But, if she thinks Ray Ray will do whatever she says, she'll be disappointed. He's come to Matty's Way the last few years, and I've never seen him do anything against his better judgment."

I hoped Rico was right. All I wanted to do was curl up in his arms, savor the beautiful memories of the day, and forget about Clarence.

I suddenly realized I hadn't thought about what Jamal might have said or thought about Clarence. My heart was opening to Rico more each day, and for once, Kalayla and I agreed. I needed to focus on the present and cherish a new love.

TALKING WITH LUCINDA

Several days before July 4th, Mattwo said, "Dogs hate fireworks, and I've had some howl and hide in the bathtub all night. My goal is to prevent that with BB."

"Mattwo," I said, "We don't live across from a park or school playing field where people might set off fireworks. Most folks head to the banks of the Charles and watch the Hatch Shell display."

"That's fine, but I'm going to explain the July 4th fireworks celebration so BB knows there's nothing to be afraid of."

I smiled and gave him a quick kiss on the cheek. "Will she be required to take notes?"

"Mock all you like, but admit it: you're proud to have the most educated dog in the city."

"Let there be no doubt about that," I said, and off they went.

For the first time in years, I had a full house, which included a man, two cats, and a dog. That might be a winning hand in cards, but sometimes it felt like a six-lane highway squeezed into a hiking trail.

Today's high would be seventy-five degrees instead of the nineties as it was for the opening. Maybe a vengeful spirit like Joey stuck his nose in the weather to irritate me. Or, one of Maureen's Irish ancestors wanted to remind her how unpleasant the heat of hell would be.

If I still lived across the hall from Maureen, we'd be hashing over the highlights of the opening, but things had changed since we moved, and she'd gotten close to Rico. I missed our time together, but there was no point in struggling against the current, especially when you liked where it was taking you.

Lucinda had invited me for lunch. Their house was a typical Cape like Mattwo's and mine, with a fence around a large backyard. Luckily, I found a parking spot nearby.

Lucinda opened the screen door and called, "Hello," while I gawked at the lovely hydrangea bushes in front of the house.

"What a gorgeous blue!" I said.

"The hydrangeas are Harmon's hobby. He'd spend hours explaining the exact amount of coffee grounds, peat moss, compost, and grass cuttings he used on them."

I walked in the front door and smiled when I saw the treasures Lucinda and Harmon had accumulated over the years. This was a well-loved home where every nook and cranny told a story.

One wall section was devoted to photos.

"The family history?" I said.

"As much as we could account for."

A glass-covered flyer dated April 21st, 1851, cautioned the colored people of Boston about kidnappers and slave catchers.

"Hard times," I said.

"Worse then, but hard isn't over," she said. "That poster came out after the Fugitive Slave Act of 1850. Come and sit. I've got hot and iced coffee or tea."

When Lucinda saw me staring at a charcoal drawing of Jamal that dominated one wall, she said, "Maureen put her heart and soul into that. She gave it to us last Christmas and said it should go to Kalayla when we pass. We didn't put it in the exhibit. Some things are too personal for public viewing."

Lucinda understood as well as I did that you hold some things tight inside yourself. Without thinking, I said, "My twins died the way Jamal did without any warning. One minute, they were alive, and the next, they were gone."

Lucinda nodded sadly. She knew that pain as well as I did.

"Jimmy got the idea they'd be great soldiers and convinced Mikie they could con their way through the Marines. They talked a good friend, Bobby Valente, into signing up with them after high school. Bobby was the one who told me how the twins died."

I wasn't in good shape when Bobby came to the Brattle Street house that day. He rang the doorbell about ten times before I shuffled to the door. My vision was blurred, and I had to open my eyes wide to decide if I was looking at one person or two.

"You don't look so good, Mrs. Barzetti. Is this a bad time?" Bobby said.

Bobby's gravelly voice was unmistakable.

"That you, Bobby? No time is a good time." I pushed the door open, and Bobby limped slowly past me into the living room. He slumped on the sofa in front of the fireplace. Bobby liked the winter watercolor of the Rocky Mountains that hung above the mantel. I told him I'd leave it to him in my will, but he'd have to fight the twins for it. He wouldn't have to do that now.

By then, my eyes were working enough to see that Bobby looked like crap. He'd been a tall kid with a gymnast's build. The twins nicknamed him Flagpole and called him Flag for short. If they saw him now, they'd have called him Bones. His skin was as tight as cellophane against his skeleton, and his veins stuck out like he was my age. You could have mistaken him for a walking corpse, and maybe that's what he was.

I shuffled to the bar where I'd left the bottle of scotch I was guzzling, poured him a glass, and topped off mine.

"Here," I said, shoving the glass into his hand.

Bobby swirled it around, sniffed it, and mumbled, "Thanks. The sooner I pass out, the better."

He gulped down a third of it and carefully placed it on the coffee table. "Can't pass out before I tell you."

Bobby sat up straight and summoned his courage.

BOBBY'S STORY

We thought there was a chance the three of us would come home even if we were royally screwed up. Jimmy and Mikie said more guys got killed at night, so we marked the calendar first thing every morning. That morning, we had fourteen fucking days left.

Bobby's body was shaking, but he wasn't crying.

You know what they were like, Mrs. Barzetti. The two of them were a team. I was the tag-along.

Bobby's words stopped, but his shaking didn't. The alcohol that fueled me for the past five months dried up. My body felt misaligned, as if some parts were in the wrong place. But my ears worked, and I heard what Bobby said.

The minute the Huey landed in base camp, Mikie and Jimmy were listing everything that sucked about being there. At first, I thought they planned to complain, but I was wrong. Remember when they asked you to send manila folders? We cut it up to make cards. My printing was good, so I did the lettering with the two of them standing over me, giving directions. Mikie and Jimmy made up a game based on Poker.

Every card meant something. Putting stuff on a card was a way of giving 'Nam the finger so it didn't beat us down. The cards said stuff like f'ing mosquitoes, f'ing leeches, f'ing gooks, f'ing C-rations, f'ing mud, f'ing humidity, f'ing heat, f'ing rain, f'ing war protestors, f'ing politicians, f'ing generals, f'ing patrols, f'ing spider holes, f'ing shrapnel, f'ing jungle, f'ing Bouncing Betty landmines.

We had cards for stuff we missed or wanted, like soft toilet paper, a hot shower, juicy steak, guacamole dip, a lobster roll, an ear of corn slathered in butter, Mom's potato salad and fruit pies, R & R with a hot babe. The best card in the deck was Get Out of 'Nam Free. Getting that was a huge deal. It meant that even if your brain got fried, you'd go home with most of your body parts.

Guys who didn't get in the game watched and made side bets, and everybody had suggestions for new cards. Playing or watching made you feel closer to going home. Stupid f'ing game.

I got up, got a glass of ice water, and clung to the bank of the cesspool I'd been living in. The one thing I could do for Bobby was to listen. I'd have scotch for company after he left. "You three always could turn nothing into something," I said. Bobby's eyes lit up for a second.

Remember how we made up lyrics to tunes we liked? We did that in 'Nam when Neil Diamond came out with "Sweet Caroline."

Guys changed Caroline to a girlfriend like Jennifer, Abigail, or somebody they thought was hot. Not Jimmy. He decided we'd found our squad song, and at chow one day, he started singing:

Skank Vietnam
Good times never seemed so far
I was inclined
To believe they never should, would, could
But now
I stare into the night and am so lonely

Bad times never seemed so bad
I hoped they never would, should, could
Skank Vietnam,
Good times never seemed so far.

One by one, the guys chimed in. We were the worst-sounding group you ever heard, so bad the guys who weren't in our squad booed and cat-called.

We didn't care. We came up with variations, most of them rude and crude. Stuff like that kept us going.

Then Bobby got quiet. I was afraid I'd lost him, but he didn't reach for his glass. I think he was steeling himself to tell the worst part.

Mikie was hyper-aware of everything around him, saw things nobody else noticed, and was the best point for patrols. He was scheduled to be on that night without Jimmy, but those two could double-team and out-talk anybody. According to them, if Mikie was the point, Jimmy had to be rear security, so they made a Barzetti sandwich. We all thought we might stay alive if they covered front and rear. They were our good luck charm.

Day patrols were terrible, but night patrols were worse, and that patrol was the same as usual. It was hot and humid, and we were searching for VC activity, straining to see in the dark. You never knew if the sounds were real birds and animals or if some VC was messing with our heads before he blew us away with a buried Bouncing Betty. We were all afraid of making some asshole mistake that would get us and the other guys offed.

It was sweltering, and we'd have gone naked, but shirts kept our ammo bandoliers and rucksacks from rubbing us raw. That night, we were carrying light. I had hand grenades, a first-aid kit, C-rations, extra ammo, an extra bolt for my rifle, water, and chewing gum in my rucksack. I was sweating like a pig, and the mosquitoes were getting a free meal, but swatting them could give away our position.

We'd been out about six hours when torrential rain pelted us so hard I couldn't see the guy in front of me. Afternoon downpours were typical in the rainy season, but night ones weren't. We hunkered down, waited for it to pass, and hoped the VC didn't use this jungle f—k to sneak up on us.

The storm lasted about twenty minutes, and I knew Mikie was moving when the guy in front of me stood up. I was fourth from the front, walking blind, but I had to keep going. We all did. The birds started squawking and gave me the creeps. My boots sank into soft ground and squished through puddles.

Bobby dug his fingernails into his palms and drew blood, biting his lower lip.

Mikie screamed, "Betty," just before the force of the explosion blew me off my feet. When my hearing came back, I heard screaming in front of me. My leg was on fire, but I knew the guys in front were worse off.

Jimmy yelled, "Hang on, Mikie. I'm coming." He bolted past me, firing wildly. I saw him stop short, and his wail of grief was worse than the pain in my leg.

I dragged myself past the guy in front of me who was sobbing and holding the guy who'd been in front of him. Jimmy was standing beside what was left of Mikie's body. His wail turned into a roar, and he charged forward, firing as he ran.

Bobby's words were halting, agonizingly slow.

Jimmy ran flat out chasing the jungle demons. Suddenly he staggered, howled, "Mikie," and fell backward. He'd hit a trip-wire that hurtled a swinging mace, a ball with spikes, into his chest.

There wasn't anything we could do, Mrs. Barzetti. They were both gone, and we hadn't seen one f'ing VC. They vanished like ghosts and left us with three KIAs and two WIAs. The guys who weren't hit did what they could to move Jimmy and Mikie close to each other. It was a stupid ass thing to do, but that's what they would've wanted.

Bobby stumbled out of the living room, and I heard the front door close behind him. I got a bottle from the liquor cabinet. I didn't need a glass.

* * *

Lucinda's face was as sad as mine. "They should have been the ones to bury us."

I nodded.

We sat lost in our memories until Lucinda said, "I wonder if all boys are the same, pushing each other, competing."

"I don't know," I said. "But my four were always at each other for one reason or another."

Lucinda said. "That day at Fresh Pond bound Clarence and Jamal like a money plant with a braided stem. Nothing could pull them apart. Jamal was like your Mikie, aware of his surroundings and anticipating whether a situation might turn sour. Clarence was the only one who could get Jamal to override his better judgment.

"Clarence was fascinated by anything with wheels and was good with his hands. He hung out at the garage down the street and worked there part-time when he was old enough. The owner was a drag-racing fanatic. Clarence caught the bug but wanted to work on the cars, not race them. He told his boss Jamal was an ace driver, so he'd lend Jamal a vehicle. Jamal wasn't interested in racing but wouldn't say no to Clarence.

"When the tire blew, Jamal yanked the wheel to avoid hitting another car. He flipped over and was pinned underneath with a broken neck.

"Clarence called us, and we went with him to tell Maureen and Kalayla. Maureen was working in her studio, waiting for Jamal to come home. Kalayla was asleep, but she heard Maureen crying hysterically and woke up. When Harmon went to talk to Kalayla, she asked why her mama was laughing. Harmon had to explain that Maureen wasn't laughing. It was an awful night for all of us."

I felt Lucinda's grief spread through my body. We were women with different skin colors, family backgrounds, and education levels. And yet, we were connected in the most basic, visceral way as mothers who had their lost sons.

Lucinda shook her head as if in resignation and said, "We have so much pain to deal with along with the joy. Maureen's opening was wonderful until Clarence showed up, and everyone, including Harmon and me, was shocked. Our boy was oblivious to our reactions because he didn't recall anything about the incident with Maureen. When the drugs didn't help his depression, the shock treatments were a last resort. We knew there might be temporary memory loss, but nobody imagined he'd forget that."

Lucinda's sadness echoed through her words, and I could do nothing to ease it. I said, "Does Maureen know Clarence doesn't remember that afternoon?"

Lucinda shook her head. "The doctors said that specific memory loss wasn't unusual and shouldn't last long. Harmon and I hoped Clarence would completely regain his memory before he saw Maureen. Yesterday, we had to explain to Maureen, Kalayla, and Rico that he hadn't. And that we didn't know when he would."

"I don't envy you having to do that," I said.

"I could see we'd disappointed Kalayla. That girl wants the truth instantly, no matter what."

"Sometimes, she expects too much. I can understand why you waited. I might have done the same thing."

When I left, Lucinda and I hugged like two close old friends.

I drove home without putting a dent in Mattwo's car. I'd have to try harder next time.

WHO'S RUNNING MY LIFE?

Rico was crashing at the apartment, which was fine with me. Yesterday, I overheard him tell Mama, "If you guys move in with me, we'd have more room to spread out, and Opa would have the backyard."

Cow turds! Lena said it was rude to interrupt other people's conversations, so I went in and quietly said, "You two can move if you want, but Opa and I have to stay here. Lena and BB need us, plus the swim club, Animal Friends, and something Ray Ray's helping me with are in Cambridge. No insult to you, Rico. Your house and the yard are okay, but Watertown is practically in California."

Rico snorted, and Mama almost smiled.

Rico said, "Five miles is not as far as California, Kalayla. Watertown High School may not have a swimming pool, but the Boys and Girls Club does. Ray Ray has wheels, and Lena does too. You usually bike to Animal Friends, and living in Watertown will help you build up your muscles for swimming."

"I don't care. I have responsibilities you and Mama don't. Grandma and Grandpa might need me for something, too." I said.

That made Mama jittery, but I wasn't giving in this time.

"Layla, honey," she said, "you heard Rico starting a conversation, not ending it. Moving in together is a big decision. Rico and I have a lot to discuss before the three of us talk."

"Yeah, but Dominic said Lena wouldn't move more than eight blocks from us. And he was happy he didn't have to tear a house down and build a new one, but he didn't tell Lena."

Mama laughed. "That sounds like Lena and her brother. You do understand that nothing is changing right now, don't you, Kalayla?"

"Yeah, sure, I understand. Opa and I are going for a walk."

Mama said nothing was changing now, but a lot could change later. I bet Dominic could find a house for us in Cambridge. And if he couldn't, Opa and I might move in with Lena and Mattwo. No matter what, Mama had better bring Rico to Grandma's house on Friday nights so they'd get used to him.

* * *

Ray Ray pulled up in front of the apartment on Saturday morning, took the stairs three at a time. Mama insisted she had to see him. She shook his hand and said, "I appreciate your help at the Gallery. I made a bag of snacks Kalayla loves as a small thank you."

Wouldn't you know, when I told Mama that the combo of good old raisins and peanuts didn't make me vomit, she thought I loved it!

Ray Ray smiled and said, "Thanks, Mrs. LeeRoyce. I'll share with Kalayla."

Double cow turds! Ray Ray made it sound like he was babysitting me instead of working for me!

"Lovely," Mama said. "I was surprised by Kalayla's sudden interest in football, but thank you for taking her to the practice."

Ray Ray glanced at me. "No problem, Mrs. LeeRoyce. I was going, and your apartment is on the way."

I grabbed Thor's biscuits, rubbed Opa's head, and left before Mama could ask Ray Ray for his references.

Ray Ray pointed to his truck and said, "You're in the front seat."

As if I couldn't see that Thor was hogging the back!

Ray Ray waited until I buckled up before he said, "I take it your mama isn't aware of our arrangement."

"She doesn't need to know everything."

"True, but you don't strike me as a football type. Saying we were going to a soccer match or track practice might be more believable."

"I exaggerate, but I don't lie unless I have to. Most times."

Ray Ray nodded and, as he pulled away from the curb, said, "Good policy. It can save you a lot of explaining later on."

"When I told Lena I was making dog biscuits, she found three sizes of dog bone cut-outs, and Thor gets the biggest."

"Did you hear that, Thor? Kalayla made big biscuits for you."

318

Thor licked his lips.

"So, where's this practice?"

"Russel Field near the Alewife T Station. It's for guys who are trying to make the team. The fact you're with me will be all over the school by this afternoon."

"Will they say I'm your girlfriend?"

Ray Ray burst out laughing, slapped the steering wheel, and Thor barked.

"What's funny? I'm good-looking, smart, and have a great personality!"

"Mostly, you are a real piece of work," Ray Ray said after catching his breath.

"What do you mean by that?"

"I mean: a) I do not date girls your age, and b) I like women who are demure, shy, and dumb."

My jaw dropped, and Ray Ray smirked.

"Okay," he said. "Maybe not dumb and shy."

"Yeah, right," I said, " and probably not demure."

Ray Ray turned into the parking lot. "Now, let's get the ground rules straight. The goal is to make sure guys know you're off-limits. Clear?"

I nodded.

"Good," he said. "We'll walk over to the field, and I'll leave Thor and you on the sidelines. If some guy hits on you, Thor will take care of it. You will do nothing, and you will say nothing, understood?"

"You mean I just smile sweetly?"

"Smiling does not factor into this plan. Let's go."

Russell Field was gigantic, and kids were hanging out around the bleachers. They waved or called, "Hey, double Ray," as we walked by, like seeing him was a big deal. He waved back and called to a kid whose arm was in a sling, "Hey Ringo, how's it going?" The kid gave a thumbs-up and grinned.

Two girls wearing glittery-short skirts, spaghetti-strap tops, and spike heels came over.

The blonde whispered something into Ray Ray's ear. He laughed and said, "No way am I lying to your mama, Deanie."

Deanie grabbed her friend's arm, and they stomped off.

"What'd she want?" I said.

Ray Ray waved his hand like he was swatting a fly. "Do I strike you as the local gossip?"

Ray Ray knew everything and everybody, and it wouldn't hurt him to tell me a few things.

"You and Thor wait here," he said. "Take his leash."

I must have looked shocked 'cause Ray Ray said, "Don't get all puffed up. Thor knows who's in charge, and it isn't you."

"Can I at least pat him so it looks like I am?"

"Yeah, that'd be all right."

"Good boy," I said, barely touching Thor. "If some jerk bothers me, I tell Thor to bite him, right?"

Ray Ray sighed and shook his head. "Did you not hear me, Kalayla? You do not tell Thor anything! He knows what to do. Your job is to keep your mouth shut!"

I opened my mouth, but before I could say anything, Ray Ray said,

"If you do something stupid, you'll cause a problem. You hired me to prevent problems? Correct?"

I looked in the other direction, made another face, and said, "Yeah."

Ray Ray filled Thor's water bowl, gave him two of my world-famous biscuits, and handed me the bag of GORP and a water bottle.

"If you pig out on the GORP and vomit near Thor, he won't like it."

Cow turds! Now, I had to be careful not to offend a dog!

Ray Ray rubbed Thor's ears, said, "Guard, Thor. Warn," and strolled onto the field.

Players from both teams shouted at Ray Ray to start on their side. He took out a coin, flipped it, and pointed to the team on his right. One of the players yelled, "Heads," and Ray Ray joined their team.

The scrimmage was wicked boring unless you get a thrill from seeing boys dump each other on their butts. Ray Ray played every position, tackling, running, throwing, and kicking the ball. At halftime, he switched and played with the other team.

Thor focused on Ray Ray, so I decided to take a stroll. When I dropped his leash, Thor growled.

"Oops, sorry," I said, picking the leash up. "Don't you get tired of waiting for Ray Ray?"

Another low growl.

"Look, Thor, don't take this the wrong way, but you could be more friendly to somebody you're guarding. Just saying."

No comment from the canine.

Thor sat, and I stood beside him. Three guys walked along the sidelines and stopped near us. The shortest one took a step toward us and said, "Hey, girlie, want to earn a buck and give us a handful?"

Before I could blink, Thor was between the kid and me. His growl amped up ten notches, and his lips curled, showing his teeth.

The kid jumped back, put up his hands in surrender, "Whoa, big fella, no harm, no foul."

His two friends hooted with laughter. One of them said, "That's double Rays dog! You want to get your balls chewed off?"

The kid made a big show of bowing to me, "No insult, girlie. You're worth a lot more than a buck."

The three of them left shadowboxing and laughing.

After they were gone, I said, "Forget what I told you about working on your attitude, Thor. It's the best."

When Ray finally jogged off the field, I said, "About time. We could have been kidnapped by aliens and turned into robots by now."

Ray Ray rubbed Thor's head and said, "I know, boy, she is a lot to put up with, but she baked first-rate treats for you, right?"

As we walked to the truck, Ray Ray said, "Friday night games will start in about three weeks. We'll go to one of them to reinforce the message. Thor and you can sit in the stands while I circulate."

"I go to my Grandma's on Friday nights."

"Your Grandma and grandpa can come to the game. Or, we can make a show of leaving at halftime, and I'll drop you off at their house."

"Okay," I said. I would have told him I was sick of him bossing me around, but I had to ask him for something else.

"You know that guy Clarence you met at Mama's opening?"

"What about him?"

"He tried to get into my mama's pants, and I want you to break his arms or his legs, or maybe both."

Ray Ray frowned, but he didn't respond.

Finally, I said, "Did you hear me?"

"Unlike you, I do not have earplugs in my ears. What did your mama do when that happened?"

"Nothing, but she's a wimp."

"What did her boyfriend do?"

"It happened last November, but she didn't tell him or me until a few weeks ago."

"Okay, so once Rico knew, what'd he do?"

"Nothing."

"And did Miss Lena know about this?"

"She was there when it happened. She stuck a gun in Clarence's face, but she didn't pull the trigger."

"Has she done anything since?"

"Not that I know of, but there's a lot of stuff that old lady doesn't tell me."

"Well, if your mama, her boyfriend, and Miss Lena didn't do anything, there must be a good reason. That means I won't break Clarence's legs, arms, or little fingers. This is not your business. Now, stop yapping so Thor can catch a few zzzs. Guarding somebody like you takes a lot of energy."

Ray Ray was as useless as Mama, Rico, and Lena. Kieran would help, but he couldn't be on the track team if we went to jail. What a pisser!

WAITING FOR MARK

Mattwo and I sat at the kitchen table after lunch, the crumbs of tuna sandwiches and potato chips on our plates. On summer days like this, BB basked in the two-sided warmth with patio tiles under her and the sun above. When the sun was too hot, she retired to the coolness of the Privet hedge, where she pretended to doze to lure a squirrel or chipmunk out for a game of chase.

"You'd think that dog was lazy if you didn't know her," Mattwo said. "Looks can be so deceiving. And speaking of deception, what do you suppose Kalayla has on her mind? Yesterday, she asked me if I had a bat, a golf club, or a hockey stick she could borrow. I'm certain she's not taking up any of those sports."

Huh! I knew that girl was up to no good!

"Maybe she thinks she needs to defend herself. Do you think they'd allow pepper spray in the high school?"

"Better you don't ask. What you don't know won't worry you."

"Yes, it will." I got up, put the plates into the dishwasher, rummaged in the cookie jar, and offered Mattwo a peanut butter cookie.

"Only one?" he said. "That's pretty cheap!"

I pointed at his gut.

Mattwo slapped his slightly bulging belly. "You've shamed me into working out. I'll harass Rico and dip into Jen's stash of treats behind the front desk. And in this case, what you don't know won't hurt you."

"Why don't you take BB when you pick up Mark at the airport? He always wanted a dog, and hanging out with BB might revive his interest."

"Will do, sweetheart. I'll pick her up after my workout."

After Mattwo left, I checked the guest bedroom. The cats liked using the twin beds as a playground and leaving a duvet mess. Mark was the neatnick of the four boys, and the tidiness in his Denver house showed that trait was alive and well.

I'd decorated the guest room with a Western theme. The duvets were a mixture of orange, turquoise, white, and beige. The room's centerpiece, an impressionist watercolor of the Grand Canyon, hung between the beds. Two Kokopelli figures playing the flute decorated the wall opposite the window.

Everything was ready to welcome Mark home for the first time in twenty-five years. He'd come for Joey's funeral and carried his father's casket with his three brothers but was gone for good before the twins died. He'd found solid ground in Denver with the Rocky Mountains protecting his back.

Was Mark as nervous about his homecoming as I was?

What was he thinking as the distance between us shrank to nothing?

Nothing was the same as it was when Mark lived here. Joey used to introduce him as the weak link in his chain of boys. JJ was his father's right hand, the twins were two sides of the same coin, and Mark was the odd one out. He never fit into Joey's world, but there was more than enough room for him in mine. I hope he felt that way, too.

SAYING YES

Midnight was quiet in this part of Cambridge and a good time for working in my studio. I heard a double knock, and the door clicked open. Rico stuck in his head, "Any brilliant and gorgeous artists hanging around here?"

I laughed. "Did you come here to help or just work your wiles on me?"

"Both," Rico said. "but it'd be more fun if my wiles came first and the work later."

I screwed up my nose. "But we'll have to empty the crates later."

Rico saluted and said, "True enough, ma'am, but you can be a real killjoy sometimes. Kalayla and Opa are asleep, so let's get this finished."

The watercolors, charcoals, and photography were in crates stacked along the studio wall. Lena and Nicole had them transported to the gallery, and Rico planned to borrow a truck so we could bring them back here.

When Kalayla overheard us discussing the logistics, she said, "Don't bother getting a truck, Rico. I asked Ray Ray to help. He loves showing off his muscles and his truck."

"Ray Ray is not a show-off, Kalayla," Rico said.

"You didn't see him on the football field. He took all that stuff to the gallery for free, but Lena probably had his truck detailed, and Thor groomed if she could find a groomer dumb enough to touch him."

The only chore left was unpacking the crates.

"Can I talk, or will my sexy voice be too distracting?" Rico said.

I slapped him on the arm. "Of course, you can talk, you fool."

"Good. So, let me ask you again. Do you want to move into my place, or should we look for a place in Cambridge?"

"Honestly," I laughed, "you are getting to be a one-note type of guy."

"When we settle this, I'll expand my repertoire."

Rico was right. I couldn't keep postponing this discussion, but if he wanted kids, it would mean the end of our relationship. I couldn't bear that.

"Maybe we should sit down," I said.

"Ouch! That sounds ominous."

"I have to ask you a question."

"Okay," Rico moved his chair closer to mine. "So, what's going on inside that beautiful head of yours?"

"It wouldn't be right to let you think or expect that we, I mean-."

"Maureen," Rico interrupted, "you don't need to explain why you have the question and what it might mean. Please, just tell me what it is."

So I did. "Do you want to have biological children? I've been putting this conversation off because I'm afraid of your answer. Because I can't have more children, I mean, I could, but I don't want to. I wouldn't change having Kalayla for anything, but I'm not the woman for you if you want kids to carry on the Eccli line. No matter how much I care about you, I can't change how I feel."

Tears were running down my face. "You should have what you want, Rico. I know you love Kalayla, but she's not in the Eccli bloodline."

Rico sat back in his chair and shook his head. "Whoa, you've got a boatload of assumptions in that simple question. Let's take this one step at a time. Do you have any doubts about how I feel about you?"

"No, I don't, but—," I said.

Rico gently put his fingers on my lips. "No buts. You know I'd like to spend the rest of my life with you, right?"

I nodded.

"Then the only question is whether you want to spend the rest of your life with me. Do you?"

I nodded.

Rico grinned like he won the lottery without buying a ticket, leaned over, and kissed me.

"I'm pretty sure the fact that I'm not married and raising a family makes my dad wonder what the matter is with me. But I took a lesson from my Aunt Lotta. She told me her mistake was trying to be a wife because other people expected her to do that. I'm not making that mistake. I work with kids, and that's enough for me.

"I've had plenty of girlfriends, but until I met you, there wasn't anyone I wanted to be with for the rest of my life. And until I met Kalayla, the idea of taking on the chaos and responsibility of a kid wasn't in the cards. That's changed. Having the two of you is a solid gold twofer in my book. So, I will ask you for the last time: do you want to move in with me, or should we look for a house around here?"

I couldn't help laughing. "You mean if Kalayla won't come, the deal is off?"

Rico tweaked my nose. "I'll take you any way I can get you, but don't worry, no matter how much posturing Kalayla does, she wouldn't let you move without her. She's single-mindedly protective of you."

I kissed Rico's hand and said, "Let's find a place in Cambridge."

"Well, it's about time," Rico said. He stood up and pulled me into his arms. "I know—the crates! But we have to celebrate the fact that we've had a conversation that Kalayla didn't overhear!"

We whirled around the studio, and then we unpacked the crates.

*　*　*

I couldn't stay in bed for another second. I left Rico sleeping, grabbed a robe, and went into the kitchen where Kalayla was feeding Opa. I felt like jumping up and down, shouting with joy.

"You're up?" she said, more as an accusation than a question. "What's wrong?"

I couldn't keep the grin off my face. "Everything is wonderful."

Kalayla narrowed her eyes. "Where do you plan to live?"

"Here in Cambridge, if we can find a place."

Kalayla threw one arm in the air, shouted, "Yes!" and hugged me. "I've got Lena and Dominic on it."

"Kalayla, Rico and I can find—."

Kalayla interrupted. "No offense, Mama, but if Rico waits for you to decide where the perfect house in the perfect neighborhood is, I'll be thirty-five, and he might be dead. And Opa might not be able to get up the stairs."

"Oh dear God, Kalayla, how can you say such things? Rico isn't going to die!"

"How do you know? Daddy died, and waiting around gives bad things more time to happen. I'm dropping off Opa at Lena's before I go to Animal Friends. She'll find a house for us by next week, and Dominic will be thrilled because he'll have this apartment and the studio to rent. Come on, Opa."

I watched Opa bound after Kalayla, defying Kalayla's prediction that she was on the edge of infirmity.

I'd call Lucinda and Harmon later. Kalayla would tell Lena and Lotta, but I'd call them too. Rico would tell his dad. I'd stop over at The Eatery. I could call my father now. He was probably having coffee and reading *The Boston Globe* before he and my mother went to nine o'clock Mass.

But first, I wanted to enjoy my coffee and savor this joy. I never thought I'd be so happy again. How could one woman be so incredibly blessed?

GETTING ADVICE

Matty's Way was closed on Sunday, but Kieran and I met there anyway. I was sitting against the side wall at the entrance when Kieran showed up in a green t-shirt that said Sandalwood Driving Range. "Why'd you ditch your Yum Yum's t-shirts?"

Kieran made a face. "Kevin's friends kept hassling me for ice cream and were going to get me fired. They think golf is lame, so I quit and got a job at a driving range. I pick up golf balls and put them in a washing machine. It's boring, but the pay isn't bad."

"Col never stops, does he?"

Kieran shrugged. "His friends won't, and he can't tell a friend from a yellow jacket. What's new with you? Learn any cool stunts?"

"I'm pretty sure I won't drown. Shanese says I'm not as bad as I used to be, and she's as picky as my step dance teacher."

Kieran slid down the wall opposite me. His legs were so long that our feet almost touched.

"Your mom's art show was awesome. Did Grandpa tell you we went again before it closed?"

"I haven't talked to him. Why'd you go again?"

"Grandma wanted to see it. Grandpa asked me in case he needed help."

"So?" I said.

"So we went."

As if that explained anything! "And what happened?"

Kieran puffed his cheeks out and blew out the air.

"I probably shouldn't have said anything. It's not like Grandma is your favorite subject."

"But you did, and now you have to keep going. What happened?"

"Grandma was in a hyper mood, like she was super nervous when we were driving there. Grandpa was his usual self. He said he'd walk around the gallery with her, but Grandma didn't want him to. When she got to the photo collage *Colleen's World*, I thought she'd stay there the rest of the day."

Colleen's World was Mama's experiment with photography, and I hated it. Three black-and-white photos shrouded in mist gave it a creepy feeling. Two photos were side by side on the top half, one of Daddy fixing a wheel on my tricycle and one of Daddy and me making a snowman. The bottom half had a single photo of an empty grave with a pile of dirt beside it in a deserted cemetery.

When I told Mama it was too depressing to hang in her show, she said, "Life is what it is, Kalayla."

Yeah, but she didn't have to call attention to it, did she?

"What happened then?" I said.

"Grandma said she wanted to leave and didn't say anything on the ride home."

I didn't know what to say, so I changed the subject. "What kind of weapon do you think I should take when I see Clarence?"

"Jeez, Kalayla, do you really need to talk to him?"

"Somebody has to, and I'm sick of waiting for Mama to do it."

Kieran grimaced. "I get that. I don't see how adults can ignore important stuff like that. Grandpa acts as if nothing is wrong with Grandma, and my dad never mentioned your mom until after I met you. How does that make sense?"

"It doesn't. I'm willing to tell Clarence what he did if he doesn't remember, but I need to protect myself if he gets mad. Could you borrow a golf club from the driving range? Or do you think a bat would be better?"

"Wouldn't Clarence wonder why you had either of them?"

"I could say I'm trying out for the girls' softball team, but he wouldn't believe I was taking up golf. A hammer might be better."

"Those are terrible ideas, Kalayla. What if I come with you? We could double-team him. He'd be so surprised he might faint, which'd give us a big advantage."

When Kieran stood up, I realized he was as tall as Clarence, and I could see his muscles. The two of us would be better than me alone, but it wasn't fair to get Kieran in trouble.

"I appreciate the offer, Kieran, but it's my problem. Anyway, I have to find Clarence before I do anything."

"The two K's have to stick together!" Kieran grinned. "Col keeps his baseball equipment in his closet, and it's a spring sport. I can borrow his bat and return it before then."

We gave each other a high-five.

Now, all I had to do was find Clarence.

MARK'S PARTY

I never was one to bite my fingernails, but Mark's party was making me reconsider. In the old days, I would have been sipping wine, but alcohol proved it was no friend of mine. BB and the cats sensed my nervousness, which didn't do a thing to calm me down. They should have been napping, not eyeing me.

When I told Mark I hoped he wouldn't mind meeting new people, he said, "Ma, I'm used to new. Don't be nervous. I love cookouts, and I promise I won't get in a fight or go sulk in a corner. I'm a big boy." He smiled and pinched my cheek.

"I'm not worried about you," I said. "I'm worried about me."

"Your house is clean, you have enough food for fifty people, and if anything is less than perfect, Mattwo will still love you. What's to worry?"

What's to worry, I asked myself.

I'd faced a thousand business situations with tough negotiations, but that was a mind game calculating numbers, projections, loss, and gain. There weren't heart risks in those situations.

But today, I felt like an anxious old woman.

What if Lucinda and Harmon weren't at ease with Rico?

What if JJ didn't recognize the business acumen that propelled Ray Ray out of poverty?

What if Amelia was aloof with guests who didn't wear diamonds and gold like her country club friends?

What if Lotta pressured everyone to adopt homeless animals?

What if Dom insisted that Mark needed to see the rest of the family?

What if Ronnie and Kalayla behaved outrageously?

The front screen door banged, and Kalayla interrupted my worries by calling, "We're here, BB!"

Opa beat Kalayla into the kitchen, scattered the cats, and launched into a wrestling match with BB.

"Get those dogs out of my kitchen right now!" I said.

"Okay, okay," Kalayla opened the slider for the canine charge. "So, you know how you told me who you invited to the party?"

She meant that she insisted she had to know who was on the guest list. "Yes," I said.

"Well, you know thirteen is an unlucky number, right? So to be sure you didn't have bad luck, I invited Ray Ray. I knew you'd have enough food for an army, and Ray Ray likes to eat, so it's a twofer. You get good luck and don't need to worry about leftovers. Smart, huh?"

I was not a numerology follower. The number thirteen didn't give me the jitters any more than the number four, also a sign of bad luck, would have.

The excellent news for Kalayla was that her impertinence did not cause my ears to smoke. "Don't try and pass that bad-luck baloney off on me. You had a reason for inviting Ray Ray. What was it?"

"You won't tell him he can't come, will you?"

"That depends on whether you tell me the truth and whether it makes any sense."

Kalayla scowled. "I invited him in case Clarence shows up. Ray Ray can take him home or something."

I didn't intend to ask what 'or something' might be. "Why do you think Clarence would come here?"

"He came to the gallery."

"Kalayla, that was a public event. This party is private, and it is not up to you who should or shouldn't be invited to a party unless you're the hostess."

"I promise I won't do it again, but please don't kick out Ray Ray."

Honestly! The mature version of Kalayla wasn't any easier to deal with than the immature one. "I will not kick him out."

"Good," she grinned. "I'll be with Opa and BB if you need my help with anything else."

Lucinda, Harmon, and Ray Ray arrived simultaneously, and when I called down to Mattwo, he said, "Send the men down here. Mark and I are problem-solving."

Half an hour later, the men were in the basement, and the ladies gathered in the living room except for Ronnie, who was outside with Kalayla. Ronnie's sister, Juliana, had called to say she'd been invited to a fabulous weekend on Nantucket and couldn't come.

Amelia, Lucinda, and Maureen were chatting about the pros of marriage, and Lotta was holding her own about the cons. I knew they'd ask what Mattwo and my intentions were, so I went to the slider and called the girls.

"Get the men up here, or we'll never eat. Then, put the snacks and surrounds on the table and bring more chairs."

The cookout menu was simple. Mattwo and Harmon would grill chicken, baby back ribs, sausages, and corn on the cob. Lucinda made a potato salad, and I made a four-bean salad. JJ's wife, Amelia, made a guacamole dip for veggies and chips. Maureen and Rico delivered a cooler with soft drinks and beer. Lotta made strawberry shortcake.

Mattwo and Harmon were grilling when I strolled over. Mattwo grumbled, "Don't let either of those two girls set foot in my shop without my permission again!"

Harmon smiled. "The girls bombarded us with questions, picked up tools, wanted to know what each machine did and how it worked. Mattwo finally shouted, 'Out! Right now, out!'

"Ronnie looked at Kalayla and said, 'If we were boys, they'd be falling all over themselves to teach us. This is a perfect example of gender discrimination!'

"Ronnie then informed us she plans to be a civil rights lawyer, and we wouldn't be able to get away with keeping girls from working in a woodshop. JJ looked like he was ready to grab a board and paddle her. If he had, she'd probably have accused him of parental abuse."

I said, "We may rue the day those two met. They'll be suing everyone in sight!" At the moment, Ronnie and Kalayla sat on a blanket with Mark and the dogs near the back fence looking as innocent as could be.

I was about to see what mischief they were hatching when Ray Ray came over and said, "Thanks for inviting me, Miss Lena. Kalayla told me she was helping out."

I snorted, "I expect by now you know about Kalayla's idea of helping out."

"The kid is funny. When we're alone, she's all mouth, but she clams up when other people are around. When she comes with me, she wears old lady clothes—no offense meant, Miss Lena—and a baseball cap. Nothing like what she's got on today."

Kalayla wore dark orange tight shorts, a lighter orange cami, and a loose-fitting black blouse. Ronnie wore similarly fitting white shorts, a white cami, and a snug red blouse. Both wore flip-flops. They were the epitome of vibrant young women who could be on the cover of a teen magazine. Lord, spare us that!

Seeing them together made me wonder if we should consider sending them to a nunnery for the next few years. They could keep each other company and test the Mother Superior's self-control.

"Did Kalayla mention Clarence to you?" I said.

Ray Ray shook his head. "Nope. I told her he was not a concern of mine and that she should butt out of adult business."

"Good," I said.

Mattwo called, "All right, line up. Let us know if you want a toasted bun."

Mark had been circulating and touching base with everyone. He pulled up a chair next to Ray Ray, Lotta, and Dom, and I heard them comparing curb-side and recycling center drop-offs in Colorado and Massachusetts.

Mattwo and I sat at the patio table with Lucinda, Harmon, JJ, Amelia, Maureen, and Rico. Ronnie and Kalayla plopped beside BB and Opa again.

We were finishing dessert when Kalayla tapped on the table and said, "Attention, everyone. Ronnie and I have a suggestion that you're all going to love!"

I sucked in my breath. No way in hell we would all love any idea those two girls had.

Ronnie said, "Mark and his partner Frankie can't get married in Colorado or Massachusetts, but they could have a Civil Union ceremony in Vermont. Kalayla's mom and Rico could get married there, and so could Grandma and Mattwo. It'd be a triple wedding. Isn't that a brilliant idea?"

The reaction to their brilliant suggestion was stunned silence. Mark's surprised expression told me they hadn't revealed their plan to him. I had no idea if a Civil Union performed in Vermont would be legal in Colorado. The girls hadn't asked if Mattwo and I had a plan, and I doubt they'd asked Maureen and Rico!

The silence didn't deter Kalayla from throwing open her arms and shouting, "Let's have a cheer for the younger generation and their fabulous idea! Hip, hip, hurray!"

Rico, Mattwo, and Lotta burst out laughing. JJ looked like he wanted to strangle his daughter, and Maureen's shocked face was so funny it made me laugh.

By that time, everyone except Kalayla and Ronnie were laughing.

Ronnie glared at us and shouted, "I researched gay rights and found out last summer Vermont was the first state to legalize Civil Unions."

"That's right," Kalayla shouted. "Girl power rocks!"

The raucous laughter got louder. You'd have thought we were at a kids' party, and Snoopy just burst out of the birthday cake!

The triple-wedding idea was a dud, but Ronnie's and Kalayla's enthusiasm was a beacon of light. I felt like giving each of them a hug and kiss.

Before I got the chance, Ray Ray hauled himself out of the lounge chair, strode to Kalayla and Ronnie, stood between them, and sang in a booming bass voice, "They are the champions. Not the losers. They are the champions of a new world!"

Not everyone knew the song made famous by Queen in the late nineteen-seventies, but Lotta and I did. When it came out, I was battling for control of Manzetti Properties, and she was searching for funding for Animal Friends. It became our theme song, our way of saying we would never give up. I hoped they wouldn't, either. The girls must have read my mind because they threw fists in the air and cheered.

I couldn't have asked for a better ending to the party!

LATE SUMMER 2001

THE SUMMIT MEETING

When I answered the phone, my father said, "Your mother wants to see you," I thought he must have dialed the wrong number, so I didn't say anything.

"Maureen," Daddy said, "are you there? Your mother wants to see you."

That was as believable as if he'd said he won the Nobel Prize in chemistry for turning an apricot into a shower curtain. Why would my mother want to see me? Had she been looking through her folder of birth certificates and suddenly discovered she had a daughter named Maureen?

"Maureen, I know you heard what I said."

Yes, I had. I should be thrilled that Colleen was reaching out to me, shouldn't I? But I felt like shrugging my shoulders and saying, "So what?" It was as if I'd opened a card that said "Love from Santa" after I stopped believing in Santa Claus.

I remember reading *Gone with the Wind* and being so disappointed when Scarlett O'Hara finally realized she loved Rhett Butler, but he no longer cared.

I understood how he felt. Even the most stubborn desire can fade.

My mother's feelings had changed, but so had mine. Regardless, if I turned my back on her, I'd be doing to her what she'd done to me.

"All right," I said, "if that's what she wants."

"We can meet you at Eddie's, so you don't have to drive," he said.

Eddie's was too close, too personal.

"That doesn't work for me," I said. "Why don't we meet at the IHOP on Soldier's Field Road?"

"Okay," Daddy said. "We'll meet at the old haunt. Your mother and I haven't been there for years."

Neither had I. Evidently, my mother had chosen a different gathering place for the family breakfast ritual after Sunday Mass.

When Rico came home after officiating at a regional Karate tournament, he said, "Hey, beautiful, how was your day?"

"You won't believe what happened."

He held me at arm's length and said, "Let me say goodnight to Kalayla before we talk, okay?"

I nodded. Rico knocked on Kalayla's door, and a few minutes later, he flopped on the sofa, took off his shoes, put his feet on the coffee table, and said, "So? Was what happened good or bad?"

"I'm not sure, but I think it was good," I told him about the call.

"Whoa! The rock and the hard place are going for pancakes and eggs! That's a huge deal!"

"So which am I—the rock or the hard place?"

"M'Lady, as long as you're on my side, you can be whichever you like."

"Come on, Rico, you make me sound scary."

"Scary? Well, let me see." He gently turned my head to the side. "Nope, nothing scary there." He turned my head to the other side. "Oh, wait a minute. Your left jaw is quite intimidating."

"Stop teasing me!" I said, slapping his hand away.

"May I prove my point by saying you were willing to take on your mother and the world when you married Jamal? After he died, you worked two jobs to care for Kalayla and didn't give up your passion for art. I'd say you are a formidable woman."

I punched him in the arm. "Why do you think my mother wants to see me?"

Rico smiled, "I don't know. What do you think?"

"Maybe Daddy told her we're getting married, and she wants to see if you're a good Italian Catholic who'll save me."

"That's one interesting idea."

I took a deep breath. "The possibility of seeing her makes me feel off-balance like I'm walking on an uneven path and might trip."

Rico said, "Maybe after she saw the images of Kalayla at the gallery, she decided she wanted to meet her granddaughter. How would you feel about that?"

"Family is too important to me to say no, but Kalayla might. She's old enough to make that call herself."

***

My father suggested an off-time so the International House of Pancakes wouldn't be crowded. When I pulled into the lot, I saw his dark blue Buick sedan parked near the front door with a handicapped sticker hanging from the dashboard mirror.

The IHOP looked as I remembered, with its bright blue roof and Open 24/7 sign on the door. I opened the door, and cool air surrounded me. I assumed my father and mother would be in the area reserved for customers waiting to be seated. They weren't.

My father waved from a nearby booth and called, "We're over here."

My mother was facing me, but I barely recognized her. She had been the most beautiful woman in the world. My stomach churned when I saw how she had changed. Her once flawless complexion was sallow, and her skin sagged as if it hadn't adjusted when she lost weight. She looked older than Lena. A walker with a seat and basket was tucked next to the booth.

My father stood while I slid in opposite him and my mother. They each had mugs of black coffee—straight up, my father used to say—next to their water glasses. A closed menu, a glass of water, and silverware wrapped in a dark blue napkin were on my side of the table.

My mother said, "We've ordered. I wasn't sure you'd come."

"I said I would. The water is fine. I'm not hungry." I pushed the menu to the table's edge.

"This is a restaurant," my mother said. "They make a living by selling food. You should order something."

"I didn't come here to argue about food, Mother. Daddy said you wanted to see me. I came to find out why."

She blinked several times when I said Mother instead of Mummie. That was what my siblings called her, what I stopped calling her when our homegrown version of the Troubles started.

"You have a daughter, and you're getting married," she said.

"Both of those things are true," I said without moving.

"Of course they're true. I don't lie," my mother said, holding her feelings in check. This was a new side of her. Angry explosions followed by withdrawn silence were the norm for her, just as shouting and storming out were the norm for me.

My father touched my mother's hand. She took a sip of her coffee.

"It's cold," she said.

The waitress appeared with a coffee carafe as if summoned by her words. "Your food will be right out." She turned to me, "What can I get for you?"

I waved my hand and shook my head.

"She'll have two pancakes with link sausage and extra syrup and butter in a takeaway box," my mother said.

I took a sip of water.

Rico would say the rock had met the hard place.

After the waitress left, my mother said, "Your fiancé is Catholic. His step-daughter should attend a Catholic school, make her First Communion, and be Confirmed."

My guess about why she wanted to see me had not been far wrong. She hoped Rico would be responsible for doing what I hadn't.

"Kalayla is going to Cambridge Rindge and Latin," I said.

"Nonsense. The girl was born a Catholic. She needs a proper education."

I didn't come here to be sucked into an argument, but I couldn't help saying, "No one is born a Catholic. Kalayla has her own beliefs."

Kalayla no doubt did, but I had no idea what they were. For all I knew, she could be a Protestant, Catholic, Buddhist, pagan, atheist, or rock worshipper. Jamal and I hadn't discussed religion with Kalayla. After he died, Kalayla and I stayed with Lucinda and Harmon, and they took her to their church.

My mother slapped her hand on the table, rattling the mugs and water glasses. "A parent should give children a religious upbringing."

"Colleen," my father said, but the waitress came with a food tray before he could go on. I knew their order by heart: my father had steak and eggs with pancakes on the side, and my mother had a single fried egg over hard with double bacon and one pancake. They both loved syrup and lots of butter.

"I think we're done here," I said after the waitress left. I picked up the takeaway box. "Kalayla likes pancakes. Thanks, Daddy."

I didn't know what to say to my mother, so I slid out of the booth and stood up.

"You may not care if you go to hell," my mother said. "But don't take your daughter with you."

"I hope I won't," I said. "But if Kalayla decided hell would be an interesting place to visit, I couldn't stop her from going."

I went from the cool inside to the heat and sat in my car with all the windows open. I hoped that seeing my mother would bring closure. All it did was remind me of old wounds and make me sad.

I thought about the orange crunch cake she'd sent with Daddy for my birthday party at Lena's, which said, "For all the missed birthdays, Mummie." Daddy said that was as much as she could do. Was it her way of saying she'd paid a price for turning her back on me? Was that a peace offering? Was she telling me I had to take the next step because she couldn't?

Long ago, my father told me, "I see the gentle and vulnerable side of your mother, Maureen. You see her frightened, well-defended side."

I'd seen the well-defended side today, but for the first time, I'd seen the vulnerability underneath it. My mother and I, the rock and the hard place, had trapped ourselves in a power struggle that neither of us could win.

What if I hadn't seen myself as the family's sacrificial lamb? What if my mother hadn't been afraid of my interest in art? What if I had told her I was seeing Jamal instead of sneaking out to meet him? What if I hadn't lost my temper whenever she tried to talk to me? What if she hadn't been afraid I'd harm the family?

My mother had taken the first step toward finding the answer to those what-ifs. I could meet her halfway.

I locked the car and went back inside.

My mother dropped her fork when she saw me. My father took her hand.

"You're right," I said. "Jamal and I didn't give Kalayla a religious background. I will talk with her and Rico about that. But, she'll be the one who decides what she believes and whether or not that involves a particular religion. She won't do what I tell her any more than I did what you wanted me to. Thank you for going to the gallery and for coming here."

My mother touched her throat as if to say she had no words, then gave a hint of a nod.

That was enough. I didn't know if she and I would sign a peace agreement, but we'd just consented to a cease-fire.

I turned, walked from the cool air into the heat, and drove home.

EARLY FALL 2001

FINDING CLARENCE

When I asked Mama where Clarence lived, she said, "I don't have his address, Kalayla. I wouldn't give it to you if I did."

Thanks a bunch, Miss Sharp Tooth. I'd find it without your help.

If Kieran and I got in trouble, I didn't want to involve my Grandma or Grandpa. Their family didn't have the talent for lying, which Kieran and I inherited from Mama's family.

That Friday night, while Mama and Rico were doing their happy couple thing, I cornered Grandpa by the snacks table and said, "Is Clarence still sitting around doing nothing?"

"Of course not, Kalayla. He's working at the same garage he always has. They couldn't do without him."

Yeah, 'cause he was probably their only mechanic. At least I found out he hadn't left town.

Grandma kept an address book beside the phone, and I found Clarence's address and telephone when Grandma was busy in the kitchen.

When I told Kieran we were all set, he said, "I'm not sure we should go to his house, Kalayla. What if his roommates are there?"

"Nobody would care what we did to that jerk."

"Jeez, Kalayla, they could be his friends."

Kieran might be right. Even if they weren't buddies, they might get pissed if we accidentally broke something.

"If we can't go to the garage, and we can't go where he lives, where else is there?" I said.

"We could meet him in a public place like the Cambridge Common. I've been thinking about it, and it doesn't seem right to beat him up for something he did months ago, especially after he spent time in a hospital.

You know what I mean?"

Yeah, I knew what Kieran meant. What a bummer. I was willing to whack the jerks at school with a bat if they gave me a hard time, but this was different. Clarence had been a real butthole to Mama, but he hadn't done anything to me. Grandma and Grandpa would understand if Mama did something, but they might not like it if I did.

But no matter how I twisted it around in my brain, I couldn't understand what Clarence did to Mama. And the only person who could tell me was Clarence.

I decided to ask him, but I wasn't doing it with Kieran, and I wasn't doing it alone. Since I was just having a friendly, information-gathering chat with Clarence, maybe Ray Ray would let me borrow Thor for a few hours.

I made a batch of marshmallow popcorn balls and took them to Friday night's game. Even though it was dark, plenty of street lamps and lights were on the field, and we were the star attraction. I didn't like it, but Ray Ray said that was the whole point. "Whenever anyone asks who you are, I tell them you're family."

"Yeah, I'm the runt in a family of giants, right?"

Ray Ray laughed. "I'll use that line when the subject comes up."

I took a couple of the popcorn balls out of my backpack. "I made these this afternoon. It's a special recipe with marshmallows."

"I get popcorn balls, and you get what?" he said, biting into one. "Humm, not bad."

Marshmallow popcorn balls were my favorite snack, so it wasn't like I made them only to brown-nose him. I planned to eat a few.

"It's kind of a long story," I said.

"We've got time," Ray Ray said.

"Thor's looking very handsome. Did you get him groomed?"

"Not that much time," Ray Ray said.

Cow turds! When I finished telling him why, he said, "I can see why you'd want to ask Clarence a few questions. So this is what I'm willing to do. I'll pick a neutral place where you can meet. I'll take you there, and Thor and I will stay in the background while you and Clarence talk. Now, hand over the rest of those popcorn balls."

***

Two days later, Ray Ray called to say he'd arranged a room at the Boys & Girls Club. I told him I didn't go there 'cause I wasn't in the habit of hanging out with other kids.

"Kalayla, if you had a gun, you'd shoot yourself in the foot before wearing a pair of shoes you didn't like."

"I would not. I'd go to the thrift store and see if I could trade them for a better pair. Anyway, you do stuff that doesn't make sense. I'd never let anybody call me Kalayla Kalayla. Why do you let them call you Ray Ray or Double Ray?"

He sighed. "A big kid like me hits the streets sooner than most kids, and my mama spent half her time trying to find me. A neighbor said she should've named me Ray Ray because she always had to call me more than once. Pretty soon, everybody was calling me double Ray or Ray Ray."

I smiled sweetly and said, "Thanks for telling me."

Now I had to call Clarence, but I kind of hoped he wouldn't answer. The phone rang a few times, and I was about to hang up when Clarence said, "Who wants to talk to me?"

"Kalayla," I said.

That probably surprised him, so I said, "You know, Kalayla, the niece you've been avoiding."

Clarence said, "I'm not avoiding you. I'm avoiding the building you live in. Bad stuff happens there."

I wouldn't have to go to the Boys and Girls Club if Clarence told me now why he'd been such a jerk.

"What do you mean bad things happening at our building? Like what?"

"Don't know. Can't remember. Bad stuff happened at Fresh Pond, so I don't go there either. I remember that."

"Why'd you stop going to Grandma's on Friday nights?"

"I didn't. I just stay out of sight when people are there. Don't want anybody saying the parents are good and kind, but the left-over son is a loser."

Clarence was being flip, but he sounded sad, and his saying he was the left-over son made me uncomfortable. Maybe meeting with him wasn't the best idea I ever had.

I was about to say we had a bad connection and hang up, but he said, "I'll buy you a Coke to show I'm not avoiding you. How'd that be?"

I didn't want to say yes, but I'd look like a jerk saying no. At least Ray

349

Ray and Thor would be with me. So I said, "Meet me at the Boys and Girls Club tomorrow afternoon. They probably have a drink machine."

"Your daddy must be whispering in your ear. He loved that place. I hate it, but I'll meet you there. They have a cold drink machine, but it usually isn't working."

***

Mama and Rico were hitting a movie after dinner, so Opa and I headed to Lena's and the old guy's. I wasn't going to hook up like they did. I was going to trade boyfriends the same as Lotta did like they were part of the Yankee swap at Grandma's Christmas party.

"To what do I owe the pleasure of your company?" Lena said.

"I wanted to talk to you in private."

Lena narrowed her eyes. Did she think I robbed a bank and wanted to hide the loot in Mattwo's woodshop?

She leaned toward me and whispered, "Do not tell me you are pregnant!"

I burst out laughing! "Don't get in a twit! I'm not shagging anybody. I'm meeting Clarence at the Boys and Girls Club tomorrow, and Ray Ray is going with me. I tried to borrow Thor and go alone, but Ray Ray said no."

"Ray Ray has good sense. What's the point of this meeting with Clarence?"

"I'm asking him why he attacked Mama. He told me he doesn't go near our apartment building 'cause something bad happened there, but he doesn't remember what."

Lena's expression didn't change. "I'm glad Ray Ray will be there. He won't overreact no matter what you or Clarence does."

"Kieran said he'd go with me, but if Clarence acts like a slimeball, I might lose my temper, and he won't know what to do. I don't want him to get in trouble."

"Do you realize how much you've matured since I met you, Kalayla?"

"Yeah, and you have, too!"

Lena laughed. "I hope you know how proud I am of you and how much I love you."

"You're not bad for a Grandma except now when you get all mushy!"

Lena squeezed my arm. "You better get home and do the homework you say you don't have!"

350

Ray Ray stopped to chat with about fifty kids between the parking lot and the Boys and Girls Club door.

The building was a combo of brick and metal panels about as appealing as the high school outside, but kids' art covered the hallway walls.

We passed rooms with glass windows, and one said After School Drop-in Program. Kids were reading, writing, or working on computers, and two old ladies wandered around, making sure the kids weren't looking at porn.

Ray Ray flicked his finger when we passed a hallway on our left and said, "Swimming pool is down there."

He stopped in front of room seventeen. "This is it. Do you want to wait out here or inside?"

When I shrugged, he opened the door. The room was a catch-all with stray chairs, one table piled with building blocks and another with an overflowing box of Lego pieces. A few weights, a couple of volleyballs, and an exercise ball were in a corner.

"Since you didn't tell Clarence about me and Thor being here, we'll wait and let him know so he can decide if he wants to stay."

Ray Ray closed the door before I could object.

About five minutes later, Clarence came in with Ray Ray and Thor. He was carrying a shopping bag and wearing a faded sweatshirt and jeans. His shiny bald head and high-shine loafers were the same as always.

"How's my favorite niece? I'm sorry I missed Christmas and your birthday. I picked this up on my lunch break. I didn't want you to think I forgot you." He handed me the shopping bag.

Ray Ray pointed to the back of the room and said, "Thor and I'll be there."

Clarence grabbed a chair, sat down, and said, "I've got a lot going on, Kalayla. I don't see why Ray Ray and Thor need to be here, but can we get going with this meeting or whatever it is?"

I was in a chair a few feet away from him. I planned to take it slow and work up to mentioning what he did to Mama. You know, do the small talk thing, like asking him if he thought shock treatment scrambled his brain or if the guys he lived with had been to jail more than once.

That's what I would have done, but before I could stop myself, I said, "Why'd you try and rape my mama?"

Clarence reared back like I'd hit him and came close to falling off his chair.

Ray Ray said, "Damn it, Kalayla!" Thor growled softly.

Clarence shook his head like he needed to clear his vision. Then, he bent over with his hands covering his head, rocking back and forth.

I stood up.

"Sit down!" Ray Ray said quietly. He and Thor moved closer to me and Clarence. I sat down.

Clarence was mumbling something over and over. I couldn't tell what it was, but I finally understood, "Why'd she have to marry him?"

I looked at Ray Ray, who had put a finger to his lips and shook his head.

Why was he mumbling like that? The way he was acting made me think of a woman I saw on Mass. Ave. She was muttering like Clarence and pushing a grocery cart loaded with her stuff.

When I told Lena about her, she said, "There's no way of knowing why her life has gone that way, Kalayla. Judging people is easy. Helping them make a new start is a lot harder."

After several minutes, Clarence stopped muttering, pushed himself up from the chair, and said, "I have to get out of here."

"You okay to drive? I could drop you off," Ray Ray said.

Clarence looked beaten down, but he waved Ray Ray away. "Thanks, but I could drive in my sleep if I had to."

Without looking at me, Clarence said, "I don't know what to tell you, Kalayla. My life's one big f–k up."

I hated that I felt sorry for him, hated that I couldn't tell him he was a jerk and a butthole and a rotten uncle and a disgusting brother. I hated that I couldn't hate him the way I wanted to. He wasn't living on the street like that old woman, but his life was a mess.

Clarence stood near my chair and waited for me to say something. I didn't want to, but I knew I had to.

"Stop screwing up," I said. "When I was a prick, Lena said I could change if I wanted to. So can you. Stop feeling sorry for yourself. Do something to make up for being such a jerk."

Clarence staggered to the door and left.

"You ended that better than you started," Ray Ray said.

Lena told me to cut people some slack, but that was harder to do with Clarence than the homeless woman. I didn't know anything about her, but I knew it would take Clarence the rest of his life to make up for what he did.

A NEW WORLD: SEPTEMBER 11, 2001

Humans and animals in New England cherish fine days like today, with bright sunshine and temperatures in the sixties. The monotony of dreary, cloud-covered skies will be here all too soon.

BB snoozed in the backyard, and Mattwo puttered on the patio. I was reviewing the accounts for Manzetti rental properties when I heard Mattwo's cell ring.

A few minutes later, Mattwo came inside and said, "We need to put the TV on. Rico says there's been an attack in New York City."

I couldn't imagine what that meant. I glanced at the wall clock—9:44 AM.

Every channel showed the same chaotic scene, with reporters trying to explain it to themselves as much as to the listeners. The Twin Towers in Lower Manhattan looked like two gigantic chimney stacks billowing grey and black smoke from the middle instead of the top. It made no sense.

When Mattwo patted the sofa, I said, "I'll get BB. I don't want her outside by herself."

"Good idea," he said, as if that was the most logical thing in the world.

The TV reporters tried to sound coherent, piecing together partial facts. A plane crashed into the north tower almost an hour ago, and a second one hit the South about forty-five minutes ago. A third plane had just crashed into the Pentagon.

"Try another channel," I said, hoping for more information.

Mattwo flicked through the channels, which focused on the smoking towers, and panicked people trying to escape while fire engines, police cars, and ambulances blared sirens and horns in an attempt to get downtown to help.

The images alternated between the area around the Twin Towers in

Lower Manhattan and the wreckage at the Pentagon in Washington, DC. The scenes were bizarre and chaotic. Dom and I attended meetings in the Financial District and knew the area well. When we didn't have a luncheon or dinner meeting, we'd get Italian subs and gelato and sit on a bench outside Tratoria Abbruzzese. The images were horrifying, terrifying.

Mattwo said what I was thinking, "Whoever planned this and carried it out knew what they were doing, like those terrorists in Oklahoma City."

Three homegrown terrorists who'd met in the army blew up a federal building in Oklahoma City using a truck bomb. This morning, three separate buildings were targeted using commercial airplanes as weapons for suicide and murder. These attacks were complicated and coordinated, the magnitude mind-boggling.

"This might not be over," Mattwo said. "Let's stay here until we know more."

My stomach churned as I thought about the consequences for the people in the buildings. "What will the survivors do if the elevators won't work and there is panic on the stairs? Even if people could get to the roof of one of the towers, commercial aircraft had been grounded, and no one could have rescued them. We should check on people here. I'll get Opa and leave Kalayla a note. Do you think they'll keep the kids in school?"

I knew I was rambling, but it was impossible to focus. I gasped and grabbed Mattwo's arm, "Oh my god, the top of one of the towers is tilting."

We watched the building fall like a high-speed elevator spewing a mushroom cloud of smoke and flying debris. The screen went grey-white. When it cleared, the remaining tower stood beside an enormous pile of rubble and billowing smoke. Nothing was recognizable.

"Everyone in or near the building must be dead," I said.

"If one tower came down, the other will, too," Mattwo said.

Questions without answers raced through my mind. Why would anyone do something so devastating? We weren't at war, and the people who died weren't soldiers like Mikie and Jimmy. I could understand why the Pentagon might be a target as the symbol of US military power, but this was beyond imaginable.

The Twin Towers were office buildings, each a hundred and ten stories high. Sightseers visited NYC to see its two tallest buildings. People shopped in the area, grandparents strolled with grandchildren, and dog-walkers made a good living. Why would anyone hurt them?

The reporter announced that hijackers had taken over a fourth plane, but some of the passengers had charged the cockpit. The plane crashed in a field in Shanksville, PA, a place I'd never heard of.

I stared at the screen in horror and saw the second tower collapse.

Mattwo flipped channels, waiting for the smoke to clear. A long-angled lens showed mangled piles of debris with fire engines, police cars, municipal vehicles, and passenger cars littering the streets close to the towers. There was no sign of life. The images were too surreal to absorb.

Cameras panned further uptown, showing dazed and disoriented people emerging from the smoke, tears creating channels down their dust-covered faces. Shoes, hats, briefcases, fragments of desks, chairs, pipes, and window frames littered the streets. Paper gliding in the wind slowly carpeted the street.

One channel juxtaposed an archived shot through the Greenwich Village Arch that showed the Twin Towers in the distance with an identical image through the Arch now. Plumes of smoke marked the location of the missing towers.

Mattwo and I watched until neither of us could bear it any longer.

"Stay here, BB," I said. "I'm going to get Opa."

Mattwo and I held hands as we went down the porch steps and hugged before going in different directions.

"I'll call when I get to Matty's Way. I love you," Mattwo said.

"Drive carefully. I love you," I answered.

People stood outside Eddie's with their faces glued to the windows, straining to see the TV above the counter. The crowd inside was silent. Someone moaned when the cameraman panned the catastrophic scene, and the reporter said it was impossible to assess the number of lives lost.

Maureen hugged me, tears in her eyes. "They're keeping the kids in school until regular dismissal time. Ray Ray said he'd pick up Kalayla." Maureen gestured at the TV. "The world isn't safe, Lena. Maybe it never was, but we didn't know it. Now we do."

I looked around and saw numb, disbelieving expressions. Invisible violence that hid behind closed doors or in another country was in full view, and we couldn't hide from it.

* * *

The days following 9/11 were disorienting. The planes that hit the towers had taken off from Boston's Logan Airport bound for Los Angeles. The hijackers had come from countries thousands of miles away. Any traveler flying from Logan that day might have walked past the hijackers or sat near them in the waiting area. No one knew what might come next. Mattwo and I stayed close to home.

Kalayla was spending as much time with us as at home. One night near the end of September, she and I were on the patio, and Mattwo was in the living room watching the Patriots.

"If you think bringing Opa here every day means we'll get a passel of puppies, you'll be sorely disappointed," I said.

Kalayla laughed. "Lotta wouldn't adopt out a rescue unless it had been spayed or neutered."

"So, I assume you have another reason for coming here every day. What is it?"

Kalayla looked up at the stars, which told me her next words would be processed baloney.

"Kieran and I talked about how wise you old people are. We decided to get some survival tips. He goes to see his grandparents, and I'm coming here."

I admit that was one of her more flattering lies.

"Mattwo and I are older than Lucinda and Harmon, but they'd be a better source of survival tips than Mattwo or me."

"I call them every day, but you live closer, and Opa can play with BB."

"If you think I have become a gullible old woman who will buy that survival tip mumbo-jumbo, you are one hundred percent wrong."

Kalayla frowned, got up from her chair, and said, "I'm going to check on the dogs."

She walked out to Privet hedge and stood there for a few minutes. When she returned, she said, "Opa and I better go home so Mama won't think a terrorist kidnapped us."

"I will call your mother and tell her you are on your way, but you are not leaving here until you tell me what is going on."

Kalayla didn't try to wiggle her way out with another lie. She said, "My daddy never came home, and those people in New York and Washington didn't either. I don't want you to die."

I should have known.

What happened on 9/11 didn't have a personal name attached to it for Kalayla, but it taught her that death could knock on any door at any time. I'd lived long enough to know life gives gifts and takes them away, and we don't get to decide how or when that happens. The fact that Kalayla knew it, too, made me want to cry.

"You can't control when we die, Kalayla, and gluing yourself to us won't change that. I'm not ready to check out, and neither is Mattwo. The best thing you can do for us and yourself is to live your life so you're proud of who you are and what you do. I didn't always do that, and I wish I had."

Kalayla nodded slowly and called Opa. To my surprise, she hugged me, kissed my cheek, and said, "I love you, Lena."

I would be grateful for that gift until the day I died.

EARLY WINTER 2002

CLOSURE WITH CLARENCE

When I told Lena Kalayla was being impossible, she said, "Why, I was just telling Mattwo how she's matured over these last months. Is she being impossible about something in particular?"

"The house! It has to be identical to your house and her grandparents' house, and it has to be close to them and you. She wants a downstairs room for ping pong, two windows in her bedroom, and a large closet. And she doesn't see why we can't move over her February vacation!"

"Humm, well, she did mention her list to Dom and me, and I told her we'd take it under advisement. Maybe you should remind her that she plans to move out as soon as she graduates high school."

"Good grief, Lena, how will I keep her safe if she moves out? If I could convince Ray Ray to marry her, he could protect her. But I don't think he'd agree to that, do you?"

Lena's eyes twinkled, and I could tell she wasn't the least sympathetic! I'd walked here hoping for advice, but she thought the whole thing was funny!

"Did you hear what you just said, Maureen? Wouldn't you agree this is a classic example of the apple not falling far from the tree?"

"I was never as stubborn as Kalayla is. Well, what if I was? She could have taken after Jamal instead of me, couldn't she? He was always agreeable."

"Maureen, as I recall, you told me Jamal didn't take you to meet Lucinda and Harmon until after you were married. I doubt Lucinda would say Jamal was always agreeable."

"You don't always have to be right, Lena!"

That made Lena laugh, and I relaxed a bit. After all, on a scale of one to ten, how bad was it? We had decided to make an offer on a house that all three of us liked, and everything was falling into place.

Even so, there were times when I wanted to shake Kalayla until her teeth rattled which was probably how my mother felt about me. I wondered if my mother had been an obedient child and done what her mother wanted her to. If I get the chance someday, I might ask her, not that I could count on her telling me the truth.

I was having lunch with Lucinda on Saturday, and I might ask her about how cooperative Jamal was.

***

"I'm glad to see you, Maureen," Lucinda said as she hugged me. "Let's sit in the kitchen."

"The house smells like a bakery. Are these pre-Christmas goodies?"

"They are. I sent Harmon to play Dominoes with the old men. That man loves sweets, and his gut is showing it. What he doesn't smell won't tempt him."

"You'll have to air the house out before he comes home to prevent that!"

"Sit," Lucinda said. "We can talk while we eat. I need to tell you about Clarence."

My heart sank. Was this connected to Kalayla's talk with Clarence? She told me nothing about it, so I asked Ray Ray how it went. He said, "Kalayla didn't scream or throw anything at him. She went straight for the jugular, which was about what I had expected."

Ray Ray didn't volunteer any specifics, but I hoped Lucinda would. I sat at the table, gripping my coffee cup like a lifebuoy.

After she sat down, Lucinda said, "You know Clarence is living independently with some other men and is back at work now. He's been calling every weekend, so we were worried when we didn't hear from him for three weeks. Harmon left several messages, and Clarence finally came to see us last Sunday. He was unshaven and haggard, had lost weight, and looked like he hadn't slept."

"What's wrong?" Harmon asked as I fixed Clarence a plate of leftovers.

"Maybe I'll eat later," Clarence said. He turned and went into the living room.

Harmon and I followed him and sat on the loveseat. Clarence was a mass of restless energy and paced as he talked.

Kalayla called and said she wanted to talk to me. I couldn't figure that out because she's acted like I was a cockroach she wanted to squash ever since Jamal died. I wanted to find out what she wanted, so I agreed to meet her at the Boys and Girls Club. When I got to the room, that big guy, Ray Ray, and his dog were in front of the door like bodyguards. Ray Ray said they'd sit at the back of the room while Kalayla and I talked. I couldn't believe it. It was like she was afraid of me and she brought them to protect her! I was humiliated and pissed at Kalayla, but I wasn't going to turn tail and run because of them.

I thought if I acted normal, Kalayla might send them away. So I went in, said hello and gave her a few presents. She didn't even bother to look at them. What'd she do instead? She hit me with a two-by-four. She asked why I tried to rape her mother.

She might as well have asked me why I decided to turn into a zebra. At first, I thought it was some stupid teenage joke. But the kid was deadly serious, her eyes intense and accusing, not spacey or whacked out. I didn't know what to say. Sure, Maureen pissed me off, but there was no way I'd try to rape her. What got to me was that Kalayla hadn't asked me if I tried to rape her mother. She asked me why I did it as if she was sure I had.

My shrink told me the shock treatments might cause memory loss, and there were blank spaces in my memory of that day. But how could I forget something like that? What if Kalayla was right? I remembered hating Jamal for marrying a white woman. I remembered hating him for dying. I remembered how much I loved him and depended on him. But I didn't remember trying to rape his wife.

What Kalayla said shoved me into a pile of crap. What if I had done what she said? How could I betray Jamal like that? I got out of there as fast as possible and holed up in my room at the house. I had to fill in those blank spaces. I remembered I was pissed when I saw Maureen with that white jock and when she told me that frumpy old woman let her use the apartment for her studio. I knew she was lying. Did she think I was stupid?

Maureen's lie nagged at me, and I remember going for lunch at a bar near the garage a few days later. I got to popping boilermakers, and my imagination got fired up. Suddenly, I was positive I'd seen Maureen in that car at Fresh Pond laughing, and egging those guys on. I wanted to get back at them, and I wanted to get back at her.

Clarence continued pacing, but his nervous gesturing stopped.

*

That's when I remembered.

I wanted revenge all my life and never had a way to get it. Since that day, sour bile had been eating at my insides, and the boilermakers let it loose. Jamal never would have believed I was capable of doing anything that low. But I was. My brother's wife—what kind of disloyal asshole was I?

I forced myself to see the shrink, and he said, "It's not a surprise you wanted revenge. Why do you think you picked Maureen as the target?"

"Because I'm a shit."

"And other than that, why did you pick Maureen?"

How the hell did I know? That guy pissed me off. I got up and walked out. I was sick of him. When I went back, I told him he was a useless jerk.

"You don't like coming to see me, but here you are," he said. "How do you explain that?"

"You're not as stupid as the shrink they sent me to during the shock therapy."

"Thanks for the vote of confidence. Any other reason you came?"

"Jamal didn't think I was a shit."

"He knew you pretty well. Do you think he was stupid?"

"Jamal said I let those guys ruin my life. He said I gave them power over me. Maybe he was right. Maybe Kalayla was, too. She said I should stop feeling sorry for myself and make up for being an asshole."

"She sounds like a smart girl. Like she might take after her father."

"She is. She does."

"Do you plan to ignore her like you ignored your brother?"

*

Clarence stopped pacing and looked unbearably sad. I wanted to pull him close like I did when he was a child. But he wasn't a child anymore.

Jamal did everything he could to help me, but couldn't do it for me. I kept thinking about what he and Kalayla said. I needed to find a way to help myself, but I didn't know how until September eleventh happened.

Clarence sat in the chair facing us, his face tense, and his elbows resting on his knees.

I realized there was something I could do to prove I wasn't a complete waste of space. I always wanted to be a fireman, but I was afraid of going for it and failing. Jamal was the one who took risks, not me. I thought maybe I could try now, but I found out I was near the age limit for firefighter training. And I had mental problems on my record. Then it occurred to me they don't just need firefighters. I was as good as any mechanic they could find who'd keep the fire engines and emergency vehicles in top running order. I talked to the guys at the firehouse where Jamal and I hung out. They told me about an Emergency Vehicle Technician training program. I'm going to enroll in it and prove I'm not a worthless piece of shit.

"Harmon and I prayed so long that our boy would find himself. And it seemed as if he was doing that. We wrapped our arms around Clarence and held on like we'd never let go.

"Clarence said we won't see him until he proves he's fit to be Jamal's brother. He enrolled in an EVT program based in New York and will move as soon as he finds a place to live. He asked us to tell Kalayla he hopes to see her again."

* * *

I was happy that the parts of Lucinda and Harmon that had split off worrying about Clarence could come home. I had no idea if Kalayla would ever want to see Clarence. Hopefully, he'd find redemption with or without her approval.

Clarence didn't mention seeing me, which was a relief. I felt as if the events that afternoon took on their own life and stripped me of choices. Could I, should I have acted differently? I can't spend the rest of my life second-guessing what I did or didn't do. And I doubt that seeing Clarence would clarify that for me.

What an irony that Kalayla is the model for Clarence and me. As usual, she did what needed doing in her way and sliced through the tangles that would have immobilized me. I am incredibly proud of her, and Jamal would be, too. I will give her a giant hug from him and me whether she wants it or not!

SPRING 2002

MOVING ON

Kalayla was giving the dogs treats when I said, "Mattwo and I got married this morning."

She whirled around. "How could you do that without me? I planned to be your flower girl and throw rose petals when you walked down the aisle!"

"We didn't walk down an aisle. We went in the side door of the church."

"That rots! Your wedding was supposed to be practice for Mama's and Rico's."

I hope I wasn't around when Maureen and Rico told Kalayla they were having an informal wedding with family, which would not include bridesmaids, groomsmen, or flower girls.

"At least we're going on a decent honeymoon," Kalayla said. "I don't see why Mama got so mad when I said her relatives in Belfast could give me awesome tips on lying. The science teacher said everything is in our DNA. Mama's is one hundred percent Irish, so lying must be a built-in trait, right?"

There was no point in scolding Kalayla for making up scientific facts or informing her that reshaping the truth was not exclusive to the Irish. I could have taught her that skill better than her mother if I had chosen to, which I did not.

"Kalayla, Rico and your mother do not plan to include you on their honeymoon."

"How do you know?"

"Maureen asked me if you and Opa could stay with us."

"Don't worry. Mama will change her mind when I tell her about the hot studs at the high school who are panting to get into my pants. Get it, panting to get into my pants? She'll freak out."

I almost choked. Good luck to Maureen and Rico. Whether or not they could withstand the power of Kalayla's persuasion and trickery remained to be seen.

"See," I said, pointing to my wide gold wedding band to change the subject.

"Maybe Lotta will be jealous and want one. I could practice at her wedding."

"Lotta is an expert on wedding protocol and will tell you you're too old to be a flower girl. How do you like your new house?"

"Fine, except Rico and I both want the basement. He says his shop should be there, but I want a ping pong table. He won three out of three when we flipped for it, but I'm not giving up. Anyway, my bedroom is cool, and Mama loves her studio. How'd you like our swim show? Pretty awesome, huh?"

"It wasn't an Esther Williams extravaganza, but was quite enjoyable. The way you groaned about learning the stunts made me think I'd have to dive in to save you from drowning."

"You're too old to swim, Lena." Kalayla smiled and pinched my cheek. "I'll see you at our Open House on Saturday. Mama is making it a big deal, and Rico is too patient. Anyway, tell Mama and Rico that teenage flower girls are the in thing now, okay?"

Kalayla and Opa went out the door onto another adventure. It was astounding how Kalayla could simultaneously be a joy and a pain in the neck. She insists she'll never get married, but I hope I live long enough to be there if she does. I'll get a place in the Guinness Book of World Records as the oldest living flower girl, whether I walk or ride in a wheelchair to scatter the rose petals. I ought to get the last word on something with that girl!

Contrary to my initial insistence that I am not a noisy old biddy, I admit I veered in that direction. Do I plan to mend my ways? Probably not. Why would I abandon a practice that has given me so much joy? Besides, Lotta will likely encourage me to continue and insist on joining me. After all, she's always been an old biddy, hasn't she?

If you enjoyed reading
KALAYLA: UNRAVELING TANGLES
please leave a review to recommend it to other readers

Thanks a lot for your time